"Into The Nothing is a true gem, and so needed in this time of awakening and change. Dr Gabriel Cousens supports the athlete in all of us to make that final touchdown. I particularly love the addition of football, because it really can teach us about the game of life. Will, focus, strength, courage and friendship are needed for the spiritual warrior, whether on the field, in relationship, or the journey of liberation. After all, it's not how many times we fall down, but how many times we get up again. At last, a book that can take us all the way from football to freedom."

—John Sullivan,
former NLF Middle Linebacker NY Jets

"The one thing I can unconditionally share about Gabriel Cousens is that he is a genuine mystic. As wild as it is, his autobiography is absolutely real and true. The teachings in this book guide and assist us on the spiritual path. I AM blessed to have him as my friend. Many will be blessed and benefit from his efforts and intentions, and the transmissions within the pages of this book."

— Jason D. Groode, Sufis Hawaii

"A romantic and fiery mystic, Gabriel Cousens takes us from the trap of the body-mind, to Kundalini awakening, all the way through the process of liberation. He does not stop there, but demonstrates the many ways in which a liberated master not only frees himself, but invites everyone to join him in the quest to know the Divine. *Into The Nothing* is a spiritual classic."

—Ayn Cates Sullivan, Ph.D.,
best-selling author and podcaster

INTO THE
NOTHING

INTO THE NOTHING

A Spiritual Autobiography

GABRIEL COUSENS, M.D.

Infinite Light Publishing & Media, LLC
Charlottesville, VA
www.infinitelightpublishing.com

Editor in Chief: Ayn Cates Sullivan, Ph.D.
Book Cover: Lucinda Rae
Book Design: Ghislain Viau

Names: Cousens, Gabriel, 1943- author.

Title: Into the nothing : a spiritual autobiography / Gabriel Cousens.

Description: Identifiers: Subjects:

First edition. | Charlottesville, VA : Infinite Light Publishing & Media, LLC, [2021] | Includes glossary.

ISBN: 978-1-947925-37-3 (hardcover) | 978-0-9970467-2-4 (paperback) | 978-0-9970467-5-5 (eBook)

LCSH: Spiritual biography. | Spiritual formation. | Spiritual life. | Mysticism. | Self- actualization (Psychology) | Holism. | Philosophy of mind. | Self-consciousness (Awareness) | Perspective (Philosophy) | Alternative lifestyles. | Holistic medicine. | Nutrition--Religious aspects. | Ontology. | GSAFD: BIOGRAPHY & AUTOBIOGRAPHY / General. | BIOGRAPHY & AUTOBIOGRAPHY / Cultural, Ethnic & Regional / General, | BIOGRAPHY & AUTOBIOGRAPHY / Religious. | RELIGION / Spirituality. | RELIGION / Mysticism. | RELIGION / Inspirational. | LCGFT: Autobiographies. | BISAC: 202010

Classification: LCC: BL73.C68 C68 2021 | DDC: 204/.092--dc23

Book Summary: *Into the Nothing: A Spiritual Autobiography* is about the wild adventurous mystical life that led to the liberation of Gabriel Cousens, MD. The book takes us through the unique process of classical spiritual awakening and liberation in several paths, including Yoga and Torah-Kabbalistic traditions, and also his experiences in the Lakota Sundance, Eagle Dance and Spirit Dance. It includes Dr. Cousens' unique teachings of spiritual nutrition, and the Six Foundations and Sevenfold-Peace, that creates a natural way of living that leads to the Holistic Liberation Way.

To my wife, Shanti
My children Rafael and Heather
& Grandchildren Rhea, Katja, and Anaïs

CONTENTS

ACKNOWLEDGMENTS

I give thanks to God who graced me with the consciousness shift within my body and my spiritual awareness into the Eternal Presence of Liberation, and who has empowered and graced me with the power to bring this spiritual understanding and energy to the world. I also give thanks to my wonderful wife, Shanti, who supported me with her understanding and love during the time it took to write this book. I express my gratitude to my parents, students, clients, and all the people involved with the Tree of Life Foundation. I also express my special gratitude and thanks to editor Ayn Cates Sullivan, Ph.D. for her thoughtful edits with the teachings and for polishing my work and bringing it to production fruition with her rainbow radiance. Thank you to Richard Grossinger for his brilliant editing insights. Thanks to Marc Ketchel (formally Swami Shivananda) who has been a spiritual friend to me since 1975, including during my seven years with Swami Muktananda, and who has helped clarify my perspective of those years, and for his excellent general editing and for writing the foreword to this book.

FOREWORD

I'm honored to be writing the foreword to this book. I have a very large library of spiritual and mystical literature that I have collected and studied over the last fifty years and I believe this book, *Into the Nothing,* is destined to be a spiritual classic. It will be welcomed and find its rightful place in the Western mystical tradition, particularly as a rare example of authentic Kundalini awakening and integration into daily life. It won't be Gabriel's first classic however, but will follow in the footsteps of his classic, *Spiritual Nutrition: Six Foundations for Spiritual Life and the Awakening of Kundalini.*

Gabriel Cousens is a mystic. He has been practicing mysticism for as long as he can remember. But what is mysticism? And what is a mystic? These may be unfamiliar terms to most Westerners, but if you like the poems of Rumi or Kabir, you have an appreciation for mystical insight and experience. Mysticism may sound esoteric, but it is simply living in direct communion with the Divine. A mystic is one who initially lives with a burning desire for the direct experience of the Divine and later becomes completely consumed by the awareness of Her abiding Presence in every moment and facet of their life.

Gabriel very openly and candidly shares what he considers his initiation and awakening moment when, in November of 1975, he received the touch of the Siddha Master, Baba Muktananda, and the descent of Grace known in the Yogic tradition as *Shaktipat.* While mystical awakening is becoming more common since Baba graced the planet in the latter part of the 20th century, Gabriel's experience is particularly unique and a primary reason this book will have such a wide appeal.

His direct encounter with the interior energy known as Kundalini Shakti, through the empowerment of Shaktipat, was the end of his searching and the beginning of an awakening and unfoldment process that would forever change the course of his life. He was now on the Path and had the first glimmers of the glories that lay ahead. The gravity of the experience was not lost on him, for he had been preparing for this moment his whole life. He knew with absolute conviction he had met the Master who could give him the keys to 'heaven' and in the process unlock the shackles which had constrained him for lifetimes.

What is unique about Gabriel's story, which he so completely reveals in the pages of this book, is what *he* brought to the process. For me, the most beautiful aspect of Gabriel's story is the fact that he didn't leave anything behind; rather, he brought it all with him. He found a way, through deep spiritual reflection and full engagement and faith in the process, to incorporate his whole life experience into what was to become his Holistic Liberation Way. It must here be clarified: this is a Path based on his own direct experience of the Divine Presence in his life. It is not a renegade departure from tradition but a reinterpreting of three streams of ancient tradition backed by scripture and historical record as well as the teachings and living example of his guru. Through his discipline and daily practice, he incorporated the teachings of the great wisdom holders of three previously disparate traditions making them his own as the Holistic Liberation Way.

Through the intensity of his search and his dedicated practice, he left no stone unturned. He had found a guru and perfect master in Baba Muktananda who taught that a spiritual seeker does not need to leave the world and live in a cave. Baba taught and gave us the direct experience that the full-blown presence of God dwells in the hearts of all sentient beings and is fully manifest in the world in which we live. We just have to open our hearts and refine the perception of our intellect in order to see and perceive the Divine play, which is what the awakened life is about. The most important ingredient in the successful awakening and unfoldment of the Kundalini Shakti is love and devotion, qualities Gabriel brought from past lives work and further cultivated under his guru's guidance in this life.

When Gabriel arrived at the ashram of Baba Muktananda in Oakland, CA in the fall of 1975 he had already heard about Kundalini and had been collaborating with his friend, the late Lee Sannella, MD, in the search for a way to awaken the Divine Power, Kundalini Shakti. He intuitively knew that awakening the Kundalini would be a major inflection point in his quest. He was already a practicing medical holistic physician and a scientist, and one who was very tuned in to the subtle energies at play in both the human body and in the external environment. He arrived with firm resolve and a well-honed capacity for extreme discipline developed through his years playing football. He later discovered that this discipline was a critical element to rapid progress on the Path. Baba Muktananda is quoted as saying, "Only discipline has value," an understanding which Gabriel wholeheartedly resonated with.

The subject of Kundalini was not a new one for Gabriel; in fact he had been in the quest for the ultimate spiritual experience for many years, which only the awakening of the Kundalini can impart. Certainly, he has been focused and dedicated to this quest for all of the more than forty-five years that I have known him.

What you will read in the pages of this unique book is the candid and transparent development of a deep and abiding communion with Divine Presence. Gabriel here lays bare the mysterious way the inner Goddess Kundalini, as the intelligence that underpins every physical and mental process, awakens and shows the Way in the great inner journey that is also reflected in the outer world for those with 'right understanding.' He shares his personal and collective challenges as a fully enlightened awareness unfolds within. He describes in detail his immersion in his Jewish tradition and the richness which it added to his life and the development of the Holistic Liberation Way. The reader will be further edified by his insights into the great Native American wisdom tradition. Finally, all will be enriched and elevated by his profound understanding and loving embrace of the sacred relationship with his wife and spiritual partner Shanti, giving full expression to his Holistic Liberation Way.

I invite you to open your hearts and minds while engaging with this unique expression of the emerging Western mystical tradition. It is delightfully punctuated by Gabriel's inspired poetry and the teaching points are highlighted on each page. The book is easy to read, and in fact will grab you and pull you into it. I'm sure you will find it inspiring and enlightening to your own spiritual journey.

With love and respect,
Marc Ketchel (Shivananda)

Introduction

HOLISTIC LIBERATION WAY...
LIFE IS THE TEACHING

Teaching: We live in the paradox of
everyday life and I Am-ness.

---

*H*aving now made seventy-seven cycles around the sun during this incarnation, it seems timely to write a spiritual autobiography. This book may be used as a teaching tool by following my life and the experiences that I have gathered while moving through the various stages of spiritual awakening. Perhaps my life will encourage you to examine where you are on your own spiritual path and ignite your evolutionary process. While reading, I encourage you to become aware of the liberation process inherent in mundane activities like football and sacred relationship. This spiritual autobiography is also an invitation to learn the basic principles behind the Eastern and Western enlightenment traditions. Enlightened I Am-ness is the powerful play of the Divine Paradox. The Divine Paradox is experienced by consciously living the dual/*non-dual* God-centered way of life.

In this autobiography I feature specific spiritual and liberation teachings in every chapter. These condensed messages are useful teachings which are designed to support a journey to Holistic Liberation. A Glossary in the back of the book includes Hebrew, Sanskrit, Yogic and other terms that might be unfamiliar to the reader. These terms are used to make the subtle point that similar liberation teachings appear in the great spiritual traditions of the East and the West. I also include what I believe is a *dharma* to share very specific insights based on direct details of my personal experience about the subtleties of the liberation process; a detailed description of the subtle body spiritual anatomy; specific details of Kundalini unfolding; the different subtle levels of the liberation states of consciousness; and some of the mysteries of the overall path of liberation. The first time a Hebrew, Sanskrit, Yogic, Lakota, French or other foreign term is used, it is italicized and deeper definitions can be read in the Glossary.

This book is an introduction to Holistic Liberation as a way of life. In brief, the Holistic Liberation Way is a path and lifestyle approach to freedom. In the bigger picture, it is everyone's eventual destiny to know the ecstasy of the Divine, both internally and while dancing in all of creation. Why not begin now?

A key message of this spiritual autobiography is the reframing of the perception of the flow of our lives as a constant teaching and as an often-hidden awareness gift of the Divine. The early chapters address an appreciation of the paradox and mystery of birth, death, and all the moments in-between as opportunities for spiritual growth and preparation for liberation. With this perspective, the challenges and everyday events of the course of our lives can be used for appreciating and understanding ourselves and expanding our consciousness from the multiple angles of our circumstances, including all the mundane happenings, from playing football to spiritual practices such as meditation.

I have discovered with a surprising sense of wonder and joy that in approaching my life in retrospect, I have found a new and expanded understanding that life is about the evolution of our consciousness toward God-merging/liberation. The rare experience of disappearing into the Nothing does not mean one is liberated. However, when one is sustained and established on a daily basis in this inner Nothing as one's primary life experience, one evolves into the life of Self-Realization/Liberation. In the process of disappearing into the nothing one loses any identification with a separate ego-I awareness as we no longer exist as a separate identity from the One.

The teachings in this book are not the sharing of external teachings based on spiritual theory. They are the actual reality of my internal consciousness through ongoing pre-liberation and post-liberation awareness from meditation, football experiences, living by the Six Foundations and Sevenfold Peace (a non-sectarian natural living path), and the constant trial by fire of everyday life. All of these traditions and experiences have given rise to the Holistic Liberation Way.

Poetry is sprinkled throughout this book and the last chapter is composed entirely of my poetry. I feel verse can often express what our rational mind cannot understand. Poetry is the language of the heart and soul.

— ⟋⟍ —

Nothing to Want

Existing in the mind,
We want everything.
In the consciousness of Disappearing into the Nothing,
There is nothing to want.
All that is left is pure awareness prior to I-ness and I Am-ness.
Our lives are our teaching.

— ⟋⟍ —

May you be blessed and may this sharing serve as teaching and inspiration for you to have the courage to regularly let go and keep Disappearing into the Nothing until there is no one left; and until eventually only awareness without an owner exists. As it says in the Torah (Exodus 33:20), "One cannot see God and live." Are you ready?

Teaching: The Holistic Liberation Way is a path and lifestyle approach to freedom on every level. Ultimately, it is everyone's destiny to know the ecstasy of the Divine, both internally and while dancing in all of creation.

Chapter 1

SWAMI MUKTANANDA: IGNITING THE SOUL ON FIRE

Teaching: The easiest way to awaken the Kundalini
is through the guru's grace of Shaktipat.

My intensely spiritual phase, the real beginning of my life, and ultimate liberation cycle began at age thirty-three and the initial stage was complete by the time I turned forty. It started with my first Shaktipat intensive at the Oakland Ashram in Oakland, California in November of 1975. At that time, I received Shaktipat from Swami Muktananda who had been acknowledged as a liberated enlightened being by his guru, *Sadguru* Sri Bagawan *Nityananda*. Swami Muktananda was a guru to tens of thousands of people around the world. He gave me Shaktipat by first hitting me with his peacock feather wand. He followed this by creating a funnel with his hand and blowing directly into my mouth. I was not expecting this, but I knew enough to deeply inhale his liberated *prana*. He then squeezed the bridge of my nose and gently pushed my head back. In the midst of this, my mouth spontaneously opened, and my tongue stuck out as far as it could go. I later discovered that these sorts of autonomous physical movements are known as *kriyas*. In this case, it is called *simhasana* (lion pose in yoga). While the lion was happening, I felt a peaceful, wavy bliss. After what seemed like a few minutes, I went into a deep meditation. In the midst of this process I intuitively felt that I was going to have my quest about the meaning of death answered, a quest that had started with my life-threatening case of tuberculosis at age one and the death of my brother, the human closest to me, when I was sixteen.

Teaching: Understanding and facing death is part of the reality of living life. It can be used to intensify our experience of the sacredness of and appreciation for life.

In retrospect, I see that my whole life up to this point had been a spiritual preparation for me to optimally receive and be spiritually awakened by my Shaktipat meditation from Swami Muktananda. Looking back, playing competitive football had been the first of many spiritual initiations that prepared me for this moment. On a spiritual level, Shaktipat was the beginning of my life.

I was born into the energy of transcendent death, an extraordinary introduction to this world. I arrived in May of 1943, during World War II, at Michael Reese Hospital in Chicago. In my first year,

I was diagnosed with miliary tuberculosis. In the early 1940s, chances of survival from tuberculosis were slim as no antibiotic treatment yet existed. Being sent to a tuberculosis sanatorium was almost a guarantee of death so, by pulling some strings with local doctors, my mother Rosalie was allowed to care for me at home. At the same time, my older brother Richard was bedridden and fighting for his life; he suffered from acute rheumatic heart disease with rheumatic kidney failure, also life-threatening diseases at that time. Two seriously ill boys slept in the same room; the bond we shared in being surrounded by potential death was as intense as life itself.

Miraculously, we both survived our childhoods.

Teaching: Death can be a liberation teacher.

I have lived long enough to share this story, which is not one of fear and survival, but of love, brotherhood, and life. In some mysterious way, my sweet, vague memories of this early time continued to prompt me to ponder the meaning of life and death. Understanding and facing death is part of the reality of living life fully, and it intensified my appreciation of the sacredness of life. What a wild way to start! God was meeting me at the portal with no holds barred. He was prescribing a lifelong quest for the meaning of death and ultimately the ineffable meaning of life. There is no explicit answer to this, but meeting Swami Muktananda and receiving Shaktipat put me on a path to the kinds of awakenings life provided in place of answers. Finding one's liberated spiritual teacher starts with an intuitive spiritual recognition.

Teaching: Facing death awakens us to life.

My family lived for the first three and a half years of my life on Grace Street (grace being what was needed at that time), near Wrigley Field, then home of the Chicago Cubs and Chicago Bears. Midway through my third year in this world, we moved to Highland Park, Illinois, a protected suburban environment. My sister Ann joined us, making me a middle child. I lived in that suburban setting until I left after high school to attend Amherst College.

Age three and a half and happy to be alive.

My parents Harvey and Rosalie were very loving and created a protective nest for us. Although suburban life was monotonous, it did not stop the cosmic play. At the age of four, I received my first inner guidance that I was to become a medical doctor. I had no conscious clue as to why, as no one in any of my family lineages had ever been in the medical profession. This Divine directive was received in a primordial, subconscious way as a deep, heartfelt, intuitive *dharmic* understanding of my life mission. In retrospect, it was my first intuitive listening and I had the call to follow the Will of God without hesitation or understanding. There was clearly a sense, even at 4 years old, that something more significant was going on behind the scenes, a feeling which I would call a sense of destiny and dharma.

Teaching: Many people experience this touch of the Divine at a young age. In other cultures, such as those in India and among the Huichol people of Mexico, the family also recognizes the calling and provides social support for manifestation of a destiny. In the West, we have to figure it out on our own.

Later, as an adult living in India, I was impressed and somewhat envious of the tremendous spiritual environment and training some Indian children are fortunate to receive. But God is also presenting us Westerners with spiritual mentorship, no matter what our environment is. This concept is known as *Guru Tattva,* "the world is the guru." Guru Tattva awareness is a way of viewing and experiencing the world that continuously supports our spiritual awakening.

Attending Elm Place, a public grammar school, I felt supported and cared for by the teachers. I also found an outlet for my energy in sports. For four years at Highland Park High School, a suburban public school, I was an honorable mention All-State football player, and a state-level tennis player. My Yogic *sattvic* being was getting expressed in the forms available. I also won the state science fair. In instance after instance, from football to science labs, I was bold enough to follow my unique gifts beyond the limits of my physical, emotional, mental, and spiritual understanding.

With parents after Amherst College a football game.

Teaching: Living one's life and life purpose
passionately is inherently empowering.

In the "growing up" process, even as a teen, I maintained relationships of reverence and love with both of my parents. In an age of dysfunctional families, this was a blessing beyond count. Not only did I feel my parents loved me, but they were in love with me with appropriate boundaries, and I was in love with them. During the time I was sick with tuberculosis, the depth of mother's love and her commitment to keeping me alive and healing me created a source of love and self-esteem that I have been able to transmit spiritually and curatively throughout my life to others. She directly and indirectly helped me understand that if I wished to survive, I needed to follow her directions. I learned to listen carefully and thoughtfully to women's words and a male-female alliance developed. My life depended on it. I continue to store and transmit Mother's healing to this day from its internalization in me, as potentized and integrated later by Swami Muktananada, Swami Prakashananda, and my other teachers.

Teaching: All of us, if we honestly examine
our childhood, will see the spiritually evolving
presence that God has gifted us with.

My elders recognized my spiritual tendencies as early as my eleventh year of life. Between sixth and eighth grade, I read one book a day, including many of the great classics. The reading teacher, Ms. White, told me that I had read more books than anyone in the school's one-hundred-year history. I was a voracious reader, driven by an urge for some mystery beyond my understanding.

Teaching: Trusting the subtle intuitive or
"knowing" flow of one's life is worth doing no
matter how unusual it appears to one's peers.

The leading conservative rabbi in the area, Rabbi Lipis, urged me to become a rabbi. He wasn't my rabbi, as he led a Conservative congregation, and our family belonged to the Reform North Shore

Congregation of Israel led by Rabbi Edgar Siskin. I knew the Rabbi
Lipis's insight would come true at some point, but I told him this
wasn't the right time. Even then, there was a strong feeling of a
beginner's mystical foresight to understand that there are layers and
timings of dharmic expression that emerge at different junctures.
Mine wasn't a clear rabbinical path like his, though it had early
Judaic benchmarks. I was headed toward a more fully focused path
of liberation.

Teaching: Our lives have specific timings and cycles;
being aware of this helps us navigate our life choices.

Seeds of the higher Torah teachings were instilled from the
beginning of my religious education, as I attended a Jewish "Sunday
School" once a week from kindergarten through sophomore year
in high school, the "coming of age" time in Reform Judaism with
its confirmation ceremony. Though acknowledged as the top
student in the confirmation class of 300, I felt I did not understand
anything about the Torah or the depths of Judaism. Being raised
Reform was like being born behind a spiritual door, shut out from
true Torah truth and mysticism. After the age of forty, my Jewish
religious training progressed to deeper spiritual levels because of
the profound spiritual inner experiences and teachings I gained in
India, which prepared me for deeper Torah study with high-level
rabbi mentors.

I did not do a *bar mitzvah* at the traditional age of thirteen
because Rabbi Siskin, the Reform rabbi, insisted upon attendance
at Hebrew classes for preparation at one specific time only, which

happened to be at the same time as football practice. There was no way I was going to give that up, as my primary spiritual experience then was playing football, not studying Torah. When I went beyond my physical limitations playing football, I came closest to experiencing the cosmic Truth beyond mind. Even at an early age, I had an understanding of the value of following my own guidance and sticking with what resonated meaningfully, versus trying to be part of the system.

As I was growing up, it was rare to share my inner world with anyone, including my loving parents, who cared deeply about me but did not have the spiritual background to appreciate or explain what was occurring. Visions of white-robed mystics in the desert appeared to me as early as 8 or 9 years old. Now I know that these figures had to do with my past lives as an Essene in the Qumran area near the Dead Sea. At that early age, I felt part of this white-robed group. Later, in adulthood, the dots connected, and I realized that I had been an Essene in past lives. At that time the power of these unusual, past life, mystical experiences were beyond my immediate comprehension. However, they subtly created a separation from my peers. I learned to keep my mystical experiences private.

Although I was raised in the more liberal Reform Judaism, the religious path wasn't taking me where I wanted to go. As a result, until the age of forty, I followed paths other than Judaism to fulfill my increasingly intense search for the direct apperception of and merging with God. Before forty, I was, however, involved in a moderate level of Jewish observance, such as fairly regular Shabbats and observing the High Holy Days. Just before I was leaving India in 1982, Swami Prakashanada gave me a directive to observe the dharma of the culture in which I was l living. On the last day of a forty-day fast in 1983, after partaking no juice or even water for the last three days, I received God's direct communication about my next dharma assignment. As I began to leave my body into the unbroken bliss of the Divine without the thought of returning, the Divine directive was to "return to my body" and "go to my roots". I interpreted this to mean for me to discover the Torah teachings of liberation.

Many years later after I became a father, neither of my children, Heather nor Rafael, participated in any formal Jewish education. Instead, we studied the seventeen-volume world-famous Torah commentary of Rabbi Ya'akov Culi (1689-1732), *Me'am Lo'ez*, when each was old enough to understand. It was their bedtime story for about three years for each young teen. I took sharing this religious and spiritual teaching with my children seriously.

Teaching: Parenting is for love, but also a dharma.

Chapter 2

DANCING IN THE ZONE

Teaching: Never give up! Instead, live ecstatically at one hundred and ten percent of your capacity.

---

*B*eing five feet, two inches tall as a high-school freshman, and weighing "a less than impressive" 112 pounds made me the smallest football player on the field. In this situation, my parents strongly did not want me to play. My brother Richard's intervention saved the day. My parents sent him as a scout to our high-school football practice, and he convinced them I would be able to play. After that, both of my parents attended all my high school football games and some of my college ones. Mother shared that the main reason she attended was to pray that I get up after each play.

My parents were professionals, and my mother had worked as a criminal psychologist early in their relationship, while my father

My wonderful father, Harvey K. Cousens, was not only a lawyer but also a lead actor in local Chicago theatre.

My loving mother, Rosalie Wahl Cousens, was a psychologist and stylish supermom.

was a lawyer in general practice. I was fortunate: they loved me unconditionally. All I had to be was my natural self. They related to me respectfully as a refined, inner-directed, spiritual, and ethical adolescent and later as a wise adult. This provided a background for my becoming a psychiatrist, holistic physician, and spiritual teacher.

Teaching: Parents' respect of the innate qualities
and strengths of their children is fundamental
to building self-esteem and self-respect.

Every evening after dinner, my father and I walked four blocks to Lake Michigan. I can't overstate the power and the specialness of this ritual because it created a close, loving bond that instilled a love that engendered solid self-esteem. This level of special connection is one of the most important gifts parents can give to their children and, half a century later, I retain a sense of gratitude for that.

As a young man, I was naturally unconventional. I had the impression that people did not know how to relate to me, perhaps because unlike most of my peers, alcohol, drugs, and young ladies were not an attraction to me. This was reinforced, actually, as I had learned since the age of 8 years old, to keep my inner world private. Over time, I became socially comfortable as an active bystander positioned on the outer edge of the popular circle. This socially learned "active bystander" way of relating has become a lifelong pattern of belonging to all the groups, yet being a member in none. My interaction was as a walker between all the worlds, not attached to any single world or social group—but only to God in a semi-aware way. This calling was instilled in me at a core level, an accumulation of past lives and soul learnings. It was a deep subliminal heeding, expressed through social life but arising from karmic impulses.

Teaching: It's vital to unconsciously and consciously develop a socially functional model for interaction with the world from a spiritual point of view. Touch but do not blend is an effective approach for maximally protecting one's spiritual life.

Although I was not openly rebellious in grammar or high school, I put my teachers on edge with complicated and often challenging questions. Although I was respectful of older authority figures, I refused to be sucked into what I perceived as mediocrity. It was fairly usual for me to come home with straight A's but critical comments from all my teachers on the issue of "self-control" (I call it "misunderstood enthusiasm"). I enjoyed sitting at the back of the class, raising my hand and, without being called, offering input or a perplexing question. Today this sort of participation by a student probably would result in their being given Ritalin to make it easier for the teachers.

Teaching: Innate activities express aspects of our archetypal past-life energetics.

During summer practice before my senior year in high school, muscle spasms developed along my left side and along my back. Because of the need to express the warrior energy within me and my love of the inner bliss of playing, I was unwilling to stop football for mere medical reasons. Chicago Bears football doctor, the late Teddy

Fox, M.D., a family friend, designed a steel brace for me to wear while playing to keep my back from arching and causing unbearable spinal-cord pain. This device made it possible for me to continue to play through four years of college.

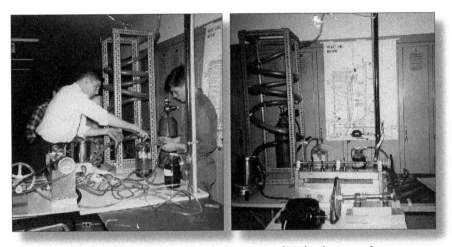

My heart-lung machine on display at High School science fair.

Teaching: Learning to play in one's life through pain is a vital lesson in persistence, endurance, and intensity that serves one well in everyday activities.

My innate sattvic tendencies (pure living and being inner-directed to the Truth of the Self) during my teenage years began to emerge distinct from my middle-class suburban paradigm. This inner-directed tendency created a sense of separation and differentiation from my peers. I did not feel comfortable with or share most people's level of understanding of life values or lifestyle, and the high school "in-group" viewed me as atypical. A pattern of "friendly bystander" seemed to work best for me.

Teaching: The Holistic Liberation Way teaches the importance of staying separate but, paradoxically connected, in order to protect spiritual unfolding.

***

When I was 16 years old my brother Richard at the age of 22 was killed in a car accident on his spring break, on his way to visit friends in Los Angeles. Before he drove away, he had come down the stairs from his room at the top of our house. I remember seeing him standing in the doorway of my bedroom. I was in bed with what had become my annual flu after football season. He gave me a loving look and a sweet "see you later" wave. It was the last time I would see him alive. His energy and light ended soon after on the physical plane, but that light, protection, and otherworldly guidance continued to remain a part of my life.

The brothers; older brother Richard holding me up.

Not only did I miss my brother, but I realized that I was mortal. I became more alienated socially, as I felt an internal soulful energy intensifying within me. Besides being a very dear friend, my brother had played many vital roles in my life. His death was and still is the most significant loss and energy transmutation of my life. It is interesting that a lifetime of awakening and liberation was activated by the energy of death. After Richard's passing, I was forced to become the strong one in the family, holding positive, healing energy.

***

A year later, as a junior in high school, I was somehow inspired to build a heart-lung machine. I know, pretty weird, even for the kid I've described. In 1959, even in hospitals, heart-lung machines were just coming out of the experimental phase. Dr. Moulder, who was doing experimental heart-lung surgery research at the University of Chicago gave me some training and the equipment needed to build one on my own. I used his used heart-lung machine pieces for the oxygenation part and developed a unique pump system with a cam shaft device to create a rhymical flow that would gently push the blood through in a way that theoretically would not cause any damage to the red blood cells. In this private mystical process, constructing a heart-lung machine became an act of creating life in the middle of Richard's bedroom. I could feel his presence there and would go into spontaneous meditation while symbolically recreating "life." My father, Harvey, a natural engineer, helped with some of the technical design aspects. The machine pulsed with its own life force, and it brought me happiness and soothed my soul.

Highland Park High School's district science fair became a motivation to complete the machine. In addition to Dr. Moulder, only one other person outside of the family knew about this science project. A dear friend, John Holder, helped me finish. We would take a break by wrestling on the front lawn—Johnny was an all-state high-school wrestler, so it was always a fun match. I realized that physical exertion was a way to increase endorphins. Wrestling brought relief from the pain of the grief of losing my brother.

My private, somewhat unconscious, healing process became public. This heart-lung project won the district science fair, and I was sent downstate to Champaign, Urbana, the main campus of the University of Illinois, for the state level of competition. My heart-lung machine received the top award there too. Many people commented on its unique phenomenon, when it was turned on, of pulsing in a way that made it seem alive, as if in an activated life-force state. I never publicly shared the deeper meaning of the experience.

Teaching: We are often given hints of important trends in our lives before we consciously access or choose them.

I visited and interviewed at Amherst, Yale, and Princeton, plus a few other colleges during spring vacation in my junior year of high school. This tour included an interview by the Yale and Princeton head football coaches. Amherst was my first choice because I found the level of lecture discussions over my head. In most of life's situations, I tended to choose the most provoking and growth-producing conditions. I also appreciated the informality of their dress code and the general lifestyle.

Teaching: For optimal emotional, mental, and spiritual growth, choose the most provoking and growth-producing conditions.

Although I applied to Amherst for early admission, I did not hear back at the appropriate time because they misplaced my college entrance application. By the time this was rectified, I had also received acceptance letters from Princeton and Yale and been offered a football scholarship to Michigan. During my college senior year, Amherst, Princeton, and Michigan were all undefeated. The top national players including ones from Michigan and Princeton, and me from Amherst, were chosen among eleven national scholar-athletes inducted into the College Football Hall of Fame. Even at that early age, I perceived it as a subtle yet powerful lesson about destiny. It was my karma to play on an undefeated college football team, whether at Amherst, Princeton, or Michigan, and to be an All-American College Football Scholar-Athlete. I was aligning with my destiny in a positive way and consciously distinguishing it from fatalism (a worldview that events are happening to one, in essence as a victim, with no influence on what is happening).

Teaching: Aligning with one's destiny asks one to develop spiritual sensitivity, especially in concert with meditation and prayer, to align consciously with the Divine Will.

I actually never considered that I was creating my reality as much as simply aligning my egoic will with the Divine Will. This approach is a matter of orientation to existence itself. At least this is believed in the Vedic, Buddhist, and Torah traditions.

Teaching: In the big, cosmic picture, there is no full free will. There is only the Will of God unfolding.

A way of understanding it on the metaphorical level is that God gives us the movie theater of our possible destinies, and we pick the movie but not the theater. In this way, there is room for the illusion of free-will choice on the physical plane, which is necessary for our spiritual evolution.

Teaching: The only real choice we do have in this paradoxical "free will" is to align our will with the Divine Will… or not… which will either elevate us on the spiritual path or deter us. God's overall Divine Will still happens, but we can make it spiritually hard or easy on ourselves by being liberated enough from our personal egos to make the spiritually elevating choice to align our will with the Divine Will.

One of the reasons for incarnating each lifetime is to resolve our past-life karmas so we can progress spiritually. In this context, another challenging lesson of my college football years concerned my lower back issue, actually diagnosed as a congenital defect known as spina bifida occulta. Karma is often associated in the present lifetime with physical pain. Successful inquiry into and healing of karmas, from the physical to the spiritual, require persistence and forbearance in the face of obstacles. I later learned that this character quality of endurance is called *netzach* (victory) on the Tree of Life in the *Kabbalah*. Expressing the power of netzach (persistence and forbearance), served me tremendously well. I observed when I held a victim consciousness, or disadvantaged or "poor me" attitude, it was a significant impediment and block to my spiritual life.

Teaching: We are all uniquely given the
karmas we need for our spiritual evolution and
liberation, whether comfortable or not.

Before each practice and game, I had my lower back taped up to protect it from arching and going into spasm. My lower-back spasm pain continued over the years and became so severe that, during medical school, I had to carry a pillow to sit on during classes.

After my father's death in 1965, my mother eventually remarried. Her new husband, Jerry Greenspahn, was an orthopedic surgeon. I was twenty-eight when he examined my back and made the diagnosis in five seconds; then he did the appropriate surgical intervention to finally cure it on the physical plane. We joked in a humorous way that he was heroic because he would have had to deal with my mother if he had made a mistake! My lower back has been pain-free for the last fifty years, with the support of daily Tri-Yoga which I learned from my Yoga instructor and eventual wife, Shanti Golds Cousens. All these family players helped me complete my body karma. The back operation was my first experience with surgery and also being a patient in a hospital. My Kundalini awakening in 1975 (which included intense lower back pain for a few days) appeared to be the final healing of this past-life karma on the subtle plane.

Teaching: Being pain-free and flexible is an indication
of a fully resolved karma complex on the physical plane.

Throughout my college years, much of my time was spent alone in study and research. I was given my own laboratory to do my biochemistry thesis research. I also built a more advanced heart-lung machine in my senior year. Although I enjoyed the challenge of the academic world, what stayed with me was an unrelenting interest in the mysteries of death, and ultimately life. After sharing some of this developing spiritual mysticism with my college peers, I quickly discovered I was alone in these realms. Ironically, this even remained an issue, although less so, when I was in Swami Muktananda's traveling ashram years later. There were a few people in the ashram, especially a few of the swamis, with whom I could share the various in-depth levels of my ongoing inner world experiences. It was important to be "seen" in this inner world. Many people feel alone on the spiritual path, and part of my role these days as a spiritual teacher is to touch people's hearts in a way that supports them, so they no longer feel solitary.

Teaching: When one feels connected to the Divine, one never feels alone but still it is beneficial to have people who understand one on the deeper levels.

One of my great teachers in my preparation for Shaktipat awakening was the power of "Guru Tattva" eyes, or seeing the world as the guru, in which even the experience of playing football became a spiritual guide. To my astonishment, I was elected both the captain of the freshmen football team and also eventually became captain of the varsity team at Amherst. I brought a spiritual love and a deep brotherhood connection to the gridiron, though I didn't understand these beyond locker-room fellowship at the time. I am convinced that this brotherhood energy was one reason we were not only undefeated but ranked number one on the East Coast for small colleges. For me, a dharmic warriorship energy became a basic football lifestyle that seemed to spontaneously transmit as an energy to my teammates. Before each game began, I prepared with what I now understand to be meditation. I entered into the game loose, relaxed, and with a calm mind. In that way, my energy was focused, allowing quick movement in any direction.

Teaching: Persistence, forbearance, and meditation-enhanced intuition are keys to success.

The same attention and energy led me to be a high-level college and tournament tennis player. I even defeated nationally ranked opponents. At a deeper level tennis had very little spiritual energy. Football was a primordial war game, an opportunity to experience the deeper Truth of who I was; even with opposing teams I shared a sort of camaraderie as fellow reincarnated warriors. When Amherst played its last game of the season against an undefeated Williams College team, I tackled their lead player, a halfback, in the first sequence of plays. He was slow getting up. Giving him a hand to help him seemed natural, and we exchanged smiles. That was subtle and rare, but never did I feel anger toward anybody on the opposing team. Even at the early age of 21, I knew innately it was just a game and we were all one. In retrospect, football was direct experiential training for the larger game of life.

Teaching: From an expanded view, healthy spiritual warriorship is about life mastery and applies to almost every situation and context.

Spiritual life is supported by knowing the playbook of natural temporal and cosmic absolute-reality laws, even on the football field. This quality is known in the Torah tradition as *mussar* which means spiritual discipline in general and specifically spiritual discipline of morals and ethics. "Dirty" playing, which includes acting without morality and ethics, depletes the potential spiritual energy of the game and of the person acting that way. The best players and teams always seemed to play the game honorably, which is the Torah quality known as *kavod*.

Teaching: Kavod or respect is about living one's life honorably as a spiritual warrior. This has become increasingly challenging in today's spiritually and morally chaotic world.

I had developed nearsightedness by the age of sixteen from too much reading, so I learned to be guided intuitively by the overall movement of the other football team, rather than seeing exactly what was going on in detail. This initiated my reliance on more of a "right brain" flow rather than a "left brain" concrete "vision," which carried over to my life in general.

Teaching: It is important to try our hardest, but yet learn to simultaneously be in a state of "letting go" with the realization that the world is forever out of our control.

Mystical football experiences began for me as a pre-teen. I would spontaneously move into a sense of oneness awareness, which was both trippy and seductive. Trance states for me were a byproduct of game intensity. They occurred during practice also, but more often in the games, as they turned intense situations on the field into cosmic revelations. The more I went beyond my physical limitations, the more I had flashes of the Truth. In a semi-aware way, I felt this expanded spiritual consciousness was growing and subtly stabilizing within me.

I had a particularly profound awakening during a high-school game against Niles Township. Niles was ahead seven to six with two minutes to go. We were on our two-yard line. Our quarterback, Mickey Panther, who had a strong passing arm, called for a down-the-middle sixty-yard "alley-oop pass". After blocking the opposing lineman's pass rush, I looked up to see the Niles player intercept the pass. The game seemed over, but then our split end, Larry Berbe, stole it out of the Niles player's hands and ran for a touchdown. We won the game thirteen to seven. Destiny had overridden the apparent situation and we went from certain defeat to a last-second win. I stood muddied, wet, and tired, on our two-yard line in amazement at the turn of events.

Another teaching came in college, with a severe left ankle injury during the previous week's game which had me on crutches for the whole week with a slim possibility of playing in the next contest against Tufts. Miraculously, I found myself able to walk without crutches on the day of the game, so my coach allowed me to suit up, but he kept me on the bench as a backup. The field was muddy, and our team seemed bogged down. The score was zero to zero, our undefeated season in jeopardy. The coach, obviously upset about the situation, in desperation finally sent me into the game. The quarterback called the next few plays with me as lead blocking guard opening holes for our running backs and we marched down the field and scored the only touchdown of the day. I was surprised at some level that my spirit and energetic power were able to influence and uplift a whole team, even from the position of offensive guard. At the end of the season, I was the co-captain of an undefeated Amherst football team, selected as All New England middle linebacker and offensive guard and the top football scholar athlete in the New England region. It was a lesson in the meaning of dharma which is "right action" in whatever context one is living.

Being among the smallest people on the team, I needed to play intensely, courageously, with focused speed and abandon. At some point in the midst of such intensity during one game, a unique insight occurred to me— "This is just a game; so why am I taking it so seriously?"

That inner question activated an existential moment that could have been paralyzing on the field. It had the opposite effect, however, leading me to play the game as if it was real… partly to survive, but more importantly to BE the living potential of the moment. This game situation reality was a training arena for my soul, and at least unconsciously for the other souls present, although it may not have been real in an absolute sense, it was spiritually meaningful. For me, every part of it was intensely loaded with experiences of spiritual transformation, God experiences, and the deepest purpose of life. Although we may be attracted to the big flash of a cosmic breakthrough (a long pass), spiritual life is usually three or four yards and a cloud of dust. In other words, spiritual life is one that requires a persistent one-step-at-a-time approach.

Teaching: We slowly, but consistently, build
our capacity to hold spiritual energy and develop
our spiritual understanding and wisdom until the
flash of the illuminated breakthrough occurs.

After my playing days, as football dissipated by morphing into life itself, I realized that daily existence was also just a game, continually providing situations for me to grow spiritually. I was committed to experience the light of God released in every situation and play. This insight became a valuable way to reap the spiritual benefits not only from football but of being put on this earth plane. Over time, I began to see everything in our so-called "mundane life" as a spiritual experience waiting to be recognized so that, as we witness its essence, we expand our consciousness. Everything was a game and more than a game. On one level, two opposing teams banged into each other, trying to defeat each other according to the rules and measure of the scoreboard. On another level, we were a bunch of college kids having fun. On a yet deeper level, we had that oneness experience. This realization of the dual planes of existence laid the foundation for the corollary understanding that my personality and the roles I, and all of us, play are cases of mistaken identity. I began to understand part of spiritual life and liberation involves waking up from this dream of the illusion of the ego and personality,

---

Teaching: The key to popping out of the matrix in
which we believe we are our roles and personalities
is to awaken to the cosmic truth of who we were,
are, and will be before the illusion of our I-Am-ness
and roles existed and, thus, who we are not.

Being a football player was a role, and our positions and plays are like personalities. The awakening is not out of the game but into, through and beyond it. On the football field, a team has the unique opportunity to experience what dynamic oneness is. A powerful example of this was in the third game of our undefeated season, we were playing Bowdoin University, a team that was not only also undefeated at that time but ranked number one, ahead of us, on the East Coast. At halftime, Bowdoin was up by eighteen to zero, an imposing and seemingly insurmountable deficit. Coming out of the half time break, my team went into a do-or-die mode. It was beyond our perceived limitations of who and what we were. We came out playing at a different physical, mental, and spiritual capacity. In my position as middle linebacker, something happened beyond my understanding. I became energetically and physically unstoppable. Soon our whole defense linked into a unified field of ecstatic ferocity beyond human endurance—a collective "in the zone" experience. Not only did we stop them on virtually every play, but, late in the third quarter, I collided head-on with their star quarterback, who was trying to escape from our pass rush. He suffered a concussion and was knocked out of the game. However, it was the turning point of the game. I am not proud of knocking him out of the game and it was not intentional. With six seconds to go, we scored the winning touchdown to win nineteen to eighteen. It was unbelievable! We had defied earth-plane odds to manifest our full destiny. As a group energized and unified with almost supernatural inspiration, leading by doing, we spiritually united in an almost beyond understanding, indefatigable, undefeatable transcendent consciousness as part of a cosmic whole.

The Bowdoin game was a lesson in control over the mentally disturbing focus of being behind eighteen to zero with only the second half left. To win this game we unconsciously called on the *Vedic* character qualities of *shama* and *dama* (control of the mind and senses) in order to go beyond our limitations and focus on the goal of the game of life, which is always God. Coming from behind and winning, though central at the time, masked the real lesson and our collective experience of the Divine in action.

Another form of oneness awareness occurred in our last game against Williams College in the previous season. We were tied zero to zero with two minutes left. We drove from our twenty-yard line in a unified trance, playing flawless football, marching down the field in unison to score in the last few seconds. These were lessons of the power of human group unity and what we can do collectively in the unifying power of our humanness when inspired by who we naturally are.

Teaching: We live in an illusory world and when we wake up, there is no illusion of a three-dimensional world but only "That."

Developing virtues through the intense experiences of football was a distinct part of my preparation to be optimally ready to receive the Shaktipat initiation. Football brought me the closest to the experience of the ultimate Truth beyond the emptiness of what is often called the "big mind", or actually any mind at all. I was spontaneously experiencing "the zone" before the concept became known. Life itself is a spiritual "game"; football, in a sense, provided the opportunity for a spiritual awakening within the game. It might not be played or understood that way by most but for me, experiencing my life through a spiritual worldview it certainly was.

The reality that the game clock is always ticking was also an important spiritual message. It is essential to take advantage of every moment in this body on this earth plane. I feel everything I do here counts. Living has become a full-time conscious effort of maintaining and expanding my spiritual awareness, wisdom, and truth. Understanding my time for the physical body on the earth plane is limited inspires me to make every moment a conscious focus on the intent of liberation. I discovered when my timing was fully aligned with the game plan (Divine Will) and with oneness in the creative flow I became more ready to open to my fullest spiritual potential and my ability to distinguish between the cosmic Truth and the temporal reality.

Teaching: Football is just a game in the "game of life," so the "game of life" is just a game and daily preparation for waking up to the real purpose of life which is to know God and merge into the Divine.

In retrospect, football honors and builds the same virtues and character qualities considered by saints and sages as prerequisites for holding the higher teachings and eventually becoming liberated. Most major Eastern and Western traditions specifically insist that one be considered mature or ripe enough to truly live by the perennial moral and ethical teachings, which are needed as a foundation for sustaining and expanding spiritual life before one can be given even deeper liberation teachings of the cosmos. Going beyond myself through the extended effort of playing football was the closest I came to experiencing the deeper Truth of who I was before my Shaktipat meditation.

The twelve years I played football from fourth grade to senior in college helped me cultivate the character qualities, strengths, and life insights I needed to receive higher awarenesses in spiritual life and become prepared to receive the awakening of the Kundalini energy from Swami Muktananda.

The actual academics of Amherst College tended to be intellectually and spiritually dry, so the experience of playing football was the balancing motivation to stay in school. Yet it was clear that after my football career ended in 1964, I would have to find other ways to be in the zone. Eventually the way revealed itself... meditation. It took me much deeper into the zone than football and into and beyond the mysterious non-dual/dual paradoxical truth of the Divine. It is, at the least, humorous that my initiation into the world of Truth started with playing football.

It often takes a subtle understanding to be aware that a certain dharma has completed itself. Letting go of obvious completed football dharmas was an empowering precursor to the bigger completed-dharma decisions that would be made throughout my life.

Teaching: It is critical for our evolution to
know when a dharma has been completed.

At Amherst College, I was mostly immersed in my studies and research. I enjoyed working late into the night and into the early morning until around 2 a.m. and getting up around 8 am. The meditative silence in the laboratory late evenings was wonderfully peaceful. It was a steady, gentle God-communion, as if I was being introduced to the life of a *sadhu* (monkish spiritual aspirant). This outward alone time was a precursor preparation for the many hours I would later spend in direct meditation for the rest of my life.

***

Teaching: Ending grieving is accepting the bigger
picture of one's destiny and trusting in God's Divine
mystery. Excessive grieving can become an affront
to God's expression of the very nature of Being.

On March 20, 1965, my father had a second heart attack. At the time of his first heart attack, I had gone home to support him. My father and I were close and still kissing on the lips when greeting and parting. I had a great deal of respect and appreciation for him but was aware that he had become increasingly depressed since the death of my brother Richard. In addition, his own father had died of a heart attack at the age of 57. This was my father's exact age at the time of his death. I saw in my father how prolonged grief can separate one from God and even from life. It is not that one shouldn't grieve, it is a matter of understanding and accepting the Divine nature of life and death.

Now at seventy-seven years around the sun, I am grateful to have lived beyond the fifty-seven-year mark of my father and grandfather as well as many of the men on my mother's side who died of heart attacks before the age of fifty, including her father and her brother. This early death pattern on both sides of my family played an essential unconscious/conscious role in my study of diet to find an optimally healthy lifestyle to prevent heart attacks. This approach included a vegan, organic, live-food diet which fortunately is also the best approach physically, emotionally and mentally for becoming a superconductor of the Divine in spiritual life. This became the basis of my spiritual nutrition teachings.

Teaching: To the human logical mind, things may seem unfair or fair, but the details of the laws of karma are mysterious, and nothing is ever fair or equal; the events of our life are only for our spiritual evolution if we understand that whatever God gives us is for the best.

A curious side note in exploring my family lineage is that my father at the age of eleven and grandfather had escaped from Bialystok, Russia (now Poland) in 1917 and walked across Europe. They left their village for a hopefully better life after years of anti-Semitic pogrom attacks by villagers and the Cossacks. They found their way to England and then to Ellis Island in New York. My grandfather restarted his Bialystok profession as a baker in Chicago. My family on my grandfather's side claims to have even invented the Bialy bagel, which I find humorous since I live on a live-food, plant-source cuisine. On my father's side I am genetically from the Levite Tribe which according to DNA tests, show thirty-seven Levite genes. Seventy members of my family on my father's side were killed in the Holocaust in Poland during World War II. In three different concentration camps, I later did ceremonies for releasing the lost souls as part of my effort to support their reincarnation evolution.

On my mother's side, my lineage includes her brother who played center on the West Point football team. My grandfather on my mother's side immigrated from Alsace-Lorraine when it was French dominated, and I was named Gabriel after my great uncle whose family still lives in that area. My grandfather was a very successful architect, contractor and interior decorator who built the Coast Guard Academy. He went bankrupt in the crash of 1929; my mother lauded his strong post-crash determination and "never giving up" attitude. She strongly emphasized the modelling of her family lineage of hard working creative spiritual warrior energies. At the beginning of my 3,700-year lineage was Abraham, the original enlightened *Ivri* (boundary crosser), and total spiritual warrior. He also demonstrated the fearless power needed to break outside of the matrix as a boundary crosser, an essential quality needed for liberation.

Teaching: Although it is important to live in the present, it's also useful to connect to one's lineage energies.

This lineage understanding was part of my developing awareness that I was and am living simultaneously in the past, present, and future. I call this the awareness of living in the Eternal Presence.

***

After Dad's death, I was so distracted I could only marginally study for my courses. I tried to immerse myself in research for my biochemistry thesis, which was original research on an aspect of the amino acid citrulline's metabolism published in *Biochemical and Biophysical* (Research Communications Vol. 24, no.3 1966). At a ceremony at the Waldorf-Astoria in New York City, I was honored as one of eleven national college Scholar Athletes. The character and quality of humility of my other ten colleagues was impressive in every interaction from talking to eating our steak meal. Not all of them were going to study with Swami Muktananda or practice veganism, but they could have, or maybe might have in another lifetime.

At the ceremony, the head coach of West Point praised his All-American awardee player, for only making three errors per "game."

It was a shock, as I had been upset about making three mistakes per year! At that moment my focus on perfectionism simply lost its place as a way of life. A famous pro-football Hall of Famer by the name of Kyle Rote was sitting next to me. He was the legendary #44 of the New York Giants. After hearing in the presentation that I had built a heart-lung machine in my free time, he surprised me by actually asking for my autograph. His sincere humility was itself liberating and inspirational.

Teaching: What we do and who we are genuinely affects each other. We have both the power to inspire each other to greater heights… or to the lowest depths. This is why the community is so important on the spiritual path. One benefits from the communion of uplifting company and friends.

At the end of my football career, I wrote my first poem as part of my transition into new phases of my life.

—✤—

Street Shoes

The shower's sullen drip
Plays its poem in his damp ears:
The foot pushes through a pile
Of jerseys and yellowed socks as he slips
Through the big door and his head clears.
Stepping through the hot dog wrappers
Flopping in a windy sea of grass and paper cups;
Silent bleachers sag a lonely gray.

The player's shadow is on the field where once
With churning cleats, he got his shots.
The crowd, in another land, roars and has its fun.
Hands squeeze into pockets for something lost,
But it is on the field, and he must walk away.
Gray slacks, a shirt, and street shoes feel light.
Neither glories nor honors can bring
It back;
It taunts, tucked in the muddy field
In the acid aired locker room;
It is felt in crunching block and ringing thud.
… The Gold of this game.
Cheering crowds and pretty words
Like street shoes lead away from it.

—〜〜—

Teaching: As in football, we must play the game of life intensely, as if real, to receive the fullest spiritual teaching and growth from each experience, yet remembering it is just a game.

Looking at the game of football, or any other sport for that matter, in its metaphoric totality, opens one up to a world of useful spiritual evolutionary metaphors associated with learning to play on the field of life in a way that elevates us spiritually. For example, the national anthem is always sung at the beginning of the game. It transforms the football playing field into a field of the Divine and the players into spiritual warriors. It was always compelling and vital to be singing in unity with the opposing team in our mutually agreed upon game of intensified spiritual practice. Singing the national anthem together symbolized a transcendent linking of our oneness amid our illusion of *duality*. The opening anthem symbolizes that we don't play the game of life alone, because we live in a social context. This becomes a song of the culture of life, liberation, and peace, in which love, harmony, and connecting with one's soul (and all the players' and fans' souls too) merges all together in a Divine field where we become One.

Teaching: The meaning of "team" is about learning to live as a unique individual in a collective oneness.

It was in this context that I experienced being a player on the holy cosmic field of life. At a spiritually refined level, I was being taught to start every action as a sacred prayer and meditation with an invocation of love. Playing football was training for living life as a spiritual warrior and ultimately for developing warrior mastery. My twelve years of football offered continual spiritual initiations in both character development and every aspect of spiritual life.

My poem, "Street Shoes" appeared in the second issue of *Io*, a journal at Amherst edited by Richard Grossinger, who later started North Atlantic Books and published many of my books years later. The inspiration for the poem came as I was walking out of the locker room onto the empty field after the final game as a period of soul-touching transition from warrior to civilian to the next stage of spiritual life warriorship. For nearly three years, I avoided any form of athletics until I found a way to be physically active that supported my health while not arousing the football energy. To this day, fifty-seven years later, I have never seen another full football game, in person or on television or ever played tennis again.

Chapter 3

BEGINNING TO DISCOVER MY DHARMA

There are classically four wheels to the dharma vehicle. The first is living according to cosmic, ethical, and moral ways in one's chosen tradition. The second is making enough money—or providing equivalent services and resources to support one's spiritual life. The third is one's specific dharmic mission (or missions) according to the time and space of one's life cycle dharma. It often includes carrying out a particular life work and way of living that elevates one spiritually.

The fourth and the most important is to know God in the form of God-merging or liberation. What was happening for me was a more active, but subtle, introduction to this highest dharma as well as the other levels of dharma which specifically guided the direction of my life's work.

Teaching: When one experiences the nectar
and bliss of the Divine within one's life work, it
is a strong hint that it is indeed one's life dharma
in the cosmic picture at that point in time.

During 1964 and 1965, while in college, I also had the opportunity to begin my humanitarian service during the summers with a teenage gang called the Valiant Lords on the South Side of Chicago. On one level they were innocent young men and women just trying to survive and who knew nothing of life's potential beyond their four to six city block territory. In the daytime, I was doing biochemistry research at the University of Chicago. After work, it was a short bus ride to Abraham Lincoln Center where I worked with the gang members. It appeared I was the only white person for a few miles around, but after a while people in the neighborhood stopped staring at me. We would often play a pick-up game of basketball to start our connection. Although a mediocre player, there was one great lesson that I received from playing basketball. Some days, I could not miss a shot, but most of the other days I was not very accurate. The gang members were fascinated by how quick I was on defense and blocking shots but could not seem to understand why I was such a bad shot. It became clear to me that like women do, guys also had cycles. I even researched it up and learned that there were indeed biorhythms based on one's birthdate. It was fascinating to begin to work with those cycles to optimize my activities. Besides basketball and listening to my tapes of all of Malcolm X's talks, the gang and I would engage in a variety of different adventures. We even got, through ties with the city of Chicago, an empty lot and created a community garden. Malcolm X was the leader the gang members could relate best to.

I actually knew Malcolm X over the phone and had set up for him to come to Amherst College to speak, but at the last moment he had to cancel because as he expressed to me, something larger than the Nation of Islam, which he had just split from, was trying to assassinate him. I had all of his tapes and appreciated the street-wise, sophisticated teaching Malcolm X provided, which expanded the gang members' consciousness beyond just survival in their neighborhood territory. It was surprising to me that none of the gang members expected to live past their early to late twenties. Because of this, it wasn't such a big deal to shoot each other or to shoot neighboring gang members, because they didn't feel they had much to live for anyway. There was a level of quiet, reality-based desperation, and it was important for me to understand this. It was challenging to help them overcome this collective feeling and is a challenging part of my dharma to help people wake up to our cosmic oneness. It is a joy to experience how many people are able to change their perspective back to the big cosmic picture and truth and open up again to the great teaching of Leviticus 19:18 of "love your neighbor as yourself".

One memorable intense highlight of my work there was when the gang stopped a spontaneous riot situation from turning violent. Abraham Lincoln Center was located across from a densely popu-lated tenement housing where this riot almost happened. One man had gotten angry, had a gun, and was threatening to shoot someone.

A large crowd gathered around him, and a bus driving through the main street, where people had gathered, did not stop in time and hit a child. The streets suddenly filled with a few thousand angry people on this hot summer evening. Our gang under my direction spontaneously decided to quell the riot, which we did very successfully by energetically and physically taking charge of the situation. It was a unique empowerment of the core gang leadership with the direct understanding for them that they had the power to be an active force for good. The police arrived on the scene a few minutes after the potential riot started and thoughtfully looked on without trying to intervene in our obviously successful efforts. We were so successful that the senior regional police lieutenant met with us afterward to thank the gang members. It was not only to thank us, but also to try to understand how we non-violently quelled the riot. It was a considerable source of self-esteem for the gang. This was an incredible transformative point in time for them. Also, during my two-year period working with the Valiant Lords, nobody was killed which is a commentary on the power of real human to human respectful and loving contact. The power to positively upgrade people's lives is humbling.

After this near riot incident, the head of the Abraham Lincoln Center, Ann, pushed me even harder to think about becoming a social worker, as she felt so positively about the work being done. But I intuitively knew it was not my main dharma in the world at that point in time and neither was being a medical biochemistry researcher, which was a major decision I was thinking about before entering Columbia Medical School. Exploring different life efforts is a practical way to draw some clarification on one's dharma.

Teaching: Understanding the timing of
one's dharma is another spiritual lesson in
the personal dharma drama question.

During my senior year of college my medical career direction seemed to be toward biochemical, medical research. For a few summers during high school and college, I had worked at Hektoen Institute of Medicine at Cook County Health & Hospital System (CCHHS) in Chicago as an assistant in leukemia research, the only white person among black professionals and one of the youngest in the group. Most of the group had come up directly from Mississippi and over time shared their life experiences with me which was quite educational. I developed a friendship with a young African American woman from Mississippi named Nelda.

One day, as we were eating lunch together on the lawn on the hospital property, we were verbally attacked and even threatened by an older, bigger, white hospital worker—blatant racism. Although he was larger, I was about to physically respond when Nelda intervened. After that, she did not want to be seen with me publicly outside of our laboratory. As a first-generation immigrant, racism like anti-Semitism was not a new phenomenon for me. Seeing street mob violence in the United States has always evoked ancestral family memories of prior demonic pogroms, Mussolini's Black Shirts, and Hitler's infamous Brown Shirts. No one taught me about this dark spiritual energy in any sort of detail, not even my parents. It's a way of perceiving that I seemed to have brought into the world from past-life memories. Nelda's haunting response to the white hospital worker's threats provided me with a contemporary insight into the insidiously

damaging effects of racism and anti-Semitism. Now, having met
people from 128 different countries, while having taught in forty-two
of them, tuning into the light and love in someone's heart and soul
beyond the appearance of five-sense perception of outer differences
is a key to successfully and safely walking in these different worlds.

Amherst College had turned out to be an excellent choice for
my overall unfoldment as an evolving intellectual person and it also
prepared me for medical school. Living in a city presented a new
opportunity for a different type of social and political growth. After
the high scientific and intellectual quality and standards of Amherst
College, Columbia University was a general and mild intellectual
disappointment. I was frustrated with the lack of classical scientific
context, methodology, and intellectual process. I found the "clinical
science" appeared to be mostly medical mythologies that we were
required to memorize. Fortunately, there were also certain clinical
professors, who understood and shared my perception of the situation, as well as some of my Amherst classmates at Columbia P&S.

While attending Columbia P&S I also lived and worked in
Central Harlem one block from Harlem Hospital and Big Wilt's
Smalls Paradise, a nightclub where Nora and I would go dancing.
Compared to the South Side of Chicago, which was an intense
inner-city survival experience, Harlem in New York City was like
going to the suburbs.

Nora and I were married in 1967. Nora worked as a physical
therapist at Roosevelt Hospital, and she was courageous enough
to move in with me in our Central Harlem brownstone, which we
shared with two other Amherst teachers working in Harlem. We
lived twelve blocks north of the Apollo Theater, where we would
walk to see performers like James Brown. Central Harlem was an

exciting, enjoyable, and politically sophisticated place in which to live. This sophisticated Harlem culture integrated us peacefully and created a supportive space to create a grammar school preventative health program for half of the Central Harlem schools. It was also a historical time of intense community political organizing for me. I was elected the first president of the Student Health Association, which represented all the medical schools in the New York Area. During this time, as part of upholding medical student dharma, I still studied hard and loved the clinical aspects of medical school. By upholding my medical student dharma, I managed to stay somewhere in the top third of the medical school class while doing my community organizing in Central Harlem. It was common to miss a night of sleep to make the timing of all this work.

The profound chronic crisis of my medical school experience was that most professors and students, with a few exceptions, did not have any grasp of the meaning of real holistic healing or any interest in spirituality. It was the late '60s, and I intuitively felt this lack of understanding, without even knowing the word "holistic." My interface strategy was to stay on the edge of this little medical society world as the active bystander. Medical school and the allopathic paradigm for healing and life in general seemed radically untenable. I fantasized about a life career as a doctor with a broader understanding but was not able to envision what it would be. The whole experience was becoming *dharmically* uncomfortable. Fortunately, a dramatic breakthrough of what to do about my career emerged in my third year of medical school during the internal medicine clinical training time. As a lowly third-year medical student there were five successive patient breakthroughs that I made that no one could solve from the resident to the staff physician. Creating breakthroughs with these "unsolvable cases" dramatically changed my career trajectory. One example of this was the case of a woman who the doctors were unable to diagnose and treat at three major medical centers in New York City before coming to Columbia P&S. They thought she had some strange pituitary abnormality. No physical diagnosis could be made. However, in an innocent and intuitively holistic way, tradition was broken by doing a unique thing. I actually talked with the patient rather than just looking at her tests. It was clear this woman was psychotically and somatically depressed. As a third-year medical student, my position wasn't strong enough to declare that this was the diagnosis, but by insisting on getting an onsite consultant from the psychiatry department, the correct diagnosis was established. An incredible psychiatrist, Dr. Mesnikoff, came to do the interview and he was brilliant. He made it very clear that the diagnosis was correct, and once they began to treat her, she did recover from her psychotic depression and her psycho-somatic diseases.

Teaching: There is value in thinking outside the box.

The other four cases were solved in the same "holistic" intuitive way with some variations. The psych consult was brought in on every single case. Each severely medically ill patient turned out to have some type of severe psychosomatic dysfunction. Although today mind-body is not a new approach, at that time in the '60s at Columbia P&S, the idea that the mind affected the body was more on the *avant-garde* side of things. Through these clinical experiences, the field of psychiatry became very attractive to me.

***

My mother's new husband was an orthopedic surgeon by the name of Dr. Jerry Greensphan, who sincerely wanted me to join his practice. Since I had a significant amount of experience with injuries in almost every joint in my body from my football and tennis years, it was a natural fit. The head of the orthopedic research department at Columbia, the famous Dr. Andrew Bassett, president of the American Orthopedic Association at the time, also strongly pushed me in that direction. However, the pre- and post-operative orthopedic surgeon locker room was a mix of golf stories, business discussion, and high school football locker room talk. As much as it was all laid out for me, I realized that this was not the most appropriate dharmic career or life choice.

Teaching: Some say: "If it's easy its good," as a dharma guideline. The deeper teaching is that it doesn't matter if it is easy or hard, it needs to be the path of service in life that best creates the situation that supports one's liberation.

And so, much to my dharmic surprise, as a third-year medical student, I began spending a lot of time in the psychiatry department attending as much of the psychiatry residents training program as possible. Several of the psychiatry residents became friends and we would hang out together endlessly discussing the subtleties of the mind and communication. At that time psychiatry seemed the most holistic approach to healing.

Fortunately, at the New York Psychiatric Institute, at that time, there was a heavy emphasis on dynamic psychotherapy and not merely fitting people into diagnosis code numbers and giving them a current drug to meet the diagnosis, as is the trend today. Making the heart connection, resonating with clients and talking to them, was both attractive and challenging. I strove to learn how to uplift and transform consciousness. From my new vantage point of the psychodynamic perspective I began to understand, feel, and conceptualize that a key essence of the healing process was making a heart connection so that the client felt cared for. This helped to create a mutual healing intent on every level. The physical emotional, mental, and spiritual integration approach to healing is still the foundation of my holistic physician's healing approach.

Teaching: The spiritual lesson is that dharma is mysterious.

During this time, I also chose to begin the powerfully evolving spiritual dharma of marriage and family. Our marriage was the start of a major spiritual dharmic path which included my commitment to our marriage and soon-to-be parenthood.

Teaching: Marriage done with the right
understanding is both about love and is a
primordial spiritual path to liberation.

***

I met Nora, my wife to be, at Wisconsin University during the summer of 1964 by "accident." I was actually driving up from outside of Chicago looking for a former girlfriend, and Nora answered the door of their communal living space. This "chance" meeting, that seemed to be unusual and a mysteriously awkward moment, did not make sense at that time. In retrospect, when I saw her my heart began to pound and I felt a little shaky. I now understand it was because I was meeting my future wife before we were "supposed" to meet. Later in 1966, we connected more as a potential couple when she was doing a physical therapy internship in Chicago, and while I was doing biochemistry research at the University of Chicago and working with the Valiant Lords at night. We continued our connection while she was working as a physical therapist at Roosevelt Hospital in NYC, and while I was attending Columbia P&S medical school and living in Central Harlem. From there, our relationship developed into marriage in 1967.

Nora and I had the same religious backgrounds, and our grandparents came from the same place near the border of Poland and Russia, next to and in Bialystok, from where my father and grandfather immigrated. We developed a gentle, loving, intimate connection on many levels, and we married in Teaneck, New Jersey where she grew up. We went to Israel for our honeymoon after the Six Day War in 1967. There was something storybook and classic old world about our developing relationship and marriage; as if Fiddler on the Roof was the music playing in the background. Beyond celebrating our new marriage, this Israel visit was an eye-opening experience and life-changing for me, in ways which did not really manifest in my work in Israel until thirty-three years later.

Nora bravely moved in with me in Central Harlem where we lived up until the time when Martin Luther King Jr. was assassinated in 1968. After MLK's death, it wasn't good to be a white couple living in Central Harlem, since people were very distraught and angry about his assassination. As a result, we moved to the Upper West Side on 103rd Street. However, my community organizing work still continued intensely in the projects of Central Harlem. I realized at that time that I was born to do humanitarian work, which I still continue to do. It seems to be part of my unique Divine expression of the Will of God.

As a Harlem resident and community organizer, I worked in conjunction and in alliance with the NYC original Black Panthers. During my organizing efforts to create an advanced community-controlled mental health center in the Central Harlem/Washington Heights area, three of my Black Panther cohorts were unfortunately killed in a shoot-out; and the fourth, a Black Panther nurse who was also part of our team, was seriously abused by the police. At our next community meeting two weeks later, she was still in post-traumatic shock and was open to my heartfelt support as part of her recovery. She and our 100-plus group of sincere community activists were very successful in winning a major victory for the community because we won the vote for a truly community controlled mental health center. I also collaboratively worked in this process with the Washington Heights/Harlem community and the regional NYC Health Department head administrator/doctor to gain his support for this project. He really appreciated the advanced concepts of community mental health and so it was helpful to bring him in as an ally as he felt that I was promoting a new vision of community mental health which was also heavily supported by the community as well. In this context I began to understand that I was developing a win/win style of community organizing which led to a series of community victories and a general sense of self-esteem and success for all involved. It was also entertaining in this particular situation to oppose my psychiatry resident friends at the New York Psychiatric Institute who were sitting publicly on the side of the status quo promoted by the New York Psychiatric Institute who was a key player in applying for and receiving the governmental funding. Although we all had to look serious during the confrontations, my psychiatric resident friends and I had good laughs later. The good news was that while I was the principal spokesman for the Washington Heights/Harlem community in relating to Columbia P&S and the P&S psychiatrists, we defeated their status quo position. This victory reinforced my general approach for creating positive change by avoiding polarity and emphasizing bonding; something like giving the Williams halfback a helping hand up off the ground after tackling him. This form of community organizing was and is about manifesting the feeling of heart-connected oneness, if possible, in the creative political process which nowadays so easily may degenerate into a negative non-productive confrontational process. My general position throughout all the successful societal change and innovation programs I have been involved in and have created over the years has been setting the intention of the highest understanding and good for all, rather than polarizing the situation with polarity politics of self-righteous, political correctness.

Teaching: The human heart connection, for long-term healing and not just symptom relief, remains the fundamental essence of individual healing and all levels of healing the community at an organizing level.

During the time I lived in Central Harlem, and with the help of $40,000 from the National Institute of Health, we were able to develop an entire innovative community/school health worker training program. The role of these community health workers was to help children at the school access healthcare in the community as well as promote community interest in preventative health. We did the training of community parents out of our Harlem home. It was helpful that the first trained community health worker was a mother who lived with her young son upstairs from me, so I was able to get a very firsthand understanding of how it was working. We started our community health worker program at PS 175 located next to Harlem Hospital. This health worker program spread to about half the schools in Central Harlem. Things were exciting in the late '60s with a lot of community social action happening all over Central Harlem and in inner-city communities around the country.

With some of the teachers at PS 175, who were friends from Amherst College, we supported community control of PS 175 which was one of the main demands in most communities. The principal of this school, Mr. Nagler, was white, and he was feeling more than overwhelmed as a near riot situation spontaneously developed at PS 175 by the parents prior to an impending nearly explosive community control meeting. I offered him a bit of coaching which helped him avoid creating opposing polarity that could potentially have cost him his job. Following this, Mr. Nagler chose to accept our plan to activate a preventative medical screening program for the more than 650 children in the school. We did this in the evenings at the school over a period of a week. The community loved it and Mr. Nagler retained his job and credibility. We also helped many of the kids through our screening program.

As the head of the New York area Student Health Organization representing students at all the medical schools in the area, I was able to develop a collective initiative to bring from the greater New York area, medical students and some volunteer doctors to do a preventative health and general health screening, including physical exams of all 650-plus kids in the school in one week of evenings. We actually found a variety of health problems and were able to identify all the kids with sickle cell disease that was not yet fully manifested, which was wonderful because we could help create a preventative lifestyle to increase longevity. It was a fantastic event that uplifted the morale of all the parents and teachers in the PS 175 community. This was a positive and successful example of community control of a school for the betterment of everyone beyond political power agendas. And to my delight, PS 175 became the first community-controlled school in Central Harlem. Dr. Doris Wethers, director of Knicker-bocker Hospital Pediatrics Department, a key partner in this project, and I co-published an article in the *School Health Journal* with our findings which completed the project. Eventually our school health aide training and service program became incorporated and salaried by the NY Health Department. In retrospect, I cannot honestly say that I consciously experienced it as a dharma as much as something I felt I had to do.

Teaching: Karma and dharma, good or bad, are only created if one is attached to the results.

This consistent success in community organizing over three years further emphasized my dharma as a community organizer that in retrospect unconsciously began in fourth grade with organizing our fourth-grade football team and continued through: being a leader/captain in college football; working with a teen gang on the South Side of Chicago; serving as the first president of the Student Health

Association which represents all eight medical schools in the New York area; and leading in a variety of organizational ways in Central Harlem. Paradoxically, this social and humanitarian activity was never recognized by me as part of my life work or dharma. This school health project in Central Harlem was a spiritual lesson in that when joyfully flowing with God's Will, one's actions do not create karma. Karma is created when there is *doership*. Positive karma may also slow the liberation process because of the lifetimes (or lifetime) it takes to receive the positive karmic benefits. From the perspective of liberation all karma, whether positive or negative impedes the liberation process. This does not mean one should not be involved in providing service in the world.

Teaching: The service one provides is only karma-free if it is not motivated by ego or expectation of a particular result.

Chapter 4

INTERNSHIP, RESIDENCY & BIRTH OF MY CHILDREN AS PREPARATION FOR AWAKENING

Teaching: Living in a way that naturally
avoids creating karma in one's life is essential
to learn on the path to liberation.

In 1969, after graduating from Columbia P&S, I took my internship at Mount Zion Hospital in San Francisco. At the time, John Phillips had written a popular song then sung by Scott Mackenzie called "San Francisco". The lyrics begins this way: "If you're going to San Francisco, be sure to wear some flowers in your hair." We arrived in San Francisco at the height of the "Flower Children" era. Although we lived near Haight-Ashbury in Golden

Gate Park, I cannot actually call myself one of the "Flower Children" and besides a little marijuana as an exploration we did not participate in this drug aspect of the "Flower Children" culture.

Our son Rafael was born in 1969 during this "Flower Child" time. Nora gave birth naturally at Mount Zion hospital and I was actively present as both a husband and father, choosing not to play the doctor/obstetrician role. We were still in the allopathic model when we decided to do the birthing with a natural childbirth doctor at Mount Zion Hospital. The birthing process went very well, and it was a wonderful bonding experience for all of us. Given the setting with me working at the hospital, Nora decided to spend the first four post-birth days in the hospital as an informal home/workplace setting. As I was working in a nearby section of the hospital, we were almost fully together for the first four days of our son's life. It was like being at home. Although visitors were not allowed, everyone looked the other way when my mother and stepfather visited. It was a very sweet time. My wife, new son and I had a beautiful time together before Nora went back to our home with Rafael.

***

My introduction into anti-globalist politics had begun in 1963 with the globalist assassination of President Kennedy. Lyndon Johnson had admitted on his death bed that he had given the order for the assassination. In this post-Kennedy assassination time at Amherst College, I became politically active around this issue and brought a variety of anti-globalist socialist speakers to the campus. I also scheduled radical speakers like Malcolm X, with whom I had a phone friendship for a year or so before his assassination. The Red Book by Chairman Mao promoted the idea that the ends justify the means. This political teaching made acceptable a level of immoral and homicidal thinking that was unacceptable to me. Over time, I began to see through all the Maoist, Nazi, Capitalistic, and Socialistic labels. With clear vision, I decided to confront the contradictions within myself and this was ultimately another major turning point in my life. I chose to stop participating in revolutionary political thinking and turned more inward toward spirituality as my deeper truth.

As in the past, my social activist direction was toward community organizing, especially around anti-Vietnam War work. Several doctors and I created a hospital-wide peace and anti-war group at Mount Zion that also protected hospital worker rights. We engaged in guerilla theater in the doctor's cafe and actually created a wonderful hospital worker talent show. Eventually, I even got the support of the chief hospital administrator in these win/win efforts. We created a Bay Area doctor's group that backed all the radical-revolutionary collectives in the area. We also supported the Black Panthers. Their headquarters was in Oakland, but their local San Francisco center was located within walking distance from Mount Zion Hospital. Our doctor's group even collectively studied Chairman Mao Tse-tung's Little Red Book.

My idealism began to fade as I realized that at least an estimated 80 to 120 million people were "killed for the good" (or sacrificed) for the Chinese Maoist cultural revolution. Approximately 50 million people were killed during Soviet Union communist revolution. I was made further uncomfortable by key American communists personally sharing with me that they were okay with 25-50 million Americans being murdered for the sake of their idealistic cause. It was at this time that I began to feel something was not right with the radical left and socialist communist theology and people who believed it. I began to recognize that the socialist left was far from aligned with my morality and my beginning spiritual understanding of our oneness of humanity. My humanitarian approach of social change was more committed to a type of community organizing that uplifted everyone and suppressed no one. Ultimately, my slowly emerging spiritual awareness pulled me away from politics, and instead I focused on waking up to God and helping others connect to their souls and awaken to God in all creation.

Teaching: The highest level of social change is commitment to the world community in a way in which no one is buried, and everyone is uplifted.

During my internship and psychiatry residency, I began to feel the political people I was working with were not as mentally healthy as felt comfortable. Although I was seriously committed and still am to the upliftment and transformation of humanity, the people I was associating with were not the ones to be doing it in an uplifting and healthy spiritual manner. It would still take another two years for me to make a significant break with politics and move toward a life focused on spiritual evolution and liberation for myself and humanity, which I see as the important higher life purpose for all of humanity.

Teaching: It is clear in the Holistic Liberation Way (or any path of true liberation) that spiritual life is more important than dualistic concepts of the world that only divide people. We are the living truth of God and are meant to bring together and uplift society.

***

At this time, I was considering what sort of three-year psychiatry resident training I wanted. I was interested in an avant-garde residency program with some very visionary psychiatrists focusing on family and systems therapy as the core of the training approach. This visionary aspect was my primary attraction beyond the standard psychiatric residency, such as at Yale where I had also been accepted. This visionary psychiatric residency represented a confluence of a circle of some of the top people in the Boston area and was based at Boston State Hospital. My residency training was the best place in the country for my holistic visionary family and systems therapy training as well as top level training in psychopharmacology as the superintendent, Dr. Jonathan Coles, M.D., was the former head of the NIMH department of psychopharmacology. It was also a major life choice to go with the highest training quality versus earning prestige points at Yale. I was also selected as one of eight people for the National Mental Health Career Development Program, a progressive national government program to develop community psychiatrists. This selection included serving in the United States Public Health Service for three years as a Lieutenant Commander, which was a graceful and non-political way to fulfill my military service during the Vietnam War.

After that internship year in San Francisco, Nora and I went back to Boston for my psychiatry residency. For a while Nora, Rafael, and I lived in Cambridge, Massachusetts where she and I were still politically active. We were being monitored by the FBI for our anti-war work to the extent that they would actually wait outside our apartment and follow us wherever we went. In becoming a spiritually focused person, I was now dedicated to the evolution of human consciousness.

My training experiences in the psychiatry residency at Boston State Hospital were the best of my educational career. The training was a full right- and left-brained experience which I deeply enjoyed. It was avant-garde family therapy and systems therapy-based psychiatry under top family therapists, including Dr. Fred Duhl, founder of the Boston Family Institute, and Dr. David Kantor, founder of the Family Institute of Cambridge. I was mentored by eight different psychiatrists from the leading psychiatric institutions in the Boston area for eight different kinds of individual psychotherapy approaches, as well as in family systems therapy. It was interesting and rewarding that all my patients blossomed no matter the psychotherapy method used. This taught me a lot about the healing process, in that the therapist and the relationship with the client seemed to be more important than a particular therapeutic modality. The family psychiatry systems-based therapy residency in Boston was the best and most outstanding formal educational experience of my life. It also made it clearer to me that as a healer, the foundation of healing was to create an optimal healing and energetic state for the clients to begin to love themselves enough to heal themselves.

Teaching: The power of one's holy intent can elevate any situation. For this to happen, we need to let go of our egoic idealized concepts of perfectionism. It is simple faith and holiness, not perfectionism, that is needed for the presence of the Divine to manifest in the healing process.

The family therapy training was a great two-year course offered by Dr. Fred Duhl and Dr. David Kantor. The benefit was immense on all levels of perception and understanding. I became very close with one of the main teachers, Dr. David Kantor. He was like a big brother and mentor. David recognized my natural aptitude and ability as a family and couple therapist and encouraged and mentored me closely into a career in family therapy. His input was one of the main foundations that supported me in becoming a holistic physician based on a systems worldview that sees the individual within the context of their social network, family, couple and individual spiritual, mental, emotional, and physical context.

For the period between 1970-1972, I also became the therapist for a variety of political collectives in Boston, as well as lesbian and gay collectives and couples, as part of support to both the straight political and Rainbow communities. It was a tremendous amount of fun doing this work and helping a lot of people. It was vital to support this broad spectrum of cutting-edge communities who were trying to live their ways of life as part of a new vision of what the world could be. Although a "straight married man," my sincere, heartfelt love and soul connection for all these various people and collectives melted through the initial fears and polarities that people sometimes brought to the situation. People got that we were unified in trying to bring through a cutting-edge vision to society, which required the breaking of old societal forms, including those within ourselves. I was an open, supportive witness to all these social experiments and, of course, I also had a great deal to learn from them. In the early '70s, as a "general" licensed minister, I even began to perform same-sex marriages, which was not exactly "politically correct" at that time. By doing so, I was performing a needed service because few people were willing to offer such marriages at that time. It was more of a supportive service than a political statement. The biggest insight from this "alternative" work was that although people idealistically thought they were beyond the traditional human dynamic interactional intimacy issues, they were not. This was particularly true with people who tried to create triangular relationships in a variety of combinations such as two men with one woman, two women with one man, three persons of the same sex, a group with a totally open dynamic, etc. From what I have seen, these combinations did not work in the long run, but there are always exceptions to this observation. However, polyamorous intrigues, both overt and covert, almost always compromise one's spiritual focus, as well as the deep intimacy process.

Teaching: Deep soul felt intimacy in a monogamous relationship is already a spiritual challenge. In triads and polygamous relationships, it is far more difficult.

I started a successful family-oriented teen center during my psychiatry residency program in Boston. We used a holistic approach which included family therapy. The biochemical side of my training was also being fed very nicely by work with Dr. Albert DiMasio, who was the head of psychopharmacology for the State of Massachusetts, and Dr. Johnathan Coles. These two superior, outstanding psychopharmacologists helped me very much in understanding the world of psychopharmacology, which was personally fascinating since my college training was in biochemistry. By the time I had reached my second year of psychiatric residency, I was so well-trained in using psychopharmacology that I began teaching it to the first-year residents under the supervision of my two outstanding mentors. Unknown to me at that time, this background foundation would become useful in my learning to work holistically with herbs and supplements in my transition to becoming a holistic physician and away from the use of any psychotropic drugs with clients. As a researcher, it was not beyond me to do the "unthinkable" innovative research. Studies showed that half of all patients taken off psychiatric medications recover naturally and tend to do better than those who are medicated. Under the supervision and the support of the hospital superintendent, Dr. Jonathan Coles, as well as Dr. Albert DiMasio, and my immediate supervisor Dr. Harold Goldberg, all the inpatients were taken off all psychiatric medications for four months. The nurses were "panicked" about this, but my decision supported by my supervisors to do this was based on the research at the NIMH and NIH level, which showed that although fifty percent would likely relapse, the other fifty percent would not need further medication and would do better long term in avoiding relapse within five years than those who stayed on antipsychotic medications. We showed that this was indeed true and literally opened the door for a lot of people to move out of their chemical prisons and out of the hospital. This choice, again, reflects an alternative bystander creative approach to life in general and in the field of medicine in particular with the overall result of helping many people. It was another seed experience into developing a natural non-allopathic drug approach to holistic healing.

***

While in Boston our 2-year-old son, Rafael, developed Legg–Calvé–Perthes disease. This is when the neck of the femur (hip bone) develops necrosis, secondary to defective arterial circulation in the hip area. He was limping and in great pain. The standard treatment would involve a cast and minimal activity for up to two years. This would have been difficult for any 2-year-old and especially Rafael. My mother, his grandmother Rosalie, was very upset about this. Unbelievably he suddenly got better. When they did an x-ray, he was completely healed. Later I found out that my mother had done a prayer to take on his disease and indeed, before she developed cancer of the pancreas, she had severe right shoulder pain. They operated on her and found that she had Legg–Calvé–Perthes of the right shoulder, a rarity. Based on everything she said, it seemed that she magically and psychically took on the disease of her grandson. It was an amazing teaching about the power of love to heal. Grandparents sometimes do these wild, loving things; indeed, my mother did.

Teaching: Deep love has the power to heal.

During a trip to India in 1972, my mother was in a severe car accident. The doctors didn't know what was going on as she turned quite yellow. When able to be moved, she immediately returned to the U.S. It turned out that she had cancer of the pancreas, and there was a tumor blocking the bile duct. At that time, pancreatic cancer was not curable in any reasonable way we knew of. She started with a few rounds of chemotherapy but decided against it because it made her feel worse. She decided to go home and live out her life. She lived a lot longer than expected and left her body in a beautiful way which will be described in detail in the next chapter.

***

The late '60s was also the time of the famous psychedelic drug movement becoming internationally public. My involvement in this world was mostly helping people who suffered bad trips. Since it was part of the social membership in the '60s, I smoked marijuana for a short time about once a week. It became rapidly clear to me that marijuana was toxic to consciousness, and so I stopped my marijuana exploration. The limitations of drugs as a "path" to bring people to liberation became obvious to me. However, during my psychiatry residency in the early '70s Nora and I did a little exploring with one "research" trip with LSD in the Boston area and a one-time group experience in Petaluma with ketamine. Part of the motivation was to understand what this psychedelic experience was about. It was also an important part of my individual and scientific curiosity and exploration for helping "flower children" through the large amount and variety of psychedelic mental health crises that were happening at that time. Even now in the past eleven years from 2009 to 2020 people are still coming from around the world for help with these issues.

Teaching: Spiritual evolution does not require
taking risks of destroying one's brain and mind
with psychedelic drugs or plant medicine.

Although not by full choice, it was relatively easy for me to become an expert in this area as there was so few people who were trained to help. But before going further into this discussion, I want to reiterate that I had limited direct personal experiences. One of my mentors who was the head of Massachusetts Mental Health Department of Psychopharmacology and who helped train me in conventional psychopharmacology, gave Nora and I some pure LSD to experience. Nora and I drove on my R750 BMW motorcycle up to the coast from Boston to Maine, where we stayed at a friend's empty cottage and spent a day nude at an isolated Maine beach assimilating one hit each of pure LSD. It was an interesting experience, lots of colors and lots of psychedelic visions. I experienced lots of changes and alterations in all my senses including when making love on the beach. The LSD also created an interesting panorama of astral plane experiences. Nora and I also later endured uncomfortable sunburns, since we weren't wearing clothes and the trip lasted for hours. It was particularly interesting at the end of the day to somehow drive the BMW motorcycle very slowly back through the woods to the cottage where we were staying. It was its own magical mystery tour.

In the early '70s, the now Dr. Alberto Villoldo was a special "explorer" friend from a shamanic point of view in these astral plane areas. We were studying with this particularly interesting medical doctor in Mexico who used a variety of drugs therapeutically. The two of us visited him in Mexico and observed his whole program of how he put people on a sequence of psychedelic drugs over a twenty-four to forty-eight-hour period to help heal their psycho-emotional traumas. It was very dramatic, and we were introduced to other drugs, particularly one interesting drug called ketamine. Alberto and I invited this Mexican psychiatrist to come up and take half of the psychology department at Sonoma State including us on this ketamine experience in my rebuilt "pyramid" garage in Petaluma, California. I actually did have a profound experience of Oneness with all creation during this session. An important insight and message that came to me during the ketamine experience was that it was my challenge to go deeper and further into the mysteries of altered consciousness and ultimately liberation than any drug could possibly go by following the natural spiritual way of life and meditation. The directive was to go beyond psychedelic drugs and plant medicines by doing the inner work where the deeper God-merged states were readily and regularly accessible and sustainable.

Teaching: When we do the inner work,
God-merged states become our main station.

As a result of this ketamine insight back in 1974, there was no more need for psychedelic drug explorations. A particular subspecialty part of my work since then, however, has been to help people repair their brain/mind complex from their damaging psychedelic drug/plant medicine use. Interwoven with this subtlety is the Kundalini or psychosis question, well-discussed by my now-deceased close friend, Dr. Lee Sannella, in his book *The Kundalini Experience: Psychosis or Transcendence*. The interface of psychedelic drugs and/or plant "medicines" (especially *ayahuasca*) with Kundalini and psychosis has also become a mystical psychiatric subspecialty of mine. The Kundalini/drug interface sometimes results in a disordering of the Kundalini flow. Kundalini is the cosmic spiritual energy stored at the base of the spine that when awakened, moves throughout all levels of the body-mind complex including the *chakras* and *koshas* (layers of the mind) spiritually activating and upgrading the whole system as part of the spiritual-physiological transformations usually associated with the consciousness awakening process.

Having been trained in entity and demon removal in the 1970s, I've noted that there seems to be a significant amount of entity invasion associated with alcohol, ayahuasca, and marijuana as well as other psychedelics. It is clear from personal discussions that some ayahuasca shamans know about this potential of entity invasion and it is also noted in the marijuana literature as well. People around the world are still coming to me for healing of this Kundalini/psychosis/demonic possession syndrome. The good news is that all levels of these imbalances including entity and demon possession can be healed.

Liberation is a different focus than that of shamans, who culturally use these plant medicines as a primary part of their indigenous lifestyle which is more focused on the astral plane. While the psychedelic/plant medicines may help to widen one's connection to the astral plane, the downside is that they may also keep you trapped in the astral plane if regularly used. The holistic path to liberation does not need external supports such as drugs. It was no accident that Swami Muktananda had a drug trophy case at the inner entrance to the Oakland ashram meditation hall, where people symbolically left their drugs and drug addictions behind.

Teaching: There is no actual psychedelic/
plant medicine path to Self-Realization.

In the same period of time, as part of my preparation to be mature enough to maximally benefit from receiving Shaktipat, another shamanic transformative experience manifested. Several months before the birth of Heather Sonya, Nora and I both had the same nightmare dream on the same night during her pregnancy. We dreamt that our fetal baby was a chicken. At that time neither of us were vegetarian. In the dream, we were eating this fetus-chicken. After that shared dream, with a brief discussion that this was no coincidence, we both spontaneously went vegetarian. We had a compelling insight into the culture of death in that it included a meat-eating consciousness. This was in stark contrast to giving birth which was and is, a life-giving process.

Teaching: A culture of death includes
a meat-eating consciousness.

I had not even heard of vegetarianism or a vegan/plant-based diet until the age of twenty-eight so becoming vegetarian, then vegan, and then live-foods was the furthest thing from my dietary consciousness. In high school, I actually won the vote for biggest eater in the high school yearbook, and it was not vegetable and fruits. As a high school freshman, after we beat Evanston, the best football team in the league, twelve to zero, I celebrated by actually eating thirteen McDonald's hamburgers. In college, before every football game, we would have a steak meal at 10 a.m. before the game at 2 p.m. After every football game, after using up so much energy, I would go to the Amherst College cafeteria and have a complete dinner, including whatever they called a steak (Salisbury steak). We had three cafeterias and all three of them got visited by me. It was a tradition for me after each game to eat three steaks and at least ten ice teas with sugar. I certainly did not come from a vegan background. Fortunately for my health, this behavior was limited to one time per week through the 1962 to 1964 football seasons; and at seventy-seven years around the sun, my blood sugar remains healthy in the optimal zone of 70-85. This funny little anecdotal story shows the power of positive motivated will power to create a healthy dietary change. It was not that hard for us to read a few plant-based recipe books, attend a few lectures on plant-based diets, and experience some trial and error to make this dietary change. This spontaneous transition to a vegan vegetarian diet was a natural, significant, God-mediated transition and formed the basis of my further transition to a 100% vegan food and 99% live-food diet by 1983. It is the diet that I recommend for becoming a superconductor of the Divine. It has become the foundational basis of my vegan live-food spiritual nutritional teachings and the diet that is best for optimizing the flow of the Kundalini.

For years I worked very hard to keep my weight up because of football. In my senior year in college I played the season at 180 pounds, which still made me almost the smallest person on the field, and clearly the smallest in the lineman positions. As a meat-eater, in 1964, I used to do seventy consecutive push-ups daily, seven pull-ups and, some days, as many as five hundred sit-ups to build muscle mass and maintain weight. So, a switch to primarily plant-based-only cuisine in one day required a certain amount of faith. Seeing myself as an ongoing physiological experiment today at the age of 77 after eating this 100% vegan and 99% live-food diet for around 47 years and exercising intensively around two times per week I am regularly doing 1000 push-ups at one time and 80 pull ups at one time which is more than ten times better than I could do at age 21 as an All-New England Football middle linebacker and guard. In addition to increased strength there is also increased flexibility compared to my football player days when I literally could not get close to even crossing my legs or touching my toes. Now this body can sit in full lotus for up to two hours and can put my palms on the ground. This physiological and lifestyle experiment helps to make the point and answers the continual inquiry if a vegan live-food cuisine can be an optimal long-term cuisine. It also makes the significant and non-theoretical point that with some effort we can become healthier, stronger, more flexible, and have more endurance with chronological age.

Teaching: With optimal diet and exercise, we
can get healthier and younger with age.

Following our vegan transformation, Nora gave birth naturally to our daughter Heather Sonya at the French Hospital & Medical Center-SNF in San Francisco. We lived an hour drive away, and even though we had training in natural delivery, we weren't equipped in several ways at that time to do a home birth. Heather's birth was a Divine happening in the middle of the hospital. The whole birth room was transformed by the positive energy and love of our interaction during the birth. Touched by the love and holiness generated in the whole process, the nurses were crying in joy. By our intent we had transformed the idealized homebirth picture into a holy sacred ceremony in a hospital that went beyond anything we could have done with a home delivery. We left after twelve hours in the hospital, post-delivery, against medical advice. Not that anything was wrong, we just were not willing to follow their protocol, like vaccinations, and felt that it was not safe for healthy babies to be in any hospital because of hospital bacterial resistant infections; and we had pre-planned to leave ASAP to avoid any harmful exposure and to return to our healthy, peaceful, environmental home space.

Teaching: It is important and relevant to bring
spiritual consciousness to one's life experience at all times
including birthing into life and the transition to death.

Chapter 5

FINAL INNER PREPARATIONS BEFORE RECEIVING SHAKTIPAT

Teaching: The physiological state of the
body influences the mind and spirit.

The years between 1973 and 1975 were the final inner transformational preparation to optimally receive Shaktipat and the awakening of the Kundalini. A whole new world of holistic healing understanding opened during these years as well. Starting in 1973, I also began a holistic psychiatry practice in Petaluma, located in Southern Sonoma County, California. Following the needs of the area, it soon evolved into a full holistic health dynamic orientated family practice, which included seeing children and adults of all ages, as well as doing individual, couple, and family therapy. In this time, it became clinically apparent that not only did the spirit and mind affect the body, but the physiological state of the body influenced the mind and spirit. Although this approach seems obvious today, at that time it was considered unorthodox, out-of-the-box thinking. What also came up a lot during this time with clients were issues with blood sugar that so many people seemed to be having, so it seemed a good idea to do a lot of work with blood sugar imbalances. My initial research from these efforts was published in Dr. Paavo Airola's book, *Hypoglycemia, A Better Approach*. My findings suggested that hypoglycemia was a much more complicated and sophisticated endocrine imbalance potentially involving some or all of the endocrine system, including the hypothalamus, pituitary, pineal, thyroid, adrenals, pancreas, and ovaries. This successful holistic approach of addressing all of these areas and also the chakra systems associated with each endocrine gland led to rapid healing with a high percentage of success. I also clinically observed that when the glandular/chakra systems were out of balance, people also had a lot more entity attacks at night; this phenomena diminished when the chakra imbalance was healed.

Teaching: Healing the blood sugar imbalances
and balancing the chakras increases the
protection of people from entity invasion.

This clinical insight was not exactly part of the modern rabbi or medical school training and my observations were leading me to a deeper and deeper understanding of the multi-level layers of the wonders and mysteries of the human organism much of which I could understand and heal, but this entity issue at that time was over my head. Because of my natural curiosity about this entity question, advice was sought of Nick Nocerino, one of the world's experts on Crystal Skulls. We hit it off immediately, and I was graced with many years of study and training from him in the area of crystals as well as entity and demonic removal from humans. Sometimes this exorcism training got intense with possessed people floating in the air and demons inside them hissing at us, resisting their exorcism. There were some very strange happenings that took a little bit to get used to. It was just like in the movies. Fortunately, our entity and demon removal ceremonies were 100% successful; and none of us got hurt or invaded. I did not realize it at the time, but my research and oral tradition suggested that the ancient rabbis usually had to be trained in these occult areas before they could be part of the grand council of rabbis called the *Sanhedrin*. Being trained in this occult area took a little courage, but it felt quite familiar and seemed necessary. When we persist and dig our wells deeply, we are more likely to hit water. Of course, we need to be spiritually courageous enough to dig deeply and drink the water.

Teaching: Going more in-depth with what may
at first appear to be simply a mundane pattern,
may reveal subtle teachings from God.

An interesting personal prophetic event occurred in the early 1970s, while taking one of the last EST seminars personally led by Werner Erhardt. I did a visualization, and three figures in white appeared, which I did not recognize until years later. They did not say anything, but each made a unique energetic connection with me. One was Avraham Avinu, the great liberated spiritual warrior patriarch and pre-founder of Judaism who I later connected with very deeply. Another turned out to be the God-merged being, Sai Baba of Shirdi, who appeared to be an old Essene who I later deeply connected with in India. The third was Crazy Horse of the Lakota Sioux.

In 1976, Sai began to appear to me a variety of times while I meditated in his *masjid* in Shirdi, India. My connection with him culminated while I was taking a walk with Swami Prakashananda in 1982 before leaving India. Sai materialized in front of me and, raising his right hand with a tremendous amount of energy coming out of it, blessed me by giving Shaktipat in my third eye area. It literally knocked me backward onto the ground. Swami Prakashananda confirmed Sai Baba's manifestation in front of me. As Sai Baba had taken *mahasamadhi* in 1918, it was special to have Swami Prakashananda as a witness of Sai's appearance and energetic transmission of Shaktipat. The third image, Crazy Horse, turned out to be the incredible Sioux warrior and mystic. I probably knew him as I may have been the first Native American western-trained medical doctor who lived at that time whose name was Dr. Charles Eastman. All three have had a significant energetic effect on my life evolution.

The early '70s were nodal times in several ways as I was unconsciously preparing for my spiritual and my deepest level of life to begin. In 1971 as already mentioned, I broke away from the radical political approach to societal change and moved toward a more holistic lifestyle with a humanitarian-spiritual focus, which has been part of my life mission since then. This was a time of transitioning more clearly into a career dharma of holistic spiritual physician/psychiatrist, family therapist, and plant-based live-food nutritionist and spiritual teacher. During the 1973-1976 years, it was also a privilege to study with Rob Menzies, who was one of the great American herbalists in Northern California at that time. Also, the importance of supplements and natural healing as part of the holistic approach was also introduced to me by my chief mentor in this area, Paavo Airola, Ph.D., the world-famous naturopathic healer. As a psychiatrist and family therapist with a biochemical background, I also found the orthomolecular psychiatry approach to be attractive. I undertook a variety of trainings in this professional area. The orthomolecular psychiatry approach evolved to a point where a client would not be taken for psychotherapy until they had received a full holistic health evaluation, and their hypoglycemia or other endocrine imbalances such as hypothyroidism had been healed, and their neurotransmitters had been rebalanced nutritionally. It was amazing how many people did not need psychotherapy after this.

My life in Petaluma, California was a professionally active dharmic time, including becoming the mental health consultant for Sonoma County Head Start, which included an approximately 300-mile radius of schools including the Pomo Indian schools in Northern Sonoma County. One of my innovations was teaching a one-year family dynamics course to the Head Start teachers so they could better work with the Head Start children and their families. I also developed and taught a similar, but more advanced, family therapy two-year course for Master's students and Ph.D. students in psychology, mostly from Sonoma State. During that time, I also collaborated with an orthopedic surgeon where we explored low back pain through the lens of the different family dynamic and other dysfunctional psychological issues associated with the low back pain. We were co-teaching this to family physician residents at

Santa Rosa Hospital in Santa Rosa California. It was dharmically fun and fulfilling to be sharing these multilayered holistic and spiritual approaches with the more allopathic medical world.

The spiritual lesson in all these areas was remembering to stay outside the box and be the unique expression of the Divine. This has relevance today as many physicians who remain "in the box" have become bored, depressed, and dissatisfied with their careers, with statistically high rates of suicide and drug use. As a holistic health practitioner, however, I have experienced an ever-evolving, joyful expression of the Divine at play, guiding me into an evolving practice of spiritual holistic medicine. It was a special time for me of fully living out and completing my need for living this idealized way of life. It was a holistic harvest of the fruits of many years of planting.

Teaching: The simplest spiritual truth is that the only real existent Truth is God as I Am that I Am. Everything else is relative "truth" that always changes as science advances or in different cultures. The key challenge is to develop the ability to distinguish between the cosmic Truth of the One God and the myriad relative ever-changing relative truths of the material plane.

For the duration of the years between 1973-1976, I became much more attracted to spiritual life and began to organize our little 8th Street block neighborhood group in Petaluma into monthly new moon meditation groups. We also developed a food co-op for our group and a community garden which was quite large. We transformed our garage into a meditation hall as it had a natural pyramid shape and was a nice place to do ceremonies and monthly new moon meditations. Behind our garage meditation hall, an astrological herbal circular garden was created, and I enjoyed sitting in the center. The creative value of a natural way of living the original Torah Way of Life, is that it leads one to a deepening spiritual life.

Teaching: By paying attention to the subtle
spiritual messages of our life, it is easier to
be aligned with the Divine Will.

One of the questions that I am continually asked is: "How does one know when to spend the energy to dig a deep well?" This is a clear metaphor for developing a spiritual path.

Teaching: There are no guarantees about when and
how to spend energy on the spiritual path, but there is
an old basketball teaching: "If you don't take any shots
(because you may miss), you'll never make any baskets."

In 1973, J.J. Hurtak and Desiree Hurtak came into my life and we have since become lifelong friends. Immediately before meeting them, J.J. Hurtak had received some mystical visions and experiences which revealed some of the ancient teaching of Enoch, who was the seventh generation from Adam. Enoch was the first being in the Biblical tradition to be taken up into heaven alive. A short time after his first book was first released on the teachings of Enoch, we set up a teaching situation at night with about thirty people for J.J. Hurtak at a local pre-school in Cotati, California. There he taught nonstop from 8 p.m. to 2 a.m. every day for six weeks. It was spectacular to go through the biblical scriptures from an illuminated Enochian perspective, but more than that spontaneously occurred. One evening angelic faces began to appear around J.J.. Everyone had passed out because of the intensity of the energy, and I was the only one left awake. I began to see illuminated energetic faces near J.J. and thought I was imagining things. But J.J. turned and began addressing the angelic beings by name. It was mind-blowing and a little frightening to see real angels. It made me aware, for the first time, of my dread of the unknown. I was afraid of this unfamiliar energetic for about an hour until it became clear to me that this spiritual fear was a test to go through. I have seen many angels since then, and so now they are a part of my reality. It is not unusual for angels to actually energetically appear at my Shaktipat meditations enhancing the spiritual energy.

Teaching: Fear of the unknown is normal and is
usually a temporary part of the spiritual path.

I have consistently observed that in the beginning people often experience fear on the spiritual path. It seems associated with the fear of the unknown, as it was for me. It is normal and often occurs as one begins to pop out of their programmed proverbial box or comfort zone. Empowered by this experience with J.J., my public acknowledgment of this spiritual fear has helped many people to pass through this fear on the path to liberation.

Teaching: Many people develop fear at a certain point in their spiritual path; it is a powerful spiritual victory to pass through this trepidation and move deeper into the unknown even including living with the fear and awe of the unknown.

* * *

In late 1974 and early 1975, my focus shifted from the life creating energetic process of birth and raising young children to the spiritually uplifting process of my mother's death from cancer of the pancreas. I began making a regular commute back and forth from the Bay Area to Los Angeles where my mother was slowly dying. It was a blessing and source of joy and love that I was able to spend this time with her over the next two years, sitting quietly with her and lovingly hanging out together. It was also a blessing she was able to enjoy her two grandchildren during this time as well. In the last three months, she began to more obviously fade out. The night before she died, my mother came to me in a dream in her silvery astral form while I slept in the nearby room. She expressed her great fear of what was coming next and asked for help, which I gave both in the dream and to her in the morning. The next day we exchanged an angelic kiss, and after a deep, peaceful smile, she went to sleep and never woke up. She died gently and peacefully on the day before her sixty-third birthday in 1975. Over the following day with guided visualization and meditation I worked in helping her soul to clearly reach the other side. It was a blessing that I, as her son, could give back to her in such an essential, spiritually loving way. Helping Rosalie pass over to the other side in a good way was also a great benefit to me in understanding more about the mystery of death. Immediately after Mother's death, my younger sister Ann chose to disappear from my life, so virtually, by age thirty-three, my family of origin had disappeared. The death of my mother was an extraordinary spiritual event for her and myself.

Teaching: Death can be experienced in
a beautiful and uplifting way.

It wasn't until later that year, with Swami Muktananda in 1975 as I shared in chapter one, that I could finally understand the deep mystical secret of death. It came while in meditation, after receiving Shaktipat for the first time from Swami Muktananda. Between Richard, who died when I was sixteen; my father, who died when I was twenty-one; and then my mother, who died when I was thirty-three, understanding the mystery of death became a major quest. I was finally spiritually ready to receive the experiential answer to this quest on all levels.

Teaching: We live in the illusion of the cosmic play of
birth and death not realizing there is no death for the Self.

As part of this journey of multiple spiritual explorations, in 1973, Dr. Lee Sannella and Dr. Alberto Villoldo, both longtime friends, and I did some experiments with carbon dioxide in which one inhales it until one loses consciousness. We were using it as a way to simulate a near-death experience. The first time I did this process, I found myself traveling down the mystical tunnel to the other side. I took this journey three times in our one-day exploration. On the last experience, I went out with a big smile. While journeying down the white tunnel, I had an illuminated vision of Yeshua (Jesus) greeting me with open arms and with great joy. That was a real surprise! These simulated near-death experiences gave me even more insight into the mystery of death, and they came closer to answering my questions about death. This type of experimentation should not be done on one's own. Dr. Sannella and I were fully trained medical doctors at that time, and Dr. Alberto Villoldo was highly trained in the parapsychological field.

Teaching: The life of a mystical explorer is on the wild side!

I engaged in ongoing research on Kundalini with Dr. Sannella, who wrote the book *The Kundalini Experience: Psychosis or Transcendence.* In 1976, we actually started the first Kundalini Crisis Clinic in the U.S. and perhaps the world. Dr. Sannella, Dr. Villoldo, and I even developed a "Kundalini machine" based on the schematics of Itzhak Bentov, author of *Stalking the Wild Pendulum: On the Mechanics of Consciousness.* In late 1975, Dr. Villoldo, Dr. Sannella, and I presented this research to Swami Muktananda at his Oakland Ashram, which was about an hour away from where we lived. Swami Muktananda had a good laugh about our research and invited us to a Siddha Yoga meditation intensive that weekend at the Oakland Ashram to have a more authentic experience about Kundalini. I interpreted this invitation as another door-opening opportunity from God, and, of course, I had to walk through it... and ultimately that takes me back to the seven-year guru cycle where this book and spiritual life started. After years of preparation, I was now ready to take this next major step.

Teaching: From a liberation perspective, you cannot lose what you've never had. With this approach and attitude, we are able to live and die as originals and not "copies." Self-Realization includes the awareness of becoming an original again.

Chapter 6

THE FIRST AND SECOND SHAKTIPAT EXPERIENCES... BLASTING OFF INTO THE BEGINNING OF MY LIFE

With my initial Shaktipat experience with Swami Muktananda after all those years of searching for the Truth I knew I had found a path that could lead me there and sustain me in it. It was a WOW!

In the Yogic tradition, Shaktipat is the giving of higher frequency spiritual energy that awakens the liberation spiritual energy called the Kundalini stored within us in its pure spiritual potential at the base of the spine beneath the confluence of the three main *nadis* in the *kanda* region under the base chakra called the *yukta triveni* (coming together of the three rivers). The awakening of the Kundalini (described as "Guru's Grace") is the necessary last switch to be activated before liberation. Traditionally the spiritual teacher who is being the vehicle for Shaktipat transmission explicitly needs the directive of his own spiritual teacher to be empowered to activate this lineage power in others in order to be an active vehicle for bestowing this grace of Shaktipat. Swami Muktananda was blessed and empowered by his guru Sri Bagawan Nityananda, the great *avadhut* to do this. After seven years as a disciple I was blessed, empowered, and directed by Swami Muktananda to also give Shaktipat. It needs to be clear that I am not the only one to be directly empowered by Swami Muktanadna to be a vehicle for this descent of grace called Shaktipat and make absolutely no claims and do not in any way claim to being his direct successor in the tradition of Siddha Yoga.

When the Kundalini is initially awakened different energetic movements and energetic flows often occur, which are technically called *kriyas*. They may occur on emotional, mental, and spiritual levels. These kriyas may include gentle pulsations or swirling feelings over a chakra area or over the whole body. There may be gentle or very vigorous physical movements; intense heat felt in certain areas; sudden changes in emotional states; spontaneous crying; rapid thought production; seeing different colors; hearing one of ten Divine sounds, called *nada;* or spiritual visions; and a variety of other lesser-known kriyas. They are evidence of the purifying and consciousness expanding flow of the Kundalini as it travels through the *nadis* (subtle energy channels in our physical body), spontaneously working through blocked areas of energy, different karmas and detrimental thoughtforms. Often the Kundalini puts the body into a particular physical posture to remove a specific energy block.

After the initial kriyas manifested, I had a vision of Swami Muktananda, in which he seemed to guide the I Am-ness into a merging with my Inner Self as a subtle experience of the Truth. From this inner awareness, my consciousness expanded into Oneness with both the outer and inner worlds before finally dissolving into the Nothing. On the way into the Nothing, the I Am-ness was completely immersed in liberated expanded *prana,* while the Kundalini moved upward into the third, fourth, and fifth chakras in their usual anatomical locations. These chakras revealed their different energies and petal formations with each chakra exposing its inner teachings. Later I learned that these petals are associated with the fifty *vrittis* (thoughts) which are endogenous (or naturally occurring) in all humans. The I Am-ness within my body witnessed four petals at the *muladhara* (base chakra), six with the *svadhisthana* (second chakra), ten with the *manipura* (solar plexus chakra), eight with the *anahata* (heart chakra), sixteen with the *vishuddhi* (throat chakra), two with the *ajna* (third eye), and an explosion up through the crown with more petals than could be counted.

Later I researched this vision and my insights seemed accurate, except for the eight petals with the heart chakra (to be explained later). As the Kundalini energy began to move upward, my eyes turned inward and upward into the ajna (third eye chakra) in what I subsequently learned was called the *shambhavi mahamudra*. This spontaneous *mudra* was part of the awakening of the third eye chakra (ajna). As the energy continued to flow upward, an ancient master sitting in full lotus appeared looking down with a subtle smile. The energy of the cosmic truth glowed forth from him and entered into me on all levels from the third eye going down to the base chakra. I experienced a whole new depth of initiation that permeated me to the deepest soul level. It's amazing to me that this was all happening in my first Shaktipat initiation.

Flying high in life.

Teaching: Shaktipat can open up a realm of experience and reality beyond understanding. A true — WOW!

Being entirely new to the ashram setting, it was not until later in the weekend that I realized this ancient, smiling master was Sadhguru Sri Bagawan Nityananda, who was Swami Muktananda's guru. This first Shaktipat meditation in the first intensive was a double Shaktipat from both Swami Muktananda and Sadhguru Sri Bagawan Nityananda and was way beyond my expectations. The energy from it burst into my crown in a circle of blazing lights opening the *sushumna* (central Kundalini channel) to the cosmos. The Shaktipat intensive opened up a realm of experience and reality beyond my understanding. Many spiritual teachers have felt that Shaktipat, and the awakening of the Kundalini associated with it, opens up spiritual vistas of a new world on a variety of planes of existence and is the final awakening gateway to walk through before liberation.

The energy of the Kundalini was so intense from the first Shaktipat, it felt as though all my neurotransmitters had been blown out. Throughout the weekend intensive these deep meditations continued to be accompanied by spontaneous patterns of fast and slow breathing, which I later learned are called *pranayama*. I also heard Divine high-pitched harmonic tones. The nada, or ten Divine sounds, are associated with the opening of the higher centers and a Yogic tradition called *Nada Yoga*.

At the end of the meditation intensive, there was intense pain in my sacral spine and lower back area that continued over the course of the next three to four days. It was not soothed by external massage or any other treatment, including hot baths. Besides being located at the classical area where the Kundalini awakened, this low back lumbar sacral area was also the site of my congenital defect at L-5/S-1. As discussed previously, I received an operation five years earlier that relieved the physical problem of the congenital defect. The Kundalini often acts to heal areas of the body where there is a karma imbalance. The result of this was the final healing of my lumbar sacral region that is still pain-free today forty-seven years later.

About ten days after this Shaktipat and Kundalini awakening, a "spiral rash" appeared starting from the base of my spine, weaving back and forth across my spine two times and ending in a flare over the left side of my neck; this lasted a few days. The centers of the palms of both my hands were also continuously hot with a roundish red rash the size of a quarter. After discussing this with my colleague and fellow spiritual researcher the late Dr. Lee Sannella we decided it was a *stigmata*, or outer manifestation of the inner awakening and flow of the Kundalini. It took about a week for these external physical signs to subside. The internal transformation, however, continued to deepen progressively over the years. I am eternally grateful for the Kundalini awakening I received from the breath and touch of Swami Muktananda which activated a full transformation of my life into a holistic multidimensional state of liberation.

By continually going to the witness/researcher point of view with these kriyas, rather than getting fascinated and seduced by them, I was protected from one of the classic ego and astral traps that people can fall into which is the potential snare of identifying with these manifestations of Kundalini. My scientific observation witness approach and sense of dharma to share this experiential subtle spiritual anatomy information in the West became a subtle blessing in this way. On researching the meaning of all these experiences, I realized that I had been introduced spontaneously to various levels of the classical *Ashtanga* eight-fold Yogic path. (Note: This is not the brand name called *Ashtanga Yoga*.) The eight-fold path included *kriyavati*, or movement of the Kundalini in the physical body. The Kundalini moved my body through various spontaneous Yoga *asanas*, also known as Yogic poses, pranayama (regulation of the breath exercises), *pratyhara* (sense withdrawal), *dharana* (concentration), *dhyana* (meditation), and *samadhi* (deep spiritual bliss), as well as Nada Yoga (Yoga of Divine sound).

This spiritual energy transmission also happens in other traditions including Judaism and Christianity. For example, it describes the energetic passing on of the energy from Moses to Yehoshua in Deuteronomy 34:9, when it describes how Moses awakened the spiritual energy of Joshua by touching him and the energy was passed into him. In the Torah/ Jewish tradition, it is called *S'micha m'shefa* or *Haniha*. In the New Testament, the Shaktipat-Kundalini transmission is referred to in John 20:22, which says that Jesus "blew upon them and said to them: 'Receive the Holy Spirit.'" In the Yogic traditions, Shaktipat is well-recognized as "Guru's Grace". This usually occurs when an awakened spiritual teacher with a great amount of the spiritual Kundalini energy flowing shares the Grace of this energy with the aspirant or a group of aspirants. I personally have done it with groups as large as four thousand since being empowered to do this through the Grace and explicit directive of Swami Muktananda. When the combination of this Shaktipat energy with the Kundalini energy of the aspirant is enough to reach the critical ignition point, the spiritual Shakti Kundalini awakens. The transmission of this spiritual Kundalini energy through the spiritual teacher may take place in a variety of ways including look, *mantra*, thought, breath, or direct touch. I have even successfully given Shaktipat to groups over the internet by look and by sound, and people have also received it from my books or from me appearing in their dreams. This level of transmission remains a sublime mystery to me.

As previously stated, the ancient Jewish equivalent of Shaktipat is called Haniha or s'mecha m'shefa. The significance of the *Shaktipat/ Haniha* initiation is a most profound and major step in spiritual life. Both Swami Muktananda and *Ramakrishna,* a great liberated saint who lived in the latter part of the nineteenth century, are quoted to have said that the complete fire of spiritual life does not fully begin until the Kundalini is awakened. That is certainly my experience.

Teaching: Spiritual life begins with the
awakening of the Kundalini.

Kundalini awakening is not necessarily linear, as it has its own intelligence. It moves where it needs to work. The first Shaktipat awakened me into being an intensely activated and committed spiritual being. It also opened me up to an ongoing, sustained, and expanded Holistic Liberation Way awareness and a spiritual empowerment awakening that opened me up to awareness of the play of Divine Consciousness in all of creation—and, paradoxically, to the awareness that God is present in material creation at all times as the hum of creation.

Teaching: God is present in all of creation.

This illusion of the absence of Divine Presence in all creation is known in Sanskrit as *maya* and in the Torah tradition as *alma d'shikra.* Thus, we have the liberation paradox expressed in two of the great spiritual paths in India of "not this; not that" (*Advaita Vedanta*) and "yes; yes" (*Kashmir Shaivism*). This awareness is also called by the liberated Hasidic master, the Bal Shem Tov (1698-1760), *Yechudim*, which is described as seeing and activating the spark of God in all of creation. The teaching of the Bal Shem Tov is for us to activate that spark in the other and then to come into a spiritual energizing and unifying relationship with it. Until this spiritual force (called Kundalini in the Eastern tradition and *Shekhinah* or *Ruach Ha'Kodesh* in the great Torah way) is awakened, most live in a state of spiritual pre-empowerment. This Shaktipat initiation from Swami

Muktananda was a major empowerment turning point in my spiritual life, igniting my soul on fire.

Teaching: From my own direct experience witnessing
the Kundalini awakening within, I have begun to
think fondly of the Kundalini as the spiritual power
of God that leads us to the heart of God.

The Kundalini awakening is an incredible blessing and occurrence. It is such a profound ecstatic spiritual birth, that the best way I can communicate about it is to share the joy and mystery of the awakening as I am doing in this spiritual autobiography. The spiritual master's touch is not the only way that Kundalini can be awakened, but it is the safest, most powerful, and most effective. The awakening may be the intense classical variety, as I have described in my experiences, or it may be moderate or mild. It occurs according to the Kundalini energy build-up in each person and what his or her internal spiritual circuitry can handle. It is important to acknowledge that the mild and moderate awakening, which often occurs, as well as the strong classically described awakening as I experienced, are all evidence of an awakened Kundalini. In my teaching approach, after a Shaktipat/Haniha meditation, it is important to have people share so that they can identify the awakening, as most Kundalini awakenings are not as blatantly dramatic as just described.

Teaching: For the vast majority of people,
spiritual awakening is gentle.

In my clinical experience based at our Kundalini Crisis Clinic—and initially working directly under Swami Muktananda on these issues, in supporting people with Kundalini awakening over the past forty-five plus years, through which tens of thousands of people have been awakened—it is rare for anyone to have serious trouble with the awakening of the Kundalini. It helps to remember that it is our own Divine energy that is awakened. It is, of course, comforting and helpful to have the awakening in the context of right fellowship with someone who is experienced with the workings of Kundalini and is carrying the lineage energy. In my work with people who have had difficulty from a spontaneous and/or drug-induced activation, part of the rebalancing is to give them Shaktipat/Haniha in a group setting, which helps to align them with the power of the lineages. This approach has been proven to be helpful in rebalancing this Ruach Ha'Kodesh/Kundalini energy.

Teaching: Once our Kundalini is awakened, we become
more spiritually empowered to see and experience
the cosmic Tantric dance of the Divine in everything.
This spiritual awakening and empowerment is one of
the greatest blessings one can have in a lifetime.

***

After recovering enough from the first intensive, I was eager to take the next intensive a few weeks later at Swami Muktananda's ashram in Oakland with another group of a few thousand people. This time, I experienced even more kriyas (postures, breathing techniques, sounds). In one of the Shaktipat sessions, my body and breath spontaneously went through all the different pranayamas (Yogic breathing patterns) that I would ever be exposed to. The Kundalini guided me through a very exhausting period of nonstop *Kriyavati Pranayama* for the duration of the hourlong meditation. Spontaneous breathing patterns completely controlled my body. I knew nothing about pranayama at that time, but after several more spontaneous episodes I became interested in studying pranayama. Presently, forty-five years later doing pranayama six days per week still remains part of my routine. In retrospect, over the years, all the kriyas and visions that spontaneously arose gave a detailed esoteric meaning to my spiritual transformation, including the experience of the distinct subtle body anatomy and energy flows that I have shared in my books starting in 1986. It seems these detailed Kundalini flows and kriyas were given to me as part of my dharma to share with people from our Western cultures. A little later in this continued expansion of consciousness in the second intensive, some of the energetic phenomena associated with the activated Kundalini appeared to move over the top of my head and down to the stomach area. It is secondary compared to the focus of energy upward toward the crown chakra, but it seems to be a detail worth reporting.

As the Kundalini unfolded in the second meditation intensive, the energy became even more powerful as it moved up my spine with hot-cold shooting pains going on in my upper back and neck. I also experienced burning pains in my thyroid area, as well as head and neck gyrations. I experienced each of the chakras as energetic petals lit up. It was initially confusing (as stated earlier) since eight petals were seen in the heart chakra, when classically as researched in the Yogic literature, there were supposed to be twelve petals. On further investigation over the years, the eight-petal form was discovered in the esoteric Yogic literature to be a vision of the spiritual heart known as the *ananda kanda* or ananda kanda lotus. In essence, this eight-petalled lotus is a deeper frequency and inner part of the heart chakra. In the second intensive the brow (ajna chakra/third eye chakra) began to pulsate as the energy culminated in an enormous explosion of white light in the head. On the inner plane I both saw and experienced the crown chakra become golden light, alternating between an inverted golden saucer and a thousand golden lights. Following this explosion, a deep inner peace pervaded as the illusionary identity with the "I Am-ness" dissolved into the Nothing. In emerging out of the Nothing, a small, silent God voice (*Kol D'mama Daka*) said, "You should learn to eat and live in a way that feeds the Kundalini." This was my first overt, direct Divine Will instruction. It was the voice of a God-seed message that started my career dharma in teaching plant-source-only live-foods as the best diet to support and activate the Kundalini and for supporting all of us to become superconductors of the Divine. This was the basis and inspiration of my first book *Spiritual Nutrition and the Rainbow Diet* published in 1986, as well as for my later book *Spiritual Nutrition: Six Foundations for Spiritual Life and the Awakening of Kundalini* published in 2005. Choosing to follow this valid Divine directive is an important message of how important it is to take inner guidance seriously. Simultaneously, it is important to distinguish these Divine Whispers from egoic or even psychotic voices.

Teaching: Divine messages need to align with the cosmic and ancient spiritual guidelines, like the Ten Speakings (Ten Commandments), Yogic Yamas and Niyamas, or Buddhist Eightfold Path. They also need to be validated by our own consciences and also by our spiritual collectives and/or spiritual teacher. All three criteria need to be aligned before choosing to fully listen and act.

Once I committed to following this silent voice of God, I began to experience and see major goodness, not only for me, but also for tens of thousands of students around the world who have aligned with this Shaktipat/Ruach Ha'Kodesh-inspired formulation and teaching of spiritual nutrition. After this "silent" Divine directive, in this second Shaktipat intensive, I became aware of a brilliantly shining two-petalled flower in my brow chakra radiating a beautiful light, filling my being with pure ecstasy and love while enveloping the total beingness. A deep feeling of belonging and total freedom emerged. My body pulsed in the ecstasy of "I am free." It was my first taste of the ecstasy of liberation. Also, during the second intensive, I began to notice auric colors around people, especially around Swami Muktananda. It was during this time that I experienced a primary, ongoing, soul-felt apperception of the eternal Truth, which, over time, has continued to expand from *swarupa* (an enlightenment moment) to *swadharma* (a sustained enlightenment awareness).

Teaching: It is important not to take a flash of Divine insight as enlightenment. Over time, as we stay with our spiritual way of life, we become more rooted and steady in these enlightened awarenesses. When these awarenesses become at least a steady fifty-one percent of our overall consciousness it then starts to be considered more of the first stages of liberation on the spectrum of Self-Realization and progressing to God-merging.

It was also in this temporary post-Shaktipat state that a long sought-after answer was given to me that I had been seeking since the death of my brother seventeen years earlier. The answer was:

Teaching: There is no death for the Self, only the physical body dies…the Self is immortal.

Receiving this direct experience of the answer to the mystery of death fulfilled my personal criteria for selecting a guru. So, with this answer, among the obvious other things happening, such as the powerful and dramatic awakening of my Kundalini energy, Swami Muktananda became my guru. During this pivotal second intensive, I moved beyond faith in God as an abstract idea to a direct experiential knowing of the existence of the Divine dancing within all creation and within myself. This experiential awareness activated an incredible level of subtle and ever-growing ongoing internal bliss. To have access to the direct experience of God's presence took me to the apperception of the direct non-verbal knowledge of God and my True Nature as the Transcendent Reality…and this was just the beginning. I intuited that I was being prepared to be part of a worldwide spiritual expansion and upliftment of planetary consciousness that was already happening. These enlightenment awakenings were not the end of the journey for me but seemed to be part of a wild beginning of an unending Shakti-push leading toward stabilization of these temporary enlightenment experiential awarenesses into a steady state of liberation.

Teaching: A liberated master can play a powerful role in supporting one's path to liberation.

Chronologically dividing this seven-year cycle with Swami Muktananda into a time sequence does not capture the true essence of the process of my spiritual evolution. The focus of this chapter has been more on the unfolding of my understanding of the inner levels of the spiritual energy as they occurred over time. This experiential report shares my respect and feeling for the power and awesomeness of the awakened Kundalini/Ruach Ha'Kodesh. It has irrevocably altered my life, yet it represented only the first major step of the spiritual awakening and unfolding. It seemed and still seems humbling and awesome to be so directed and specifically empowered to be fully living in liberation and sharing this unique part of my dharma.

Teaching: The world was created so we could experience the Oneness of God; and so that we could have an ongoing direct non-dual experience of God as One; and to become Self-Realized; and then eventually God-Realized. It was also created for us to be in constant non-causal gratitude, non-causal celebration, non-causal peace, love, and joy in living the Word of God.

With this profound and straightforward understanding about death, I began sharing this understanding along with meditation at most of the hospices in New York State, the northern East Coast, and also in Northern and Southern California. These hospice lectures and meditation represented the giving back completion of this quest.

Over time, while all of this was going on my deceased brother Richard continued to communicate in dreams and meditations. And sometimes in other unique ways such as in the early 1990s when a very powerful psychic from New York City (not unlike the Oracle from *The Matrix* movie) was coming to meet with me. The psychic got delayed on her way from the Bronx and was about to give up when my brother Richard physically appeared to her and said it was critical that she meet me; and so, she continued on her journey determined to meet with me. That was the first thing she shared in our initial meeting. She had no previous awareness of any of this information. I had not talked to her or met with her before this, except to set up a meeting place. Her experience was a confirmation that this connection and constant support from Richard was ongoing. We are not the only ones here.

Teaching: We live in a multidimensional universe with many levels of souls and of entities around us all the time that we do not usually see, but may feel or sense.

Chapter 7

KUNDALINI AWAKENING: REVEALING OF THE SUBTLE INNER ANATOMY

*A*fter experiencing the profound grace of this Kundalini awakening, my inner fire urge for the Divine pushed me to pursue this path of liberation in a maximum in-depth way. This directly included staying with Swami Muktananda at his *Siddha Peeth*, a powerful Shakti ashram in India near a little town called Ganeshpuri; and to travel with him as part of our travelling ashram community of a few thousand people on his world tour. Little did I know that my seven years with him would also be the last seven years of his earthly life.

> *Teaching:* When the door opens on the path to
> liberation that is the time to walk through.

Nora and our two children, Rafael and Heather, were also on the tour with me. We lived in the Ganeshpuri Ashram about sixty kilometers from Mumbai, as well as several ashram settings around the U.S., such as the South Fallsburg Ashram in upstate New York; the Oakland Ashram in California; Santa Monica, California; Honolulu, Hawaii; and Miami, Florida. We never felt settled in any other location. It was a boon that Swami Muktananda was so supportive of householders living this Yogic path of liberation. I appeared, however, to be the only householder allowed to stand with the swamis during *darshan*, where people would line up each day to meet with and ask personal questions of Swami Muktananda. This enabled me to hear all his personal teachings and advice to the ashramites and visitors which was an empowering spiritual education. This approximate one hour per day darshan experience, meditating six hours daily, chanting four and a half hours daily, and my four-and-one-half hours of guru *seva* (service) as a holistic physician, as well as being a father and husband, was about all I had time to do. I was grateful that Swami Muktananda supported and created the spiritual space in general as well as the ashram space for householders to become liberated, and not just the swamis. Contrary to many ashramites, including Nora, Heather, and Rafael, I was extremely comfortable in India, even in 120-degree Fahrenheit weather and could have permanently stayed in India. However, it was not my dharma to stay because of the children and what I intuited about future service that needed to be done in the West.

Over the next few years with Swami Muktananda, my daily energetic transformative inner visions were nonstop. The time I spent in meditation rapidly increased from one hour daily to up to six hours daily as my physical and subtle vehicle developed the capacity to handle the energy. Meditation in itself became both a general and also specific consciousness-transforming experience from the many subtle plane experiences which appeared to me. It was literally my food and a major source of spiritual teachings. For example, for a period I had a repeated vision of a white *Shiva Lingam*. On the highest level, the Shiva Lingam represents the merging of *Shiva* (sacred male) and *Shakti* (sacred female) into the cosmic Oneness. That repeated vision over time transferred its symbolic truth into my consciousness in a mysterious and permanent way that illuminated the full Oneness of consciousness.

Teaching: The merging of the inner male and inner female leads to the awareness of the non-dual Oneness with all creation, God, and the Self.

During our stay at the Ganeshpuri Ashram, although not seeking it, I experienced many astral plane deities who also appeared in meditations giving particular teachings. There was no need for me to study Hindu mythology because it all came in meditation without asking. Some, like Shiva, came quite frequently and with specific teachings, and, thus, I was inspired to do a Shiva *puja* (act of worship) in the Shiva temple in the Ganeshpuri Ashram at 2:30 a.m. before meditation each day. The swami sleeping in the temple got used to being awakened by me to begin the traditional ceremony with *bilva* leaves placed ceremonially on the Shiva Lingam. Most of the gods and goddesses in my astral plane visions were easy to recognize and also gave specific teachings, but one in particular took about three years to identify and to understand. It was a persistent vision of a male body with three heads with Shiva being one of the heads. The point I am making however, and for whatever reason beyond my understanding and choice was that the teachings and spiritual power of the Hindu gods and goddesses was somehow being downloaded into my consciousness or possibly released from my unconsciousness into my conscious awareness. It was very real.

It was during these early years with Swami Muktananda that I met Swami Prakashananda Sarasvati, who in 1969 was the first Swami Muktananda declared liberated. He was like the Divine Mother. I met him one day, in the Ganeshpuri Ashram, when I felt this tremendous forcefield of love behind me. I turned around and saw this mystical motherly man with thick glasses standing behind me about ten yards away. It was an instant connection. Often, I would visit his ashram in Saptashrungi for a few days at a time and later his two-room house in Nasik on the grounds of the gigantic Rama Temple. There were just a few Westerners around him, and our time together was a continuous sweet darshan. Over time he became my guru "uncle," which worked as he was in the same lineage and was deeply devoted to Swami Muktananda and the Divine Mother. At Swami Prakashananda's ashram in Saptashrungi, I discovered a tree with three equal trunks and asked about it. Swami Prakashananda explained that it was the energy of *Dattatreya*, the primordial guru, made of *Brahma*, Shiva, and *Vishnu*. This explained my frequent visions of the three-headed figure. It was Dattatreya.

Hanging out with Swami Prakashananda on the front steps of his two-room house in Nasik, India.

Although the experiences of all these deities happened mostly at the Ganeshpuri Ashram of Swami Muktananda, occasionally it happened at our home in Petaluma in our little forest on our land where we were living after Swami Muktananda had left his mortal body. One of the most remarkable experiences was with goddess *Lakshmi*, the goddess of physical and spiritual wealth, good fortune, and prosperity on every level. She is also the Shakti energy or consort of Vishnu both physically and spiritually. She appeared at the end of a sunrise fire ceremony, known as the Agni Hotra, as a full traditional goddess figure and recognizable being. She moved closer and closer; and we had a total merging on every level, as well as sexual. Her full energetic, feminine spiritual blessings entered me, and she still remains part of my beingness, expressing in a variety of subtle ways. Lakshmi was the last Hindu goddess to visit me. Her Divine appearance was distinct from a vision. It was a direct astral plane materialization like I experienced with Sai Baba of Shiridi. This visitation from Lakshmi further prompted my physical and subtle bodies to unify the sacred male and female energies within. Additionally, the experience of the multiple Hindu deities having real existence on the astral plane was amazing, transformative, informative, seductive, and almost overwhelming.

Teaching: The merging of female and male internal energies is a critical transformation that happens on the path to liberation. It is part of ending the inner duality in the overall merging back to the Oneness.

There have been two other such astral plane materializations in my life since then as well as the receiving of Divine energy from these. One was of Sai Baba of Shirdi, who left his body in 1918 as previously explained which was witnessed by Swami Prakashananda. The other was a being of light who materialized in front of me and identified himself as Abraham. This amazing and subtle initiation occurred in 2008 during a seventy-two-hour self-directed dry fast initiation in the land of Israel in a desert semi-cave above Arad. This physical appearance lasted about thirty seconds. His appearance radiated and infused Oneness, love, and the power of being a blessing to Am Israel and the world through spiritual service to humanity. His awesome presence initiated me with the deepest experience of universal love and kindness, which I still feel today. It was a complete immersion in the Abrahamic love empowerment directive to walk before God, be whole and be a blessing to the world. I experienced this as a full initiation into the Abrahamic way and mysteries.

The earlier *Tantric* merging experience I described with the goddess Lakshmi revealed another mystery to me. It was regarding gender identifications. In the liberation process our inner masculine and feminine balance as well as our outer male and female balance also needs to be restored. Shanti, my marriage consort partner since 2000, embodies some of these Lakshmi energies and thus has had a substantial positive effect on actively bringing the feminine energies into my life and subtle bodies in a way that was transformative and balancing. The essence of the mystery that Lakshmi revealed, from a liberation perspective, is that the whole egoic personality, which includes our physical genetic male or female body identifications, as well as our emotional and mental identities, is a case of mistaken identity. That is, because we are "That," prior to consciousness, in which no illusion of gender exists.

Teaching: Gender identity is a case of mistaken identity. Prior to consciousness, we are *That* in which no illusion of gender exists.

An American friend well-connected to Indian culture thought it would be fortuitous for me to see if I was listed in the *Bhrigu Samhita,* or *Book of Bhrigu.* These prophetic books are written in Sanskrit and are held privately by two separate families—one in Mumbai and another in New Delhi. Family members are trained from generation to generation to read the patterns revealed in the book. As it so happened, a highly skilled and well-trained person from the New Delhi Book of Bhrigu family was in the area. My friend arranged for the Indian reader visiting from New Delhi to come to my home to give a reading. Fortuitously, the reader was able to locate me in the *Book of Bhrigu.* If a person is found in it, the text reads out their full destiny in detail. His reading was incredibly accurate starting with my miliary tuberculosis at age one, through notable childhood events, and the death of my brother at sixteen years; and included when I got married and the ages of my two children as well as being a holistic physician with all the career details as well as my interest in spirituality since the age of eight. He also forewarned that Nora and I would have some relationship difficulties associated with emerging lifestyle differences associated with our spiritual paths which did result in a divorce as he forewarned in the mid-90s. The expert confirmed that my Self-Realization did happen in this lifetime and even gave me the exact month and year it happened which was in August 1981. He also told me that my reading pattern configurations in the *Book of Bhrigu* were almost identical with one of the avatar incarnations of Vishnu known as *Rama*, the King of Dharma. This was interesting because as I previously shared, the Goddess Lakshmi who materialized and merged with me after the morning fire ceremony *(Agni Hotra),* is known as the consort of Vishnu. Sita who is an incarnation of Lakshmi was the consort of Rama. In this way Lakshmi is thus connected to Rama, an incarnation of Vishnu. It is beyond understanding at this point in time what this fully means, but it all seems positive and aligned with my dharma. The *Book of Bhrigu*-trained reader became very excited with my reading's deep correlation to Rama, and he literally spent an extra three hours going over the details of my reading, as well as directing me to a cave, for some more insights, where Rama was taught by his guru, the revered Vedic yogi Vasishtha. I have not yet visited this cave but have its location and how to get there and definitely plan to visit. I speak more about this experience in Chapter 17: "Illusion of Free Will, Releasing Lost Souls and More Spiritual Adventures."

During my initial Shaktipat, the whole subtle anatomy of the seventy-two thousand nadis, the three principal nadis (*ida, pingala,* and *sushumna*), as well as the visions of the chakras petals and energetic knots were literally revealed to me. The compelling, energetic Shaktipat experience during this initial Shaktipat meditation was all referred to in the *Book of Bhrigu* reading; and that I would also share these teaching experiences to people in the West. As the Kundalini energy radiated itself up through the different knots (*granthis*), theorized by my inner mystical scientist to be regulators of the different intensities of the Kundalini energy, I experienced these three knots in three places: below the base chakra knot (Brahma Granthi), the heart chakra knot (Vishnu Granthi), and the third eye knot (Rudra Granthi). During the first two years after receiving Shaktipat, I became more familiar with this energetic and, as the Kundalini increased, I experienced that the Kundalini has different levels of energy intensities. The level of energy called *Prana Kundalini* was experienced from the base chakra to the heart granthi (or heart knot). From the heart to the third eye, I experienced a more refined level of energy, called *Chit Kundalini* which seemed the most strong and full bodied, and from the third eye to the crown, there is a subtle powerful energy called *Para Kundalini*. The granthis, or knots, as I experienced them, regulate the flow of these energies. If these energies are not regulated appropriately by the knots, the Kundalini flow can become imbalanced. These details were outlined in this ancient book. It was an honor and joy to see that this was and is part of my life dharma which I am actually doing right now in this spiritual autobiography.

In Sanskrit, the word *nadi* means "stream, channel, or hollow stalk". The nadis are the subtle energetic channels through which the Kundalini flows. In the very first Shaktipat as the Kundalini flowed up my central *sushumna nadi* from my base chakra to the crown of my head, I also observed three tubes or channels within the sushumna, the central channel in which the spiritual Kundalini is supposed to fully flow. As all this was happening, I was both deep in meditation deeper than I had ever been and paradoxically acutely alert in both the witness and an acute amazement state. Later when I researched this, I discovered these three were called inner sushumna channels the *vajra nadi* which is solar, fiery and yang energy, the *chittra nadi* which is lunar watery and yin energy, and the more subtle *brahma nadi*, which ascends to the crown chakra.

During my seven-year enlightenment cycle (starting around the fifth year), the brahma nadi (which appeared to be the most refined energy and the only nadi to go upward past the *rudra granthi* knot in the third eye, reaching up toward my crown) became activated. In this slow and repeating process, somewhere above my third eye and the space between the right- and left-brain hemispheres there appeared another energetically defined space. My consciousness was perceiving and experiencing what I discovered is called the *Ah Cah Tha triangle*, which is referred to in esoteric anatomy as a special chakra between the sixth and seventh known as the Soma or *Amrita Chakra,* which I had never heard of. It is also called the nectar of the moon or nectar of immortality release area. Inside of the Ah Cah Tha triangle I observed a luminescent crescent moon, and within that were the images of two blue beings, which I later identified in my literature search as the female and male images of *Kameshwari* and *Kameshwara*. Kameshwara is associated with *urdhvareta* or the upward flowing of the semen, which I experienced over a six-month cycle both physically and as a flow in meditation. This urdhvareta continual upward flowing semen experience temporarily ceased the downward flowing sexual energy and created a transformative, spontaneous celibacy period.

Upon the Kundalini energy reaching this Amrita chakra consistently in meditation, a sweet tasting nectar began to drip down into the soft palate of my mouth, which lasted for weeks. It did not matter what I ate or even if I had sinus congestion. This Amrita chakra sweet tasting nectar did not open during my first Shaktipat meditation, but sometime in the second year after my Kundalini awakening. At that time, however, I did not see any Amrita chakra or Ah Cah Tha triangle, I was simply tasting the nectar. If later research into the Vedic scriptures had not wholly validated these inner visions and direct experiences, I would have been sure it was my imagination, but I could not simply have imagined all of this. Not only was the power of Kundalini transformational to me personally, but it was also given to me as a sacred inner mapping to share with the Western World as a dharma.

Teaching: Every little detail of one's life, if interpreted with the intention to understand and elevate spiritually, becomes the revealing of the secret God code meant specifically for us.

Understanding the dynamics of Kundalini and the Kundalini Crisis as it is activated in a person has been a unique dharmic role for me both as a spiritual teacher and psychiatrist. It has empowered me to help people transform through the usual rare but potential Kundalini Crisis or actual psychosis or sometimes a mix. At the time of this writing, in 2020, the Kundalini/psychosis syndrome seems mostly associated with drug/medicinal plant usage after the Kundalini has awakened. It is probably for this reason that neither the yogis nor the Torah scholars recommend the use of psychedelics or plant medicine as a path of liberation. Too many people do poorly mixing the two. The path to liberation needs no props. Using props like psychedelics may interfere or even block the path to liberation, as well as create the illusion that one needs to use plant herbs and have astral plane visions to evolve spiritually.

Swami Muktananda enhanced part of my outer spiritual learning and Kundalini expertise process by assigning me the responsibility of working with anyone who became overwhelmed in general by the Shakti power in the ashram, or even temporarily psychotically over-whelmed by the interface between their psyche and the Kundalini. So, whenever there was a person with a Kundalini Crisis within the two thousand or more people who were usually traveling with the ashram—they were often referred to me. This was a tremendously powerful training and service to offer on a 24/7 basis. However, it was not always convenient.

One time, after our family finally had an apartment in the Ganeshpuri ashram, at two o'clock in the morning there was a frantic knocking on the door. When I opened it, I saw two strong male ashramites firmly holding another ashramite who appeared to be out of his mind. It was a straitjacket scenario out of a mental hospital, a full chaotic scene. In general, most people in the ashram were relaxed about the wildness of the Kundalini unfolding and, thus, very tolerant of most situations, but this person's behavior had gone entirely out of control. Not exactly knowing what to do and only partly awake at two in the morning, I hugged him for more than a few minutes and absorbed all that wild, chaotic energy coming through him. I hugged him until he calmed down and came to his senses. Surprisingly, after absorbing all that chaotic energy, I was unaffected. It was a direct experiential teaching that my energetic field could burn up *samskaras* (deep psycho-emotional scars) and the karma of individuals with imbalanced Kundalini, bringing peace to the situation. Later it was discovered that this psychotic 2 a.m. visitor had decided, since he was in India and doing so well with the Shakti, that he'd come off his antipsychotic medications on his own. Unfortunately, he had become grossly psychotic amplified by the Kundalini. He was put back on his medication, and I began to adjust his medication to help him find the minimum dosage that would not obstruct the flow of the Kundalini while keeping him sane. This is a somewhat tricky procedure, but a valuable service to render as the anti-psychotics, antidepressants, and anti-anxiety medications may significantly interfere with the evolutionary power of the Kundalini.

God certainly has dramatic ways to make a point. This 2 a.m. teaching shifted my whole understanding of how I was empowered to work with Kundalini and Shaktipat, in general, as well as the Kundalini psychosis syndrome, and, later in exorcising entities and demons. Always witnessing and taking avid mental notes of the never-ending cosmic teachings, I had an even deeper and more profound gratitude for the spiritual lessons I was receiving in the presence Swami Muktananada.

At a later stage in my spiritual development, based on these earlier experiential teachings, I also realized that in the act of giving Shaktipat to small or even large numbers of people, my soul-fire could burn up at least some of their samskaras and karmas; and my soul-fire even grew stronger through transmuting these energies. I also became aware that part of my soul-fire energy was passing into them, but instead of becoming soul depleted this process somehow amplified the cosmic soul-fire coming into my vehicle. More importantly, when Swami Muktananda directed me to give Shaktipat in the month before he left his body, I felt prepared to take on this dharma on every level. It became clear that the karma burning associated with giving Shaktipat was not my imagination and I had been cosmically empowered to do this. As a scientist, it is always good to have validation for one's theories.

After the first year in India, I was given an additional task of working with people who were unable to do their ashram tasks because the intense Shakti or spiritual energy of the ashram was too much for them. The ashram had a rule that if one could not perform one's ashram tasks for three days, they had to leave. It was hard to have people coming from all over the world and ask them to leave if they couldn't pull their minds and behaviors together. Initially, this dharma was both unpleasant and uncomfortable until I began to understand that in spiritual life part of the evolution involved creating a healthy integration of the spiritual energies with life in the material world.

Teaching: We need to be able to hold the balance
between the earthly domain function and the
spiritual domain so that they eventually become
integrated as one whole life expression.

Swami Muktananda's subtle teaching was about supporting a fully integrated multidimensional person functioning in all the different planes of existence from the material to the spiritual planes, yet simultaneously not identifying with any of them. Living in a quiet God-centered sublime ecstasy of the inner Self while appearing normal to outside observation has become an essential part of the teachings gained from Swami Muktananda and part of my spiritual learning lesson of this initially uncomfortable assignment.

Because of these experiences and my practical and psychiatric training, as previously mentioned, I started a Kundalini Crisis clinic with Dr. Lee Sannella in 1976 to serve spiritual aspirants from many traditions around the world. We served many people from different traditions who were having a Kundalini Crisis, and who often had no reference point for understanding what was happening. These confused souls found themselves in situations where some thought they were going crazy. Some were trying to meditate and were having physical kriyas (postures, breathings, sounds), and their masters were hitting them with sticks because their movement was not in alignment with the teachings of their tradition. Often, after a little counseling, many of these people were fine.

An additional immediate lesson here is that sometimes the Kundalini can spontaneously awaken for a variety of reasons. Kundalini awakening may occur after years of intense meditation and spiritual practice regardless of the particular religious tradition. There may be other reasons for the Kundalini being activated. More than one woman had a Kundalini awakening while giving birth. One person even had a Kundalini awakening when a brick fell on his head. The ways of God are mysterious.

In Dr. Lee Sannella's book, *The Kundalini Experience: Psychosis or Transcendence,* he discussed the critical diagnostic question which is: "How does one determine whether a person is psychotic or is having a spiritual awakening?" In addition to the experiential training received under the spiritual supervision and observation of Swami Muktananda, these trainings and experiences over the years have helped me refine the ability to make the distinctions of that subtle and difficult question.

Teaching: It is important for the spiritual welfare of a spiritual aspirant to have someone determine whether a person is psychotic or is having a spiritual awakening… or both.

Most of the clients I have seen since 2015 are people who have had a Kundalini Crisis set off with an ayahuasca-induced energetic conflict. This level of crisis may happen amongst people with previously awakened Kundalini, who later took ayahuasca; or in people with a history of ayahuasca use, who had a Kundalini awakening. In all these cases the ayahuasca seems, in some way, to have activated the crises. On some physical and subtle level, there appears to be an energetic conflict between these two energies, often resulting in some imbalance. Although this statement is from my direct clinical experience and not theory, it appears this Kundalini-ayahuasca conflict may only happen to a minority of people. Some people seeking my help have actually been off-balance for several years with their Kundalini/ayahuasca crisis. In working with them, the very first thing I do is to give them Shaktipat to reestablish the healthy flow of the Kundalini energy with the grounding power of the lineage. Often this is enough to realign their energetic system. There's much more to it, from a clinical perspective, which isn't the point of this spiritual autobiography, except to say that there is a potential negative interface between Kundalini energy and ayahuasca, and actually most all external drugs and toxins which may slow or create a Kundalini flow that is significantly out of balance.

Teaching: Shaktipat by a spiritual master with a lineage helps to reestablish the healthy flow of the Kundalini energy.

It was not an accident that Swami Muktananda had a trophy case where people gave up all their cigarettes, heroin, marijuana, LSD, cocaine, alcohol, other herbal psychedelic medicines. In other words, ayahuasca is not the only potential disruptor of spiritual unfolding.

Teaching: When the spiritual energy awakens, there is no need to have drugs, and they may interfere with the overall energetic expression and function of the awakened Kundalini.

The key understanding is that liberation occurs on the higher planes beyond the mind and shamanic awakenings on the astral plane. Kundalini helps us connect to the higher planes beyond the astral plane. The plant medicines tend to take one primarily to the astral plane.

Teaching: We live in a complex, multidimensional world; and when we are initiated into its multidimensional nature, it is easier to directly understand that we are multidimensional beings living simultaneously in all these worlds.

An additional piece of critical, but less public, information is that, in my direct clinical observation with thousands of people, the users of psychedelic, synthetic, and natural herbal plant medicine and synthetic drug usage are more susceptible to entity invasion. Over the years I have exorcised many people from entity invasion associated with drug use, especially from ayahuasca and marijuana. Entity invasion associated with marijuana usage is discussed in detail in John Mini's book *Marijuana Syndromes: How to Balance and Optimize the Effects of Cannabis with Traditional Chinese Medicine.*

Teaching: The explicit role of the Kundalini energy is to expand consciousness, to empower, purify, and transform the spiritual anatomy into vessels that can hold the energetics of liberation. The use of psychedelics and plant medicines and synthetics, from marijuana to ayahuasca, may cause damage to the subtle spiritual anatomy such as the *nadis* and *koshas* (layers of the mind) and/or block the expansion of consciousness beyond the astral plane, which is the plane where these plant medicines and synthetics primarily operate and take one to.

Chapter 8

MORE ON MY LIFE WITH SWAMI MUKTANANDA (1975-1982)

Teaching: It is an honor and spiritual privilege
to grow very close to spiritual teachers and to
bathe in their wisdom and loving Shakti.

Occasionally Swami Muktananda would take us on a spiritual pilgrimage called a *yatra*. Once we went to Sai Baba of Shirdi's *mahasamadhi* shrine where powerful energies emanating from his shrine began hitting me immediately. The term, mahasamadhi is the final leaving of the body in this lifetime. In this tradition, it is common that the bodies of the spiritual saints are packed in salt to physically preserve them so that they can most powerfully continue their spiritual frequency transmissions. This was the case with Sai

Baba of Shirdi, who left his physical body in 1918. The energies I experienced opened several doors of understanding for me. In addition, Swami Muktananda's devotion to *Sai Baba of Shirdi* was observably impressive. He felt that Sri Nityananda and Sai Baba of Shirdi had the same highest level of God-merged consciousness.

Teaching: God-merged consciousness
is only attained by a rare few.

These two illuminated beings were key inspirational mentors for me on the astral plane.

Being very drawn to Sai, I would go to the town of Shirdi regularly via bus and would stay for a few days at a time and would meditate for my usual six hours per day while sitting by the ceremonial fire that Sai Baba had started in around the 1880s in the outdoor building called the *masjid*. It was approximately a two-meter by the two-meter fire. This is where Sai Baba would meet with his students. It was my habit to sit against the wall within about two feet of the raging fire in the scorching Indian heat. Mostly Indians, rather than Westerners, were coming to Shirdi at that time in the late '70s and early '80s. Although meditating that close to the fire for so many hours looked like an austerity, it was comfortable since on a soul level I merged into the cool blue light inside, while at the same time I burned karma under the fire power of Sai's grace. Sometimes when coming out of meditation, I would notice that people had turned my body into a *puja*, a site of worship. I would be covered by all sorts of offerings such as flowers and other things given to me while I sat there in meditation, oblivious to the outer play. That was a little bit of a surprise, but it was a positive message. For whatever reason, I was the only Westerner allowed in the masjid at night to sleep, usually under my prayer shawl on either a light mat or the raw cement floor; I loved the energy of the masjid and was happy to spend both the day and night there. It was a special home for me.

It certainly helped that one of the local spiritual leaders there, Shivanasan, a sadhu (holy man) who seemed to spiritually radiate and glow, took me under his wing. He shared some of his Sai Baba of Shirdi stories, and he gifted me with a large bag full of sacred ash, called *vibhuti*, that Sai had manifested. Just being near Shivanasan gave me lessons in humility and spiritual simplicity. He lived in a little space just big enough for him to lay down at night. One day after completing my six-hour meditation by the fire, Shivanasan literally took my hand and led me to a cave-like house in the village of Shirdi. There was a tall man inside who looked at my hand and said without asking anything, "Sai is your *Ista Devata* (primordial guru). You will even transcend the consciousness of Swami Muktananda and reach the highest levels of liberation. You are part of the energy of Sai Baba of Shirdi." The tall man also said that I would become a spiritual master and my wife would teach the women and help the women; and I would work more with the men. It was amazing that he outlined a specific role to play that appears to be coming true. The tall man also predicted that part of the power of my spiritual work would be modeling sacred male/female intimate relationships. I was to demonstrate enlightened *Shiva/Shakti*, He-Adam/She-Adam, and Aba/Ima re-energetics, thus restoring the underlying Oneness of the male/female harmony, as well as providing a model of the intimate courage it takes to surrender to the Divine. This mysterious tall man never even asked if I was married. He appeared to have the power of omniscience and prophecy. At that time there was some personal concern because Nora, who had her own spiritual interests, did not have any genuine interest in playing that female partner spiritual energy role, but the idea that I would become liberated and reach high levels of liberation was compelling to me.

After this unusual encounter was finished, I asked Shivanasan, "What was that about?" He explained that this tall man was called the "Mango Man." He explained that in the late 1800s/early 1900s there was a lady who was unable to have children. She came to Sai Baba crying for help, and after a year or two, he said: "Bring me some mangoes, and that will be the number of children you will have." So, she brought twelve mangoes, and he blessed her. She gave away six of them to other infertile women, and she kept six and had six children herself. One of these was the Mango Man, so he was born as a miracle. He was a semi-mythical figure in the Shirdi community. Shivanasan told me, "Whatever he said to you will come true." The spiritual energy of Sai Baba of Shirdi, who may have been the one who appeared in a vision as an Essene when I was 8 years old, was and continues to be a tremendous influence in my life.

The other primary spiritual master/guru-uncle God gifted me with was Swami Prakashananda who (as previously mentioned) I connected with during the second visit to Swami Muktananda's ashram in India. In my experience, he was the first person in the ashram besides Swami Muktananda that felt liberated. Swami Muktananda had indeed declared Swami Prakashananda liberated in 1969. I had immediately felt a very close bond of love with him without hearing him speak a word. Although he had retired warrior energy, and he actually personally knew and marched with Gandhi, he was like a loving mother.

Over the years, he became an amazing personal guru-uncle. He was not in any competition with Swami Muktananda, as he was part of the same lineage, but held an entirely different energy of *agaram bagaram* (self-effacing with humor), distinct from the fierce Shiva energy of Swami Muktananda. Swami Prakashananda also had an ashram and a little orphanage up on a mountain, called Saptashrungi, directly below where the goddess Saptashrungi according to legend had granted a boon to a devotee by becoming a figure merged into the mountainside overlooking his ashram. I received informal Shaktipat from Swami Prakashananda in a variety of ways. For example, at night when staying at his little home in Nasik, I had the opportunity to rub his feet, and during the day when I stood near the foot of his reclining chair, I received his energy as he blessed the variety of people—from children, to villagers, and local swamis who daily passed through.

With age, Swami Prakashananda also began spending more time in Nasik, in a little two-room hut next to a large Rama temple. I would often visit since it was a relatively short bus ride from Ganeshpuri to Nasik. In a humorous, gentle and loving way, he imparted great spiritual wisdom to me in every visit. It appeared he was also the local, regional guru, and many of the Indian sadhus would visit him regularly as well as many of the local villagers from the area. Some Westerners from Australia, America, and Europe would also occasionally come. He did tour Australia but refused to go to the U.S. for energetic reasons

Swami Prakashananda's deep motherly enlightened love and compassionate healing energy spoke for themselves. It was an honor and spiritual privilege to grow very close to him and to bathe in his wisdom and loving Shakti. Also, in Nasik lived a family called the Rajans, a medical family devoted to Swami Prakashananda. I was in the outer circle of this group of devotees and friends around Swami Prakashananda. Eventually the Rajans ended up caring for him until he took mahasamadhi in 1986. I am deeply grateful for the time God gave me to spend with him, which lasted about eleven years until he left his body; and also, the tremendous wisdom and loving support he gave to my liberation process including his multiple times of acknowledging me as liberated.

***

Back at the Ganeshpuri ashram, my sensitive 5-year-old daughter, Heather began to cry every time we went past a particular area in the ashram near an adjacent field, which we passed by each day on our way to the 4:30 a.m. morning chants. Although my day started with a 2:30 a.m. puja ceremony and meditation, I would go back to pick up my family at 4:30 am. My daughter's crying happened every single day for a few weeks. Finally, I became a little exasperated with Heather (Ganga) and took her back to our space where our family lived to try to understand what was happening. Our place was one room with four beds filling the room. Nearby was a small room and a shared bucket of water, for our family and others living in the family dorm, for washing and showering. It was a bare and simple setting, but the kids were doing well with it. At 5 years old, Heather had no idea of what was happening so talking with her was not helpful. But something was obviously wrong, so, I took her to Swami Muktananda. He said that an evil spirit had moved into the field next to where we were walking, and Heather was negatively affected by it. Then he taught me what to do to get rid of it and then added, "Well, go out and take care of it."

It was nice that he had so much confidence in me, which was more than I had at that moment. It was my first experience in directly dealing with a particularized demonic force on my own. While not something I particularly wished to volunteer for, by Guru's command, I did what Guru told me to do and went into the literal battlefield and did the special demon removal ceremony with Vedic chants, prayers and focusing my personal energetic force in commanding the demon to leave. Obviously, I survived, while the demon did not. The next day Heather (Ganga) was fine. After that, we had no problems of this sort ever again.

Teaching: It takes spiritual courage to banish a demon.

This type of mystical, shamanic, and liberation learning frequently occurred around Swami Muktananda. Every situation became a Shakti-filled consciousness transformation. In this case, I had to find the spiritual courage to walk out in the neighboring field and banish a demon. Little did I know that this dharma of casting out evil spirits and demons would be part of my dharma in the future. Nor did I ever imagine that I would have the skill, power, or courage to banish demons and resurrect lost souls stuck in the darkness chakras of the planet. It was this direct experience in a field next to the Ganeshpuri ashram in India with the empowerment blessings of Swami Muktananda that inspired and prepared my soul-energy to be spiritually strong enough to offer this shaman warrior service in the world.

***

Each day during my time at Swami Muktananda's Ganesh-puri ashram the other ashramites and I would gather for spiritual discourse with Swami Muktananda. It is called a *satsang,* and some-times it was also a gathering, as previously explained, for darshan which is a time in which people can be in the presence of the guru. I, however, rarely spoke verbally directly to Swami Muktananda more than a few times per year. Most of our communication was both explicit and non-verbal mind to mind communication. I have no doubt that Swami Muktananda was explicitly, by the specific tasks he assigned to me, giving me the basic and fundamental Vedic and Kashmir Shaivism wisdom and intellectual training; but also subtly training me for my spiritual role on the planet from founding the Kundalini Crisis clinic; to becoming an expert in and sharing the subtleties of Kundalini; to empowering me with the skills for diagnosing Kundalini transcendence and/or psychosis questions; to facing and casting out demons; and ultimately to empowering me becoming a fully liberated spiritual master on all levels, including giving Shaktipat. My basic approach was to keep showing up and "go for it" in full surrender. The bigger and most important message was the wise, clear, artful, loving and subtle way Swami Muktananda was preparing me for liberation and for my life mission/dharma of helping to spiritually awaken the planet.

—⁓—

Inner Voice of God

When the silent whisper
Of the inner voice of God
Speaks
There is neither leading nor following;
There is only
That unfolding
In full grateful surrender

—⁓—

Chapter 9

MOVING FROM COMFORT ZONE TO SPIRITUAL CHALLENGE

Teaching: Keep showing up and "go for it" in
full surrender with the spiritual teacher.

Swami Muktananda's made it clear that he believed children were capable of a great deal more discipline and focus than most parents ever considered possible. The children in the ashram, for example, were expected to come to the morning chanting at 4:30 a.m. in which the whole community participated. It was also his policy that children, no matter their age, if they felt ready, could participate in the two-day, eight-hour per day Shaktipat meditation intensives. It just had to be their choice. Our son Rafael, who was 8 years old, took the Shaktipat intensive sitting with me and did well in receiving Shaktipat and integrating the spiritual teachings of both the intensive as well as the spiritual lessons that came from living in the ashram. Heather, who was 5 years old and now called Ganga, (a name given to her by Muktananda) also decided to take the intensive after Rafael did. She sat with me dressed in her sari on the men's side amidst all the male energy and did amazingly, even heroically, well on all levels. In the morning Shaktipat meditation, she began to have almost nonstop kriyas and turned beet red from the awakened Shakti Kundalini. She was so exhausted after the morning that I carried her in my arms and placed her on the windowsill of the meditation hall to nap during lunch. As the ashram was a 100 percent safe place for children, as much of the community both knew and was protective of all the children, there was no concern about leaving her there for the lunch break. She was still asleep after the break; and she woke up and courageously completed the full two-day twice a day eight hour per day Shaktipat intensive.

Based on this ashram experience, all children, no matter what age, are invited to participate in my Shaktipat meditation programs if they are willing to sit quietly wherever in the world I am doing a Shaktipat meditation. It has been interesting to discover that even when giving Shaktipat to pregnant mothers, their babies in the womb begin actively moving around in response to the Shaktipat. In my book, *Conscious Parenting,* I make a strong emphasis that parents appreciate their children's capacity for receiving spiritual teachings, experiences and their ability to concentrate and meditate as early as 3 years old as my children were encouraged to do.

Swami Muktananda was fearless it seemed in all areas, which was a great inspiration as part of my spiritual warrior empowerment. My nature was and is very much both that of a sattvic purist and a *rajasic* spiritual warrior as well. It was quite acceptable to me that my Shakti-driven meditation and *sadhana* which evolved very quickly into six hours daily and the rest of the ashram was a wonderful spiritual nourishment. However, this was not exactly what everybody did at the ashram. As in the outer world, there are always distractions one can find. My participation in the outer ashram life both socially and politically was minimal; and people at all levels seemed to understand and respect my Shakti liberation driven intent and left me alone. I was there for one thing and one thing only... which was the empowerment of the inner ashram dharma, the natural sattvic way of living that has the explicit purpose of leading to awakening and liberation.

Teaching: Learning to be alone and slightly separate
from one's social world is important for spiritual life.
A key understanding is: "touch, but do not blend".

My food choices were also sattvic but the meals at the ashram consisted mostly of spicy hot vegan dishes cooked in what tasted like motor oil, so this food was hard to eat and worse to digest, especially if one planned to meditate within the next hour. The males and females were in separate parts of the eating space and we sat on the ground and ate off banana leaves with servers dropping food onto our banana leaves. From the position of a doctor, I successfully lobbied for a special room with bland, oil-free food. It was a big victory that made many people happy. This may sound trivial but to make this happen in the ashram required mastering the art of pushing for something without pushing for it, and without appearing to be attached to the results.

Swami Muktananda's nature was hot *rajas*, which in *Ayurveda* would be called a strong *pitta dosha*. He was fiery and fast, and that was a little bit of a challenge for my sattvic nature. For example, one day, I was moving slowly, having just come out of a deep two-hour meditation and struggling to come fully back into my body so I could walk to my *seva* responsibilities. I saw him walking fast around fifty yards away from me with a whole train of people behind him trying to keep up. From a sattvic state of post-meditation consciousness, I felt a slightly judgmental response to his hot rajasic energy. He obviously felt my thoughtform, because he stopped, turned around, and glared at me and then sped away. In that glaring moment I immediately let go of my sophomoric sattvic intolerance, and I was much freer to move between the different states of life, which are called the three *gunas*: *sattva*, rajas, and *tamas*.

Teaching: In spiritual life, every moment matters; as each moment may be utilized as a nodal point for spiritual transformation.

Gunas can roughly be described as personality tendencies and patterns. The teaching point I am making is that with the power of one glance from the guru, I was freed up from being stuck to living only in an idealized limited purity consciousness which in Yogic terms is called a mind-set of "tamas in sattva", so my soul could now freely manifest the healthy expressions of all the gunas in proper balance, timing, and when appropriate to the situation.

Now at 77 years of age, I remain in gratitude, while examining how this seemingly simple sattvic-rajasic transformative moment of interface with Swami Muktananda prepared me to be comfortable with all the rajasic, or active, work to be done after leaving the ashram which I have indeed done and plan to continue to do over the years.

After this liberating specific energetic Guru's wisdom transmission, I began to experience increased freedom and a natural alignment with the Divine Will. I understood the spiritual teachings of the three gunas (sattva, rajas, and tamas) in an entirely new way. Although tamas usually means drugs, junk food, white flour, white sugar, thievery, and low life, it may also mean being stabilized in an aspect of a particular guna expression. For example, in working with the gunas, the quality of tamas was used by me to support being fixed (*tamasic*) in my commitment to spiritual life (sattvic). It was challenging for me to let go of my previously fixed but spiritually limited position and to be open to this new freedom. Using this new non-judgmental understanding of tamas, I was able to maintain and sustain a state of *swadharma*, or cosmic beingness, in any guna. Self-Realization includes the ability to move in any direction and use any of the guna energies.

—⚏—

Cup of Liberation

The cup of liberation is always empty,
While being endlessly filled with the light of God.
If one's cup is filled with the tasteless, sour, bitter wine
Of pride, jealousy, and egoic identifications
Or any concepts, hopes or opinions,
The Divine cannot fill one's cup,
For it is full of one's own wine.

—⚏—

Teaching: Spiritual life, at its deepest level in our world society today, requires being a heroic spiritual warrior who is willing to act through any of the gunas as needed.

Initially after meeting Swami Muktananda, we did not immediately go on tour with him full time and continued to live in our idyllic completely off-the-grid lifestyle on our land in Mendocino, California as well as being part of his traveling ashram community. Nora had a significant amount of resistance to joining Swami Muktananda's travelling ashram. I respected her feelings and knew that we had to reach a collective agreement in order to move in this direction.

We had already moved from Petaluma, California up to Mendocino County, about 12.5 miles from Elk on the road from Boonville. We were probably the only drug-free little commune in the whole area. We built our own ecological home, which ran on electricity from a huge deep cycle battery that charged up when we drove our car. Then we plugged our house into that battery in the car for our 12-volt electricity. Our children went to a school right out of a storybook. It was a one room school in an old-fashioned, little red schoolhouse for all grades in the small village of Elk, overlooking the ocean. Half of my time was spent working with clients and the other half working in our organic garden. During this time, we also ran a Swami Muktananda spiritual center for the broader Mendocino community with regular weekly meditations. It was relatively easy, however, to maintain strong spiritual practices in this semi-isolated country environment. Living one hundred percent off-grid meant no public water , electricity, city sanitation, or telephone; it was a creative, "back-to-the-earth" dream setting.

This was a special family-centered time for ourselves and our children. Initially, we did not even have a phone and cell phones were not available at that time, which led to some difficulties with clients not being able to reach their doctor. Making a phone call required riding on my R750 BMW motorcycle fifteen minutes into Booneville. One day, on my motorcycle with my son Rafael I rode to Boonville to make a phone call. Although we were only going about fifteen miles per hour as we went down the road, we hit some gravel going around a curve and flipped over. Raff was okay, as was the motorcycle, but I lost about nine percent of my total body skin, mostly off my back. My shirt was in shreds and mostly missing. From a medical point of view, losing nine per cent or more of your skin is considered a semi-emergency and possible hospitalization. After recovering from this fall, I drove slowly with Raff back to our home. It was my last motorcycle ride. With a focus on spiritual life, there was no need for me to take any unnecessary physical or health risks, including riding a motorcycle; so, I sold it. It was not my style to go to the hospital or stay and get loaded with antibiotics, so I relied on herbal knowledge to make a full upper and lower body back poultice, which was changed three times each day by a variety of community members. Aside from not being able to wear clothes or do physical labor for two weeks, I healed well. However, I still have some slight scars on my back in the areas where the skin loss was the equivalent of third-degree burns.

Teaching: Taking care of one's health on all levels to maintain an optimally functioning body, mind, and spirit is a fundamental teaching for a holistic spiritual life.

We enjoyed a comfortable lifestyle, living part time in Mendocino and being on tour with Swami Muktananda. We used the best alternative devices for off-grid-living. It was a lot of work, however, and not exactly the "simple life on the land" fantasy, but it was a beautiful time for our whole family. For example, each day I would rise early in the cold morning to meditate for a few hours. My daughter Heather, who was 3 years old at that time would cuddle in my lap under a pile of blankets during the meditation. This created a very gentle and sweet bonding between us. However, during this idyllic time, I strongly felt my intense yearning to merge with God was not being wholly fulfilled in this setting, nor did it appear that it was ever going to be the right space to support my intense desire for the Divine.

Discussing with Nora that we had to permanently leave this abundant new-age joyful comfortable communal lifestyle and go on a full-time spiritual journey with Swami Muktananda was a significant challenge for our faith and relationship. All I could think about was merging with God. I knew it was my life purpose. We had been given the grace to fulfill this counter-cultural, eco-spiritual, fantasy lifestyle. But now spiritual circumstances had changed, and it was time to create the space for a more intense, spiritual growth cycle by spending full time with Swami Muktananda.

Leaving our comfort zone in Mendocino was complicated. When we returned from the first extended family visit to India, the Kundalini Shakti's extreme upward flow from my first chakra into the second chakra and moving upward from there into the brain created a period of spontaneous celibacy. This was very stressful for Nora and for our relationship. The *urdhvareta* (upward flow of the semen creating natural celibacy) could not be brought down by any sexual activity. It was an extended sexual upward flowing kriya that had nothing to do with any Yogic philosophy but an actual physio-kundalini transformation going on within my physical and subtle bodies. Even having a sexual thought created extremely uncomfortable pain in my first and second chakra area that extended about ten inches upward in the sushumna. Finally, after about six months, I wrote to Swami Muktananda about it, and explained the situation. In Swami Muktananda's reply, he said to Nora, "Your husband's an idiot." He added that it was only for swamis to be entirely celibate, and that her husband needed to return to the guidelines for Yogic householders, which was to have sex around one time per month. His humorous, Shakti-filled communication seemed to be a blast of energy that completed this physio-kundalini kriya. He was actually acknowledging that my part in the sadhana physiological inner transformation was complete. His humorous comment also opened a door for us to go on tour with him full time, which we did.

There usually are a few times in the spiritual life where the door opens, and if you do not walk through, the cosmic moment is lost perhaps even for that lifetime. That was a key concern for me, as this principle of walking through the door when it opens is more critical than many understand for life in general and spiritual life in specific. A number of people I have counseled have lived their lives in regret for not taking the opportunity when the Divine Will offered it. Committing to live in Swami Muktananda's ashram full-time was one of the most life-transforming moves I have ever made. It has powerfully shaped the rest of my life.

Teaching: Having the courage to walk through the door when God opens it is one of life's great teachings and messages. It requires a willingness to live life with abandon.

During the initial several years with Swami Muktananda, I had many visions of the different Hindu gods and goddesses as well as of Swami Muktananda, Sri Bagavan Nityananda, and Sai Baba of Shirdi (as previously explained) as well as a variety of physical kriyas. After a few years of six hours per day of meditation, the different visions significantly decreased, and my mind entered into a Divine silence filled with white light; and over time my meditations became repeated experiences of merging into the white light and eventually merging into the Nothing. The primordial guru energy was transforming me through the influence of Swami Muktananda, Sri Nityananda, and Sai Baba of Shirdi, which created a great sense of gratitude. It was as if God's whole cosmic power was blessing my soul. My soul energy daily moved into the Oneness of the white light, not only during meditation, but even while jogging. Over time even my individual I Am-ness began to regularly merge into the white light. Classically, this state is called *sankalpa samadhi* in the Yoga literature. Alive in an awake universe, life became a dance of spiritual poetry.

Teaching: The practice of regular meditation continually invited me to dissolve into the Nothingness, prior to time, space, and the illusion of "I Am-ness" which permanently expanded my awareness beyond the limitations of the mind while living in the paradox of everyday life of I Am-ness.

Nora opened to things that were right for her, yet all along ashram life wasn't her thing. Fortunately, she understood that it was something that this wild horse soul-fire had to do intensely as I was like a bear after honey. I was pushed hard by the Divine Urge! This Divine Urge is a fundamental part and blessing of the spiritual path. Actually, at that time, my choice was not so philosophical. I simply had to follow this Divine calling despite having a family with two children, a whole wonderful community in Mendocino, and a very comfortable and economically stable "eco-spiritual lifestyle." I have much gratitude and honor for her to this day for making the choice to go on tour with Swami Muktananda.

Teaching: By ignoring the Divine Urge, we often miss our highest dharmic spiritual opportunity for this lifetime. Missing one's spiritual opening opportunity is a spiritual tragedy that people often do not often realize until it is too late.

In the process of surrendering and going for it, the Divine urge grew even stronger. The Divine Urge also empowered the spiritual soul force perseverance. For this reason, developing the power and persistence of spiritual warriorship is crucial. The path of spiritual evolution has many tests along the way that are there to strengthen us spiritually. Unfortunately, there are many "dead bodies" along the way, as there are those who see these tests as obstacles and choose to drop out. Swami Muktananda's Shaktipat awoke this latent Kundalini energy within me into the full fire of the Kundalini force.

—⚬—

Light

Light
Light
Light
Closing the eyes there is light beyond radiance
Opening the eyes there is amplified light
Everywhere there is light
In all forms
In the absence of all forms
In the Tree of Life Consciousness
There is only light
Not even the Tree exists

—⚬—

City of Yah

When you live in the suburbs of **Yah,**
Complaints, gossip, self-seeking, greed,
Resentment, criticism, and reacting are
A normal part of life.
Come live with me in the City of Yah
Where the eye becomes single
and there is only the light of wholeness, love, and joy –
dancing unabashedly in our souls.
Come live with your soulmate underneath the Tree of Life
In the city of Yah,
And forget the suburbs.

—⚬—

Incredible Light Energy of Being

Half asleep and fully awake,
The energetic body filled with indescribable, blazing Light
Explodes through the total Being,
With a delectable fullness
Of Joy,
Of Peace,
Of Contentment,
Of Love,
Occurring without reason or cause,
The natural human state
Existing as the matrix of Beingness within
As phenomenon and prior,
In the silence of the night,
In the silence of meditation,
Rises like a thousand blazing suns
And settles down,
But never sets in the activity of the day.
It is always background and often foreground
To an underlying matrix
Of ecstatic, non-causal well-being, peace,
Love, beauty, contentment, and joy
Emanating twenty-four and seven,
Residing as Infinite Light of Divine Presence
Uplifting me as the One in every moment of every action
Blazing forth as the Nothing of Awareness
In the silence of the Divine Presence
In the stillness of the mind and body

As the day unfolds through the night half asleep and fully awake
The ecstasy of the Divine Self
Is beyond cause, comprehension, and I Am-ness.
It is Yah's permanent Grace to everyone.
Incredible Light Energy of THAT
The Light of I AM THAT
Is all that ever Was, Is, and Will Be.

—ɱ—

Chapter 10

INTO THE NOTHING

Teaching: It requires a certain level of fearless
surrendered consciousness to allow oneself to detach
from physical senses and drawn into the white light.

By around 1978, white light seemed to regularly pour out of my
heart chakra and envelop my entire being and consciousness.
My awareness would move in and out of merging into the white light.
At first, it was a little disorientating trying to do things like walking
or jogging, but, over time, the energy began to localize within me
as a constant column of white light emptiness and simultaneously
as a source for radiating the primordial white light of God which
had become stronger over time. It is part of why I could have two
hernia operations without anesthesia as well as dental work, including
cavitations, (where an infected part of the jawbone was scooped out

and then filled in) and teeth being pulled, all without any level of anesthesia. It just requires consciousness to be drawn into this white light while detaching from physical senses. Technically this is called *pratyahara* or sense withdrawal, which is the fifth level in the path of eight-limbed Yoga.

After the white light internal activation and stabilization, my consciousness also began to merge into the black void, technically called *nirvikalpa samadhi*. In this process any sense of my persona or "self" began to dissolve. The void became an illuminated black fire of nothingness, and only a subtle, non-dual, empty "I-ness" remained. At some point, this I-ness became so merged into the void that the illusion of a separate I-ness disappeared and there was no one left even to experience the void. The first experience of dissolving into the black void lasted approximately forty minutes per the clock as observed before entering meditation and coming out. This occurred about four years after the initial Shaktipat. My physical vehicle stopped breathing according to those who discovered me. Nora discovered my body and thought I had died and my soul had departed while sitting in lotus position. She called other ashramite neighbors in to decide what to do. Fortunately, she and they were wise enough not to disturb me in this spontaneous deep samadhi state.

Afterward, these states of consciousness continued, in which my breathing would stop during meditation, as the I Am-ness disappeared into the Nothing. At least Nora and the ashram neighbors could be at peace about these states. In researching it up on the outer plane, the subtle organism had spontaneously switched over to what is called *sushumna breathing* in which the central nada channel through which the main energy of Kundalini flows, begins to take in the cosmic prana directly in its pure form rather than as oxygen from the air. This is how some yogis can live after they have been buried alive. In the Torah tradition, this illuminated black fire is called *hoshek* which then emanates as light. Over time my consciousness began to merge more regularly into the primordial Nothing prior to creation in time, space, and I Am-ness and eventually consciousness moved even prior to the dual/non-dual, something/nothing duality, *yesh-to-ayin* (Torah Tradition) unity. This deep level of Nothing is the experience of an Eternal Presence or "I-ness" prior to time/space/I Am-ness, yet simultaneously including all variations of past, present, future, yet beyond it. It is very difficult to describe, especially when the I-ness disappears and only the deep Nothing is left without even the existence of "I-ness"

Things were spontaneously getting more Shakti-filled intensity to the point where I felt I might just physically explode. My primary goal was simply to keep showing up and not interfere with this intense Kundalini process. The subtle imagery of my spiritual poetry is inspired by these direct spiritual experiences and is my right brain way for this profound spiritual transformation to be expressed.

Sustaining Liberation

Liberation cannot be sustained by a separate I Am-ness.
One must be lived by liberation;
And in that paradoxical situation,
There is no one to be lived.
Smiling in Emptiness
Don't try to experience
What Gabriel has experienced;
Simply realize the Truth
Everyone's realization
Will have its own
Individual and unique
Melodies, tones, and expressions;
Realization is Oneness
Yet one's experiences
And expression of liberation
Will vary per one's
Karma and dharma.

---ɷ---

Being Loving

To be loving
Is not necessarily to be comforting.
To be loving is to share absolute reality;
That is comforting
For those who are ready.

---ɷ---

Absolute Truth

Absolute Truth
Includes duality
In the sacred mystical mysterious, paradoxical
Walk between the B'limah and the Mah.

---ɷ---

Fragrance of Liberation

The perfume of liberation
Is right under our nose.
Are we ready to inhale it?
Or do we need to think some more?

Supreme Reality Shines
The supreme reality of who we are
Shines in all things
As all things.
We are the dance of illuminated Maya
Celebrating all creation.
Come join the dance.

True "I-ness"
The liberated one
Resides as the eternal witness
Energetically engaged,
Yet paradoxically completely free
Of the dual and non-dual
Levels of understanding,
Olvayasatya
At peace with all levels of existence.
The True "I"
Is "I-less,"
While remaining
As the "I-ness."

—〰—

Truth Silences

Dancing in the Truth
Silences all categories of Thought
The illusion of real
And unreal disappears
And there is only That.

Total stillness arises,
When the vrittis of the mind cease
And all resistances to life cease
Without resistances
There is no mind
To know
Only That is left.

When all concepts
Are gone,
Only the mystery remains,
And requires
No mind
To know.

—⚏—

Chapter 11

FREE WILL IS AN ILLUSION, BUT WE HAVE CHOICES

Teaching: Our life pattern has a series of options at certain key times which affect the course of our spiritual evolution.

---

*A*t the Ganeshpuri ashram, I kept myself generally separate, but did become good friends with two swamis: Swami Shivananda (Marc Ketchel) and another one known as Swami Vivekananda (Brother Charles). Swami Vivekananda had lots of inside stories to share about Swami Muktananda that helped me better understand how to learn spiritually from Swami Muktananda on the outer planes. Swami Vivekananda was one of the few people who understood the non-dual and prior to non-dual experiences that I was undergoing, as well as the liberation awareness that emerged out of the Kundalini activation. I was very grateful to have Swami Vivekananda's feedback to help me process what was happening. It is important to associate with sincere spiritual friends actively committed to their own liberation process.

Swami Vivekananda was also an expert astrologer who astrologically predicted the exact days of the timings in which my beyond-samadhi, dissolving into the nothing nirvakalpa samadhi experiences began. Using his astrology system, he also correctly predicted the month and year when I would be acknowledged as enlightened. Other astrologers and the previously discussed *Book of Bhrigu* readings have retrospectively specified these same enlightenment times as well. One of the spiritual gifts of Vedic astrology, as well as the *Book of Bhrigu*, is that they take away the illusion of doership and, in essence, the idea of "free will" in terms of the flow of one's life. Yet, paradoxically, the illusion of being free is needed by most people on the physical plane to support their spiritual evolution. This is because it's important for most people to feel they have free will choices in regard to the flow of the Divine will. The process of making the illusionary free will choices actually empowers us spiritually to either move toward the light of God or away from it.

Teaching: We are not trapped in our astrology pattern but have the "free will" to choose a path on the astrological cosmic spiral pattern that aligns with our highest octave of spiritual expression; or also to our lowest octave.

My astrology was ridiculously accurate, and it reflected exactly what was happening in both my inner and outer life. Aside from what I have just shared, my seven-year Jupiter or "Guru" cycle corresponded precisely with the seven years I spent with Swami Muktananda from ages thirty-three to forty. Paradoxically people need to be mindful of the danger of becoming fatalistically attached to their astrology. We do have bifurcation choices along the way. Instead of choosing to be with Swami Muktananda during this time, I could have chosen to study with a more experienced holistic physician or continued to live a comfortable "back to the earth" life in Mendocino with Nora and children.

Teaching: It is more important to be attuned to our Divine plan through our inner intuition than through studying astrology. Astrology may be helpful in terms of developing certain insights and validating our life patterns, certain timings, and how we can best align with Divine Will.

As previously expressed, during my time with Swami Muktananda I hardly spoke with him directly. However, I was certainly in full communication with him on a constant basis on the subtle planes of the mind. I also knew he was actively attuned to and looking after my soul's spiritual unfoldment, both consciously and unconsciously. After a while, my mind became subtly fused with Swami Muktananda's, especially in his presence. I regularly directly experienced the peace of his empty mind. It was an active form of becoming One with the Guru.

I had an opportunity early on in the seven years with Swami Muktananda to be involved more personally with him through his medical care and thus serve his outer form, but it quickly became clear to me that this was not ultimately the right path of service or spiritual growth for me. Since I was one of his personal doctors for a short time, I was given Swami Muktananda's blood to do some blood tests and was inspired to take the special opportunity to put a drop of his blood on my tongue. Within a few minutes, I reached an incredible, expanded state of wild liberated consciousness, which continued nonstop for three days. It was a serious state of altered, elevated, and expanded cosmic reality. It was a fantastic "taste" of what was to come. His liberated soul energy entered my soul not only by his breath prana from my first Shaktipat but also now by the soul energy of his cosmically awakened blood.

Be like the Eagle

One cannot
Follow
Any spiritual path
Like a lemming
To enlightenment.
There are no liberated lemmings;
The lemmings
Have all
Leaped over the cliff
Into the abyss
Of their concepts
And belief systems;
While searching
For the illusory cultural safety of the masses
And their mass belief systems
Of spiritual normality.
Be like the eagle

Who dares
To fly over the cliff
Of concepts and beliefs
Of the masses
And flies
Alone
To the freedom of the Self.

—⚇—

Teaching: The spiritual path requires a readiness
to completely let go of the illusion of control, and,
paradoxically, realize in the three-dimensional
illusory world of free will, there is no choice.

During our second extended visit to Ganeshpuri, as parents Nora and I used to switch off with watching the kids in our room on Sundays, when everybody would come out from Mumbai and gather for an extended morning darshan. On a particular day when it was my turn to supervise our kids in this safe setting, I went up on the roof for a short meditation during their nap. Apparently, I fell into a deep samadhi (bliss state) in the blazing sun in one hundred twenty-degree plus weather for several hours. It was not my intention to do so, as many would consider it a dangerous thing to do. Swami Muktananda was sitting in darshan in a completely separate part of the ashram, and in his subtle astral plane way saw what was happening. Suddenly a person fell off a bicycle in a minor accident, requiring no medical intervention. But Swami Muktananda said to one of the swamis with a sense of urgency, "Go find the doctor."

There was no medical reason for a doctor to see the bicyclist as he was fine. The purpose was to protect me from sunstroke. People were sent in a rush to find the doctor and were directed by our children to the roof where they saw me in an ecstatic state, externally oblivious to what was happening. They pulled me out of the samadhi state and away from the blazing sun. Knowing that my spiritual teacher had directly protected me was special. When you are swimming in the deep end of the samadhi process, it is very reassuring to have your spiritual teacher looking after and supporting you as this is a vulnerable time in relatively uncharted territory.

As my daily schedule evolved, meditation became more and more a major happening as it was one of the most powerful amplifiers of the Kundalini Shakti adding additional cosmic fire to my soul-fire. The intensity of my spiritual awakening and of the Kundalini forced me to completely surrender to the cosmic flow; the six hours of meditation per day was not an elective choice. It took strength on every level to maintain this meditation intensity. My second two-hour set of meditation was in our little apartment or outside on our little balcony under the mosquito net where I sat without any clothes on except a little shawl at noon. Additionally, I entered meditation again in the late afternoon for two hours in a cave under Swami Muktananda's apartment, which was completely pitch dark. Inside, near the entrance, there were a pair of sandals that belonged to Sri Nityananda (Muktananda's guru). Every day I would touch my forehead to these sandals before meditating. One day, as my forehead touched his sandals a blast of light came out of the shoes. It knocked my body backwards onto the floor, and I felt a weird energetic sensation in my back. Fortunately, it was completely dark, and no one was disturbed by this cosmic initiation. I simply lay there until I could reorganize my body from this cosmic event and sit to meditate. I had just received the cosmic Shaktipat of Sri Bhagawan Nityananda for a second time.

In the seventh year the transformative love of the Shakti became more than intense. The reflective message here is that there is a point in sadhana where the Shakti-Kundalini Will of God may become such a flame that the separate I Am-ness has no choice but to surrender to the Divine Will. Besides the personal choice to show up, all doership disappears and God's Shakti becomes the Divine door opening. In this state of consciousness there was no "I amness" to be in control of or identify with; and the illusion of free will was long gone. There was only the Divine flow aligning my soul-fire with God's Will. Every thought or identification of the illusionary appearance of my own life had literally disappeared. No feeling of the illusion of choice on any level remained. Along with the understanding that I was not, nor was I ever, in control of the bigger picture of my life, a profound, ecstatic permanent emptiness seemed to illuminate every cell of my body. A major permanent shift in consciousness had happened.

Some of the scriptures tell us that the last step before liberation requires the Guru's Grace to move the Para Kundalini energy up from the third eye up into the crown establishing a permanent flow. The Para Kundalini which normally emanates from the third eye region is the most refined and powerful energy of the three levels of intensity of the Kundalini (prana base chakra), Chit (heart chakra to third eye chakra), and Para (third eye to the crown) Kundalini. Because I did not regularly verbally communicate with or have an everyday personal relationship with Swami Muktananda, it was natural to wonder how my activation and final liberation blessing was to take place or even if it was to happen. Yet during that seventh year my inner voice was explicitly telling me that it was time for this final initiation to occur. The energetic answer was soon to come. One day when I was sitting down for my usual two-hour noon meditation on the balcony of our little apartment, an externally directed urge arose within me to go and sit and meditate in the small meditation area outside Swami Muktananda's room. It was rare for me to do that because my noon meditation was usually done alone, but I responded to this directive at that moment… and I got up and went to the meditation area outside of Swami Muktananda's room.

As soon as I sat down for meditation, Swami Muktananda in actual physical reality came out of his room and walked directly over to me. He put his hand on my head and began to pull the energy in an upward flowing direction without touching. I could feel his hand directly over the top of my head. As he pulled up, the energy felt like it was going from my third eye energy all the way up into the *sahasrara* (crown chakra). In this direct initiation process from Swami Muktananda, the Para Kundalini now felt fully activated and connected to the crown chakra. The final initiation had specifically been given in a very direct physical way; it was beyond expectation. My interpretation of this whole event was that Swami Muktananda had specifically summoned me on the astral plane to come to sit outside his room to physically receive his final initiation.

As soon as the activated para-Kundalini energy moved up into and above the crown chakra, it looked and felt like a golden rod extending up from the middle of the brain, exploding and expanding in light as one solid energy filled my head. Everything inside me opened and expanded unimaginably into an illuminated steady emptiness that still remains. As soon as the energetic initiation finished, Swami Muktananda turned around and went back to his room. No words were exchanged. This was the perfect example of Guru's Grace.

Teaching: I have never been the operator of my life,
except the conscious choice to realize that I was never in
control and to let go of any illusion of being in control; yet
paradoxically it is my choice to choose to cooperate with the
Shakti unfolding and thus to surrender to the Divine Will.

After this, the experience of nectar dripping down from the soft palate into my mouth, giving the Divine taste of *Amrita*, began to occur more often. Visions came of the god Kameshwari and the goddess Kameshwara in the Ah Cah Ta triangle between the right and left hemispheres of the brain in the area between sixth and seventh chakra. There was also a strong ongoing awareness of the Oneness of all and seeing the Divine glow dance in all creation and experiencing a remaining subtle "I-ness" existing within all creation as part of this Divine dance.

In a state of subtle I Am-ness, I was primarily aware of the existence of a "separate subtle ego unique soul self" as the witness and not as the ego. The everyday state of most people is an "I am this or that identity" such as: I am a male or I am a holistic physician. It is an "I am... something" identity.

Teaching: The personality is a case of mistaken identity.
It is this limited awareness that leads to so much pain
and disharmony in the world as it is identified with
various aspects of the ahamkara or overall ego state.

In this new state of awareness, however, I no longer felt separate from the Divine or all of creation. A subtle "I-ness" existed as the play of consciousness in all. It was no longer a *swarupa,* liberation moment, but had become an ongoing reality of sustained liberation, swadharma. This "I-ness" is a partially merged Self-awareness into the Divine in which only a sense of an individualized soul spark is still left. This is the last step before merging into the Nothing. The subtle "I-ness" awareness is necessary for serving in the world on the physical plane. This final initiation from Swami Muktananda transformed my soul awareness into a relatively steady state of *sahaja samadhi* of non-causal love, non-causal peace, non-causal Oneness, non-causal contentment, non-causal passion, non-causal compassion, and into a flame of a full-on alive soul-fire. It has become the baseline, permanent steady state of my everyday consciousness.

Teaching: Everyone's liberation process is unique yet conforms to a general pattern in which the normative "I am this awareness" transforms into the "I Am-ness awareness,"and then transforms into the "I-ness awareness," which then merges into the Nothing... and there is nothing left. At the deepest level of this flow there is not even any sense of being a separate I-ness.

In order to integrate this paradoxical awareness, I had to learn how to "slightly" disappear into the Nothing and still function physically in the world. The challenge is to remain simultaneously conscious of the inner eternal Divine light illuminating the internal emptiness alternating from the Nothing in which there is no I-ness, or Prior-to-Consciousness, to I-ness awareness while dancing in the world.

It took about ten years oscillating in this awareness until another shift spontaneously happened, in which the polarities of the Nothing/Something became apperceived as the paradoxical unity and integration of the Nothing and simultaneously the Something. It includes the nowness of past, present, and future, as well as the paradoxical play of the Something and the Nothing. It is the Eternal Presence beyond the idea of the limited nowness of the present moment. I call this the Eternal Presence awareness. It simultaneously includes these multiple liberation paradoxes.

Teaching: Everything has already happened,
and paradoxically nothing has ever happened,
and nothing will ever happen.

This Eternal Presence awareness slowly became the deeper steady more permanent level of liberation state for me in the cosmic evolutionary continuum from Self-Realization to God-merging. The apperception of living simultaneously as the multiple paradoxes of life continuum while being unified in the awareness of the Eternal Presence best approximates this aspect of the enlightenment state.

Chapter 12

SELF-REALIZATION

Teaching: The urge for spiritual liberation is
the ultimate primal urge of all human life.

During this seven-year cycle, I did not read books by other spiritual teachers for both lack of time and because I choose to follow the advice Swami Muktananda received from his guru Sri Bhagawan Nityananda which he followed for the last six years of his sadhana: "Stop reading books and only meditate." However, in the seventh year, I spontaneously picked up a book by the Self-Realized being, Sri *Nisargadatta Maharaj*, who lived in Mumbai, and I was surprised to see that I had already apperceived the essence of Sri Nisargadatta's profound *Jnana Yoga* (path of self-knowledge) teachings through direct inner experience and the knowingness that had been illuminated rather through the Jnana Yoga mind approach.

This whole spiritual autobiography and its poetry has been about the liberation process. Self-Realization is beyond the mind/time/space/I-ness continuum and thus not describable and has a unique quality for everyone. Yet there is a common frequency-awareness energetic that is recognizable by other liberated beings such as Swami Muktananda and Swami Prakashananda who recognized this in me.

The outer descriptions, such as not identifying with the ego-self or feeling the Oneness, only slightly point to Self-Realization. Being in actual awareness of the Divine Self as the Truth of who we are and are not, is part of the awareness of Self-Realization, another part of this is constant Oneness with All That Is. I witnessed myself walking in the world as the witness to all and as a multidimensional walker between the worlds, not identifying with any but part of all. In Self-Realization, one is totally free to move in any direction even including choosing to be actively and passionately involved in all of life according to one's dharma.

Teaching: Self-Realization does not mean being detached, but instead, being passionately non-attached, and in Oneness with all of creation and to life.

In Self-Liberation one becomes fully alive, and fully and incomprehensibly connected to the Divine as the inexplicable will of the Divine. In a high-tech world, which some people feel is trying to make us into obedient slaves, the Self-Realized ones are the alive, awake, authentic souls on fire that can inspire all to become awake and stay awake. We are all born originals, but most die as copies. In this context, part of my life purpose has become to help people reactivate their primordial connection with their soul as the spark of God which is the original truth of who they are so we may become originals again.

Teaching: A Self-Realized being lives and dies as an original.

Liberation is a pathless path continually filled with dual/non-dual paradoxes. In the process of liberation, the instinctual drive toward liberation/freedom (*t'shikut deveikut*) is activated. This drive is the most primal instinct and inner drive that we have as humans. It is more powerful than Freud's death urge *(Thanatos)* or sexual urge (*Eros*).

As I had done every few months, I shared my evolving awareness and experiences with Swami Prakashananda, a Self-Realized being who had been acknowledged as liberated by Swami Muktananda in 1969. To my surprise, his assessment was: "You are liberated." He seriously announced this with a look of joy in his eyes. I was not ready yet to believe him. The acknowledgment seemed so big; and in a certain way took me by surprise, as much of what I was sharing with him had become so much a normal part of my new level of consciousness I did not see it as significant. This is another reason why it is important to have a liberated being as your primary spiritual teacher. A few weeks later when I made another visit to his home in Nasik, he again pronounced me liberated in front of my son, Raff, who was meeting Swami Prakashananda before Raff returned to the U.S. Yet again I was not fully ready to believe him. At this time, my family needed to return to California for the school year; and we had finally run out of money. Since I needed more integration time, I chose to stay in India for another month having fun living on two dollars a day.

After sending the family back to the U.S., I again went to visit with Swami Prakashananda. He affirmed for the third time, "You are liberated." There was an Indian woman there named Amma Jyoti, who translated in more detail Swami Prakashananda's eloquent, poetic pronouncement of my newly Self-Realized state in a lovely way. Swami Prakashananda then explained that I needed to spend private time with him to integrate the meaning of what had taken place over my lifetime up to this point and the meaning of what he was now telling me. This time, I was ready to hear the awesome truth of what he had declared.

So that we could talk, relatively alone, away from his devotees, we took the Bombay train to New Delhi. While on the train he shared many lessons and teachings about integrating the energies and aware-ness of Self-Realization. One of the most practical pieces of advice he gave was: "Wherever you are in the world, it's important to uphold the dharma of that place." He continued, "For a Self-Realized person, we know that dharma of a particular place is an illusion, but paradoxically our role as a spiritual teacher is to uphold the dharma of that place, or spiritual chaos may happen in the minds of your students."

One may ask why such a simple teaching is so important in our world today? In liberation awareness, contrary to just intellectual understandings, all ideas are truly and deeply experienced as just simple concepts of the mind.

Teaching: Crazy wisdom can be healthy when the spiritual teacher breaks some dharmic concepts, if it is done in a way that does not harm anyone in order to create a teaching experience for students.

From a liberated perspective dharma is simply a collection of social and personal mental concepts. When this is illustrated by the spiritual teacher in a gentle way that causes no harm or confusion but as a creative wisdom experiential teaching to help students get the point that all is a concept, it can be very helpful. The danger, which has happened for more than a few spiritual teachers, is that they become seduced by the explanation of "crazy wisdom" to justify adharmic (unrighteous) actions and potentially create a fall for themselves. This often happens when sexual boundaries are not honored. Swami Prakashananda hinted that I wouldn't be teaching only in the Yoga/Hindu format. He said, "So wherever you go, holding the dharma of a particular culture or religion is a most important thing for an enlightened Self-Realized being to do. Because if you uphold the dharma, you will create a situation for other people to be inspired to uphold the dharma." This is necessary for sustaining spiritual life and supporting the liberation unfoldment of the students, as well as uplifting humanity. Crazy wisdom is when the spiritual teacher acts in a way that breaks the social rules to show the student that they are just concepts.

Teaching: A Self-Realized person must uphold the social, ethical, religious and spiritual dharma of the place in which they live in order to inspire and elevate humanity.

After our train ride, Swami Prakashananda said, "You need to sit with Swami *Janananda*" (the other main liberated disciple of Sri Nityananda, besides Swami Muktananda). He then made arrangements for me to be with Swami Janananda for an hour. Fortunately,

Swami Janananda was staying in the town of Ganeshpuri at that time, so I walked to see him. When I arrived, Swami Janananda was in a single, humble room lying on a bed. There was a luminous silence surrounding him. I sat down in an empty chair beside his bed. No one else was present. Swami Janananda appeared to have reached a God-merged level of liberation, which seemed close to that of Sri Nityananda and Sai Baba of Shirdi. It was awesome sitting in his presence. Though he was lying there on a bed in deep samadhi, he acknowledged my presence. I just sat quietly next to him, absorbing all the awareness energy. There was nothing to say. His energy was beyond extraordinary.

After my experience with Swami Janananda, Swami Prakashananda explained that there was a difference between Self-Realization and God-Realization or full God-merging. With this perspective in 1982, I realized that I was a newly liberated soul, just beginning this great next journey of the unfolding of Self-Realization. Swami Janananda had reached the highest stage, and Swami Prakashananda placed himself in the middle of this unfolding enlightenment process toward full God-merging.

—◊—

Jewel of Liberation

You cannot capture, steal, or earn
The radiant Jewel of Liberation
One can only be consumed by it
So that one's separate identity
Is replaced by the empty silence of the perennial cosmic illuminated Truth.

Chapter 13

THE PARADOX-FILLED PATH TO LIBERATION

Teaching: When a person is in the blissed-out Oneness of
the cosmic Truth, all judgments disappear. The separation
from the illuminated essence of the guru fades and one
enters into a Tantric relationship with all of creation.

The teaching of holding the dharma also came at a unique
time where it became public that Swami Muktananda had
been sexually inappropriate with some of his female devotees. I was
so merged in the Nothing that it didn't have much impact on me
at that time, but several swamis questioned me about my visits to
Swami Prakashananda. They asked, "Where are you going? Where
are you at with this issue?"

It felt like a loyalty test. I made it clear that I was not interested in engaging in any ashram drama including this one with Swami Muktananda. There was and is only one reason to be at the ashram, which is liberation; and it was helpful to receive guidance from Swami Prakashananda about the unfolding liberation process, as Swami Muktananda was with thousands of others. It was important for them to hear that I was not willing to be trivialized by these external events. After this, they chose to leave me alone. However, a certain level of subtle discrimination about worldly situations needs to be made so I did have to look at whatever teaching there was for me in this situation. The Self-Realized One understands all moral and religious dharmic rules are "holy lies" and all thought-forms are merely moral and intellectual concepts, yet to a certain extent for the sake of the community, they need to be honored in a most conscious way. Integrating this paradox is essential in the unfolding of the liberation process for the enlightened spiritual teacher. In the spectrum of Self-Realization, we are inwardly free of all dharmic concepts and, yet, paradoxically, must follow them.

Looking back at this ashram situation from the perspective of a holistic physician, I have a more holistic compassionate medical understanding of what may have been going on for Swami Muktananda. His semi-public indiscretions began in 1975-1976 after he suffered strokes, probable multiple silent brain infarctions and seizures, angina, and a heart attack, as well as having type-2 diabetes over an extended period of time. Type-2 diabetes is associated with an increased incidence of strokes and heart attacks. Seventy-five percent of deaths from type-2 diabetes come from heart attacks—all of which Swami Muktananda experienced. Potential ongoing silent brain infarctions can also cause subtle damage to the brain areas affecting personality, including moral and ethical behavior. However, this does not mean to ignore the adharmic seriousness of what had occurred, but to give a holistic empathetic medical perspective on the situation which was upsetting to so many people. Given all this, from a holistic, spiritual, and medical perspective, he may have been suffering from some subtle changes in his superego function around sexually holding the dharma. As I mentioned previously, this is not an uncommon occurrence following a chronic type-2 diabetes degeneration scenario, including a post-stroke and heart attack sequence. In other words, it is not unreasonable to believe that his subtle chronic degenerating medical condition, which fortunately did not seem to affect his spiritual awareness and tremendous Shakti energy, may have played an essential role in what appeared to be his adharmic (unrighteous) activity in the last few years of his physical body's life.

Another undermining result of perfectionistic thinking is the tendency for dualistic thinking, which may create an unrealistic and dysfunctional self-perception. I certainly felt that in myself in regard to this situation. People often want their spiritual teacher to be the perfect parent, which is not the way it ever works. In the Torah tradition, all the leaders, including Moses, had some imbalances, so there needs to be a more nuanced expectation. However, the Eastern religious thought-form of "the guru is perfect" as part of the general teachings subtly imply that the guru never gets old, sick, or has medical problems. This of course happens in Western Traditions as well. It is a setup for a lot of anger if the guru is not perfect at any age, time, or level of health. The unyielding Truth is that every human will get old and die. Perfectionism often creates an excessive self-judgment that separates us from the Oneness. This situation forced me to look at this tendency in myself as well.

Teaching: Perfectionism can be an obstacle on the spiritual path because it creates an unrealistic self-view that usually undermines one on every level because no one on the physical plane is perfect, and the path to liberation is a pathless path filled with non-dual paradoxes.

Swami Muktananda was heroic up to the time of his leaving the body in the intensity with which he gave out the Shakti and was present almost every day for darshan, no matter his state of health. He continued to lead regular spiritual intensives, which took a lot of energy on every level up until a few days before the time of his taking mahasamadhi or death. He kept up a high intensity of spiritual teaching and Shakti energy throughout the last seven years of his life. I was fortunate to visit him in a private darshan just two days before his mahasamadhi and receive his full blessing and liberation acknowledgement.

I have given this message a lot of consideration, because it is important to help people not become discouraged on the paradox-filled path to liberation. It is a call for spiritual maturity, which all the paths of liberation require. It certainly impressed me on the importance of Swami Prakashananda's advice to uphold the dharma. The whole situation was unfortunate including for Swami Muktananda, whose actions put a stain on all those twenty-two-plus years of sadhana and the extraordinary enlightenment energies he shared with so many thousands of people. I am also grateful for the powerful lesson his adharmic actions taught me about the importance of holding the dharma.

Teaching: God's Will has nothing to do with easy
or hard, it has to do with being surrendered to God's
Will, whatever it may be—whether easy or hard.

There is another paradox on the spiritual path that is worth
mentioning. When a person resides in a liberated state, using the
term "I" is a paradox. At times I speak of the "self" in third person,
as Gabriel or the "I-ness," but since I am inviting the reader on the
journey to awakening, I have chosen to use a first person self-identity
in order to continue sharing my experience and awareness in a more
assimilable and familiar way.

Teaching: Every step on the path of enlightenment is a trial
of consciousness. The physical spiritual teacher is a milestone
and support along the way, but each of us who are in it for
the whole way need to walk alone into the "Promised Land."

In the last two months in the Ganeshpuri Ashram, I was explicitly
instructed and empowered by Swami Muktananda to give Shaktipat
and to spread the teachings. Swami Muktananda also gave me his red
and white peppermint-striped cushion that he had been sitting on for
years in the darshan courtyard. This was a great blessing and a clear
statement of empowerment. It stays hidden but in daily use today.

In the seventh year of my guru cycle, what was left of my identity
of a separate ego-self began to go spontaneously into complete
dissolution on a regular basis in meditation. The dissolving into
the Nothing experience is not the same as experiencing an "I-ness."

The "I-ness" still remains in the void of *nirvikalpa* samadhi. In the disappearing into the Nothing meditation experience, there is a literal disappearance even of the "I-ness". These states of disappearing into the Nothing became more and more sustained for periods of time while in meditation. In coming out of meditation, the "I-ness" would emerge as a reflection of my true Self. Outside of meditation I began to be able to be physically active in a sahaja samadhi state which means maintaining the "I-ness" awareness while merged in the whole light within. I am sharing these subtle states of consciousness for the same reasons I shared the spiritual anatomy.

Years later, I tried to research this disappearing into the Nothing experience in literature. I discovered an eleventh century Sufi mystic who described disappearing into the Nothing. In Hebrew Torah tradition there's a word, *histalkut*, which can be interpreted as disappearing or dying into the Nothing. Some of the Safed, Israel sixteenth century enlightened mystics, also describe something like this happening. My teaching here is that these experiences do have historical precursors in at least the Torah-Kabbalistic, Sufi, and Yogic traditions. The histalkut or disappearing into the nothing experience is deeper than the traditional death experience. Those who have had a near-death experience often describe leaving the physical body in a distinct subtle body and moving down a white tunnel. Histalkut represents a deeper apperception of the mystery. There are no tunnels; there is no astral form; and there is no you. While there's no death for the Self at one level of reincarnation, at another, deeper level there is a death of the Self as the differentiated Self becomes merged with the Nothing prior to time and space in the Eternal Presence. It is paradoxically profound.

With this level of liberated consciousness happening, and sustained, which had been the main point of spending intense physical time with the guru in an ashram setting, it seemed time to leave the tour. The head ashram doctor had actually offered to have the ashram cover all expenses if I stayed, but there was also the family dharma calling, as Nora and our two children had already returned to California several months earlier. It was effortless bliss to live in India; and the Indian Yogic/Hindu culture felt like home. It was a full comfort zone for me. Muktananda's astrologer, Chakrapani, told me that I had many past lives in India confirming my intuitive feeling. Yet my heart wisdom said it was not dharmic to stay.

Teaching: Some New Age teachings say that if it's easy, it's good, but that's not necessarily aligned with the cosmic truth. Knowing one's dharma involves connecting one's heart, mind, and soul to God's Will whether it is easy or hard.

The weekend I left to return to the U.S., Swami Muktananda was having a Shaktipat intensive in Mumbai, which I attended before flying back to the U.S. In taking my leave prior to the Mumbai intensive, in a private meeting, I thanked Swami Muktananda and told him directly that the purpose of choosing him as guru and the whole point of spiritual life (liberation) had been fulfilled and how very grateful this soul was. As I mentioned earlier, although there was no sense of self, some sense of ego-self is necessary to help the reader follow the storyline. Since we had mind-melded in communication for years, Swami Muktananda knew that this soul energy was asking for his explicit acknowledgment that the Self-Realized state had happened for me. He had a big smile, and he directly acknowledged this soul energy's liberation. He also gave me a Blue Pearl gift, as a symbol of his recognition of the Self-Realization that had happened. I touched my head to Swami Muktananda's lotus feet and then departed. My last few days with Swami Muktananda were truly poetic. After giving his final intensive in Mumbai, while I was flying back to the U.S., Swami Muktananda was permanently flying out of his body. Although many people wept in grief, I felt great joy for him and for my incredible completion of this seven-year Jupiter/guru cycle.

Teaching: The Holistic Way of Liberation is a never-ending wild ride. Our role is to keep showing up. Self-Realization cannot be earned; it is an act of Grace.

Chapter 14

RETURN TO AMERICA

Teaching: Live simply as a way of being rather than doing.

Returning to the U.S. after my seven-year guru cycle brought up a variety of issues that are certainly relevant to me today. Excusing violent political actions as a justification for "uplifting humanity" completely misses the bigger purpose and meaning of life. The key remedy for me was not to sepa¬rate my conscious soul connection from the perennial, moral, ethical, and spiritual teachings of the *Vedas*, the *Niyamas* and *Yamas* of Patanjali's Eightfold Path, and the Torah Way of the Ten Commandments. Although not completely conscious of why I made the decision to leave radical left politics it took faith in my deeper understanding of the meaning and purpose of my life to make this decision. After my seven-year guru cycle it became even clearer to me that the path to supporting people reach their highest spiritual, social, economic, political, and personal happiness potential was to help as many people as possible to spiritually wake up. Since then I have been involved in working individually with people and in groups, promoting national and international peace meditations and more than 100 humanitarian projects in twenty-six nations around the world.

Patagonia mountain view home.

The next stage in my life, symbolically began at age forty in 1983. We had used up all our finances and all our savings on this seven-year journey; it was now time to start over to support my family and create the next phase of our life together. It wasn't difficult to start a holistic medical practice. We bought a house in Petaluma and created a whole spiritual community with regular public meditations and teachings. Swami Muktananda's empowerment blessings were taken to heart and I began to be a vehicle for the transmission of Shaktipat on a regular basis in leading meditations.

In the process of returning to Petaluma and American life, my first step was to focus on spiritual life with family. Nora and I had an excellent foundation of sixteen years of marriage and our seven years of being with Swami Muktananda. The children and Nora seemed quite happy to participate in this process. After writing my first book, *Spiritual Nutrition and the Rainbow Diet*, in 1986, which people in the live-food movement and spiritual people throughout the world experienced as a breakthrough inspirational book, my life became more public. I still have requests to autograph this book over thirty-seven years later. In time, I began to teach spiritual nutrition seminars both in the U.S. and around the world that included spiritual life teachings and Shaktipat meditation, as well as about vegan live-foods as a way to become a superconductor of the Divine. Initially Rafael and Nora were part of the "away" team for this work in speaking around the world.

It was also a quiet period in our lives, which meant Nora and I could give more attention to our relationship. We wanted to help our kids reintegrate into the public world, as both our children were going to public schools. In the process, we also built our own home on 200 Spring Hill Road slightly outside Petaluma. It was a multi-layer hexagonal structure and a hexagonal mediation and Yoga hall that could hold one hundred people. These were gentle times for us to create a householder spiritual lifestyle. After my return, I also began to develop a more formal body of spiritual teachings that has continued to expand. My inspiration was to cut across all boundaries of spiritual teachings of all traditions and to arrive at the essence of holistic spiritual life and liberation; in essence, creating a holistic path to liberation. This non-sectarian Holistic Liberation path is based on a natural way of living that leads to liberation. It is called the Six Foundations and Sevenfold Peace and is a path for creating a quiet mind and transcending the mind. It was about inspiring people to develop a way of life that supports the unfolding of the Kundalini energy and waking up spiritually.

Teaching: Spiritual experiences were and are phenomena that point toward the Truth but are not the Truth. They only give a taste of the Truth. The Truth is not a time-limited experience. It exists prior to time and space.

---

* * *

Arriving back in America, I noticed how obese and materialistically oriented so many Americans appeared. Compared with the spiritual culture of India, it seemed many people were out of touch with the real purpose of life: gratitude, joy, love of God, and ultimately merging with God. Going between these two very different worlds had in the past evoked a little bit of emotional and psychic trauma within me, which many other people have felt returning from an ashram to the United States. This time seemed different. The cultural conflict did not seem to have an effect, as this "self" was only reveling in seeing the dance of the Divine in all things and people.

Although we had used up all our savings in that seven-year cycle; it was well worth it. What a "great deal" at a low price, as what I received was beyond what any money could buy. Upon returning, I immediately went into a private practice of holistic medicine and began to quietly align with the next phase of my life including my new role as a spiritual teacher and a giver of Shaktipat. I also started referring to myself in the third person on occasion as a spiritual teaching, which I do in this poem, because I understood that the "ego-self" is a case of mistaken identity. This ego-self had burned up and become a soul-fire. In this book, however, the choice has been to primarily speak in the first person, which is not so foreign to people.

—ɯ—

The Price

People come to Gabriel
And tabulate the price.
Gabriel went to his Guru
Never asking the price
And left with no money,
But with the extraordinary radiance of the Truth.
It was so inexpensive,
Yet, priceless,
And the grace of liberation
Has made Gabriel the wealthiest
In the world.

—ɯ—

In retrospect, the path of ever-expanding liberation was a day-in and day-out process, which I did not experience as "spiritual practice," because it was and is a most enjoyable way of living life. In the Torah path (which I learned about later in my post-liberation evolution cycle starting in 1983) my practice included: *mitzvot* (good deeds), *simcha* (spiritual joy), and *achdut* (direct apperception of the Truth). My return to America in 1982 was also a powerful time for this soul-fire to complete an exploration of the optimal diet for spiritual life. My understanding of the Six Foundations & Sevenfold Peace also emerged out of my inner transformation during my seven-year guru liberation cycle. It was more formally articulated in my early post Self-Realization stages and is an organized, non-sectarian summary of the natural way of living that leads to liberation.

After returning to America, a surprising daily and progressively increasing experience of disappearing into the Nothing continued to grow, further resulting in the stabilization of swadharma (steady state of enlightenment). During this time all levels of my holistic individual and family dharma were being upheld. I am not sharing a spiritual secret here. The way of liberation has been the same for thousands of years. There are no shortcuts. Living in the Truth never stops. There is no self to have the feeling of having arrived, or that there is no more evolution. Thinking one has arrived is where many gurus and spiritual teachers have fallen into trouble. As the Bal Shem Tov used to teach, pride is always waiting to take one down. With a humble heart, Rabbi Nachman of Breslov (the great-grandson of the Bal Shem Tov) took the position that as soon as he reached a new level of realization, he would begin again, as if he was taking his first step into holiness. Humility based on Oneness awareness and the power of the Six Foundations and Sevenfold Peace, including *vairagya/histalvut* which means seeing God equally in everyone. It is the crucial antidote to the trap of pride. Living in the Truth never stops expanding.

Teaching: There are no shortcuts. The way of liberation has been the same for thousands of years.

This "soul-fire" is not a perfectly accurate term because after liberation there was no longer any real sense of a separate self. With each post-liberation meditation this soul-fire became incrementally free from the limitations of egocentric tendencies, belief systems, and stories of the past, present, and future. Perhaps these tendencies are never gone entirely, but even at the first stages of Self-Realization, they began to hold significantly less power.

An important purpose of Shaktipat activated meditation is to burn all one's impurities, *vrittis* (activities of the mind; transpersonal bio-energetic mechanisms through which the mind expresses itself as thoughts, tendencies, emotions, and desires), and *samskaras* (fixed vrittis/thoughtforms). This helps create a quiet thought-free mind that we transcend as we "disappear into the Nothing". This is the ultimate purpose of the Six Foundations and the Sevenfold Peace. My entire Holistic Liberation path has been a slow, steady waking up from the dream of "I Am-ness" of the mind, which is an egoic noose around one's neck. It is the primal illusory dream into which we are born. In the post Self-Realization process, one begins to paradoxically live both in and progressively more and more out of the mind matrix; no longer believing in the matrix or any level of societal or personal stories of past, present, and future.

There were often little, but highly significant, pre-enlightenment messages along the way. Once, while meditating on the little balcony of our apartment in Ganeshpuri overlooking the field where a farmer was plowing with an ox, I came out of deep meditation and looked at the field partially blocked by the balcony railing. This soul-fire simply stood up above the balcony railing and "saw" the whole vista. It was a surprisingly simple yet powerful metaphorical breakthrough into liberation consciousness. Liberation includes standing up and witnessing the entire picture and experiencing the Oneness in the Tantric merging. This simple physical and metaphorical "standing up and seeing the Truth," no longer blocked by the limitations of the mind was a simple happening that was an actual experiential shift in consciousness in which the narrow vision of the ego no longer limited the liberation of my consciousness. After this simple happening, consciousness more clearly began to control and guide the ego. This simple "standing up paradigm shift" was the breaking of the glass ceiling of limited ego-controlled consciousness. It was an "Ah Ha!" moment. Although this shift happened in a moment, I was aware of the years and lifetimes of spiritual effort that had just fructified in my ability to "get it".

As already stated, in the first two years of spiritual life, after receiving Shaktipat, there were many visions and teachings by the gods and goddesses who appeared in meditation. More primarily this soul-fire received the teachings in meditation from Sri Nityananda, Swami Muktananda, and Sai Baba of Shirdi, along with repeated visions of a white Shiva Lingam (the merging of the male-female elements into one) transforming into Sri Bagawan Nityananda and then becoming the Self. Ultimately and humorously this shift and expansion in consciousness, was a result of some sort of "Divine behavior modification" based on repeated experiences of the Truth from all these different inner meditation experiences. As this awakening process unfolded, and as I slowly let go of more and more beliefs and egocentric tendencies, it became easier and easier to see and be the bigger picture:

Teaching: The message of the spiritual
path is to wake up and stay awake.

Swami Muktananda told an inspiring story along these lines. He went to Sri Bagawan Nityananda after many years of searching to ask a spiritual question he had found in a book. Sri Bagawan Nityananda said, "Throw away the book and go meditate." My approach during this time was only I Am That I Am in the Oneness of That. In my overall spiritual unfolding, I have been influenced by the Yogic, Hindu, Taoist, Native American, and, later, Torah and Kabbalistic teachings, but they were not at the core of my unfoldment. My primary path to liberation was to receive as much Shaktipat as possible and meditation, meditation, meditation. Supporting this was Shakti-filled talks by Swami Muktananda, as well as personal discussions with Swami Prakashananda, and swami friends and peers. The ashram also had several levels of teachers' theory courses that I took to become a teacher, and so I also developed an intellectual background in Advaita Vedanta and Kashmir Shaivism along the way. Paradoxically one can't eat, technique, pray or even meditate their way to liberation. I was being lived by the non-generic Six Foundations and Sevenfold Peace way of life that I (in retrospect) naturally began to do, which helped purify and quiet my body-mind and build the spiritual character and vessels to hold the ever-increasing spiritual energy which allowed me to transcend the mind. There, of course, is more to the path. It is called grace and alignment with the Divine timing and Divine Will, rather than any level of doership.

Teaching: The paradoxical truth is that we can't attain what we already are... and grace is key to this waking up.

The liberation process and the Divine don't play by human rules of spiritual practice. One cannot technique their way to God. The wild unfolding awareness of liberation can't be stuffed into a safe box of the conceptual mind. It just wasn't the way it was happening. The mysterious unfolding of the Kundalini Shakti was beyond the glass ceiling of the mind. Analogously, the good spiritual traveler has no intention, has no plans, and is not intent upon arriving, and the good scientist has freed herself of concepts so that the mind is open to what is. In this way, the power of the spiritual life and the spiritual path was gently clearing the concepts of the mind, so this soul awareness could be open to what is.

As simplistic as it seems, my intention was primarily to be one of those who kept choosing to show up and be ready to die into the Truth... and simultaneously keep some level of general intent on liberation. No matter what level of Self-Realization I attained, the next step was and is always one of being a beginner at the next level of awareness in the process of evolving from the first stages of Self-Realization to God merging.

I regularly had to and still do call on whatever level of spiritual courage I could muster because there were times when it was severely exhausting to burn so continuously. This soul-fire energy made an inner decision that even if this "self" was to burst into flames and disintegrate there would be no stopping. Indeed, it felt like, at times, there was only so much energy the vehicle could hold. This soul-fire resolved to meditate until there was nothing left. This was not a technique. I was merely trying to keep up with the Shakti/Kundalini/Shekhinah/Ruach Ha'Kodesh energy unfolding and pulling this soul-fire along. My path is not a sophisticated, intellectual, approach to spiritual life.

In this paradoxical process, spiritual life isn't a problem to be solved. I was not a person to be liberated, and this particular soul-fire certainly wasn't interested in ego escaping from the pain of the internal and external world or the "wheel of karma." The message, which came by just sitting in meditation, was to rest in the Divine Presence in the "I-ness" of the Eternal Presence. At an essential level, this soul energy cannot say it was seeking anything, as much as it was being driven by the Divine Urge (*T'Shukat Devikut*) and enticed by the Eros of the Divine Kiss (*Neshiki Elokit*).

Over this seven-year cycle this soul-fire lost the illusion of an ego-self and found the cosmic Self. Paradoxically when the "I-ness" disappears into the Nothing, the individuality, which is our creative expression of the Divine, also disappears into the emptiness. All that is left is the surrender into becoming the unique expression of the Will of God...and to keep surrendering until there is nothing left in this endless dissolution into the nothing. This was the essence of my wonderous pre- and post-liberation reintegration and understanding of what was going on.

Teaching: Awareness never has "experiences" because it is prior to experiences. The big Self, as "I-ness", is constantly present as the hum before the emergence of time, space, and beingness. The true "I" is indeed "I-less" while paradoxically remaining in the "I-ness".

In the playful unfolding of the spiritual path, it's important to have spiritual teachers, spiritual friends, and other earnest spiritual aspirants, who create a context of support and guidance because, along the way, there are always blind spots to one's awareness. The spiritual teacher can help one see the blind spots and address one's doubts.

Teaching: One of the other roles of the enlightened
spiritual teacher is to convey the certainty of liberation
and that we exist prior to consciousness.

There may be strong energetics between student and teacher, and it's vital for both the teacher, who's more in charge of the situation, and the student not to have their relationship evolve into a sexual relationship, which unfortunately happens on many paths more often than one would expect. This could be a substantial potential downfall for teachers as well as students.

The overall point of the practice of meditation is to merge into the Divine. There were subtle potential traps that I tried to avoid. I felt somewhat seduced by the many ongoing, amazing spiritual experiences and visions continually happening in meditation. The experience of the Truth emerged from the day in and day out meditation over the years, which helped this soul-fire awaken from the illusory dream, including the seductive dream of the spiritual experiences. Grace was and is the other wing of the bird. Meditation dissolved the illusionary "I-ness" so the soul-force could see that this self wasn't going anywhere, and nothing was happening. In fact, nothing in the big picture is ever happening.

Teaching: From the awakened perspective
nothing has ever happened, nothing is going to
happen, and it's already happened because we exist
beyond time, space in the Eternal Presence.

Over the years, after this soul-fire was acknowledged as liberated by both his acknowledged liberated Guru Swami Muktananda and his acknowledged liberated "guru uncle" Swami Prakashananda, the next task was integrating the liberation process as it continued to expand. This evolved into understanding this soul-fire was and is a multidimensional being; a walker between the worlds connected to all worlds and yet not part of any of the worlds. This subtle, mysterious walk is the key to the enlightenment integration. All levels of existence eventually become as one integrated whole.

Teaching: Part of successfully walking between the
Nothing and the Something is being aware of Divine
timing and being willing to follow one's dharma
or right action in harmony with Divine time.

***

In 1983, I undertook a forty day fast, with the last three days without even water and entered the experience of existence in endless bliss of the Divine. On the last day of the fast, this soul-fire was actually leaving the body, attracted by the overwhelming infinite bliss of the Divine, but a heavenly voice whispered, "No... Turn around and go back." The voice gave an additional assignment... "You have to return to your roots." The voice also said, "You can return to this state within three days whenever you choose."

I accepted my dharmic assignment for the next stage of my journey and I returned to the body. It was very tempting to let go, but I am wholly committed to following the dharma of the Divine Will.

> *Teaching:* When God speaks to you, one
> is best served by listening and doing.

The power of this still small voice of God directed me to reconnect with my Jewish roots, which had been in the background since
the age of sixteen. The *t'shukat deveikut* (Divine Urge) had been even
more powerfully activated, taking me into a deeper steady *deveikut
(God-merging)/chey'rut* (enlightenment) awareness. The message was
that it is now time to share these deep Torah awakenings to help
activate Am Israel and particularly those who are no longer able to
find the spiritual light they hungrily sought within the traditional
religious systems. It was time to study deeply and to look for a rabbi
to help me. Unfortunately, no rabbi I contacted had any idea of what
I was talking about in general, any idea of the spiritual state that this
soul-fire was living in, or even anything about Kundalini.

> *Teaching:* It is sometimes difficult to find the
> spiritual light in traditional religions.

As a result of the new dharma assignment, I had a bar mitzvah
in 1984 and ultimately became a rabbi after twelve years of Torah
study in 2008 under Rabbi Gershon Winkler. Shanti and I have been
traveling to Israel since 2004, twice yearly, leading spiritual fasts and
giving a variety of spiritual nutrition teachings, vegan teachings, and
enlightenment Torah teachings in Am Israel. We have also led other
workshops in Israel for Israelis and interested people from outside of
Israel from over twenty-five nations.

A major teaching from seven-year guru and post-guru cycle is that specific goals and intentions, even on the spiritual path, can lead to building ego and, thus, limit our capacity for enlightenment and expanding in the post initial Self-Realization state.

Teaching: With specific goals and intentions, we limit our openness to the wildness of grace and dharma necessary for liberation and expanded post Self-Realization consciousness into God-merging.

Standing in front of the TOLF where I became a rabbi in 2008.

Knowing one's dharma is not necessarily easy; and not everyone is blessed to be so explicitly guided by the Divine Will. At 4 years old I knew I wanted to be a doctor, whatever that meant. From fourth grade through college, I simply had to play football, and I knew, without a doubt, when it was time to stop playing tennis and football. The choices just had to be listened to. Even when first receiving Shaktipat, a slight but audible whisper said, "You should learn to eat and live in a way that supports the Kundalini." This soul-fire chose to follow those holy directions and from that has come thirteen books, including *Spiritual Nutrition and the Rainbow Diet, Conscious Eating and There Is A Cure for Diabetes.* Following this God-whisper led me to discover and begin to teach that a one hundred percent plant-source-only, at least eighty percent live-food, cuisine was not only the best diet for spiritual and physical life but was one that uplifted the whole planetary network of life. Humorously enough, I never imagined writing even one book. From the books, the energy gathered and evolved to create the Tree of Life a plant-source-only, organic, eco-spiritual holistic health healing and spiritual community in Patagonia, AZ in 1993. Years of being exposed to thousands of people from one hundred twenty-eight nations around the world was not my choice, plan, or expectation. This soul-fire's personal preference would have been to spend hours meditating and supporting the family with a few holistic consultations per day. It was very easy for me as a holistic physician in Petaluma working three days a week and meditating the other four days, to live abundantly beyond any economic level received at the Tree in Arizona. But the Divine Will moved me out of that comfort zone and into a situation where I was receiving $300 a month from 1993 thru the year 2000, with the rest of the earnings going to support the community and living in a very frugal setting. In aligning with the Divine Will, this shift to Patagonia, Arizona was the dharma, and it needed to be done. The results of honoring this dharma have uplifted the consciousness of tens of thousands of people, which of course is the beauty of following the Divine Will. This dharmic lifestyle was not a heroic choice. It was simply following the Divine Will as it came through and having the courage to let the chips fall as they may.

In 2000 when Shanti and I were discussing marriage, I told her, "Don't think just because I am a well-known holistic doctor and spiritual teacher that I have a lot of money." There were no savings, and, at that time, I was earning $600 a month with all the rest going into staff salaries and the community needs. It was not a typical marriage proposal, but Shanti accepted with joy, love, and her style of spiritual warriorship, which impressed me. Our marriage is primarily about love, spiritual partnership, sacred relationship, spiritual warriorship, and sharing a bigger spiritual mission, rather than becoming a materialistic unit for reproduction. Shanti is clearly the woman described by the "Mango Man" at Shirdi.

***

A powerful and simple path to Holistic Liberation is the Six Foundations and Seven-Fold Peace which is the natural way of living that leads to liberation. Paradoxically, it is a path to be lived without focusing on liberation as an intentional goal but as a background understanding and general intention to live a God-centered life. It is a wonderful way to live, and it takes away the pressure that egoic goals create, including the desire for liberation. In this way, my life has become a life of meaning without an explicit purpose or goal.

Teaching: The liberation path is paradoxical, as is liberation
awareness. To know yourself is ultimately to lose yourself.
It is the pathless, paradoxical path of "lost and found".

This soul-fire path has been more about being willing to jump into the unknowable river of Shakti and hoping some part of this "I-ness" knows how to swim. It has been more of a leap of faith into destiny that was, and still is, beyond understanding. It's about letting one's cup run over without being concerned about where it spills, even if it spills on you. The key enlightenment integration for any level in spiritual life is the mystical walk between the *B'limah* and the *Mah,* the Nothing and the Something. In that way, we then begin to see that the world is not an illusion but, in a more enlightened way, a multi-leveled reflection of the light of the Divine in all of creation. It is an illuminated dance of the *shekinah* (Shakti), sacred feminine in the world. The daily path is to respect, sanctify, and grow spirituality from the details of daily life and study, while simultaneously feeling the devotion and love of the Divine. The love and joy of God remains at the center of my life, additionally balanced by gratitude and awe of the Divine. A lot of people don't realize this, but many great enlightened beings such as: Sri Nisargadatta and Sri Ramana Maharshi, as well as Swami Muktananda and Swami Prakashananda, even after they had reached enlightenment, all maintained, as I do, their dualistic *bhakti* or *deveikut* (devotional practices) so that they could increase the *rasa* (love inspiration energy) inspired by that love and devotion for the Divine.

Teaching: A subtle aspect of the non-dual/dual paradox is that we can be both dual and devotional, while dwelling in the non-dual Oneness.

Chapter 15

THE SIX FOUNDATIONS AND SEVENFOLD PEACE

Teaching: The Six Foundations and Sevenfold Peace
are a natural way of living that quiets the mind so we
can transcend the mind which may lead to liberation.

The Six Foundations, which I formulated, and The Sevenfold Peace, which I modified from a liberated perspective for this period of time from the modern Essene teachings of Dr. Szekely, are discussed below.

The Six Foundations

1. **A diet of 100% vegan and at least 80 percent live-food cuisine:**
   My personal diet is close to 99 percent live-food, but 80 percent
   over a few years works well for many people. It also includes
   spiritual fasting two times per year for seven days. The goal is to
   help transform the body and subtle body energetic channels into
   becoming and maintaining itself as a superconductor for the Divine.

2. **Building prana, chi, or nefesh:** Building one's lifeforce is accomplished with Yoga asana, pranayama (breathing practices), *Ophanim*
   (sacred positions of the Hebrew letters), Tai Chi, Chi Gong, and/
   or Sacred Dance. When the prana, chi, or *nefesh* are expanded,
   consciousness is naturally expanded. I do TriYoga asana and
   pranayama six days per week on a regular basis. Doing TriYoga daily
   balances the vrittis (thought forms associated with each chakra),
   the chakras, flow of Kundalini in the nadis (subtle energetic channels and nervous system), the blood and lymph flow, maintains
   muscle flexibility and strength, and brings electrical energy into
   our mitochondria which are the energy factories within the cells.

3. **Service and charity**: In both Yogic and Torah traditions, selfless
   service practices keep our hearts open to the world. It also burns
   karma.

4. **Working with a liberated spiritual teacher.** A liberated spiritual
   teacher can support the unfolding of one's spiritual life, if one
   is ready for it. An advantage of working with a spiritual master
   is their power to help awaken one's spiritual energy, Kundalini/
   Ruach Ha'Kodesh. A spiritual teacher can encourage one's development of spiritual virtues, assist in cultivating the subtle spiritual
   wisdom needed to progress on the spiritual path, and help one

to burn their karmas. The spiritual master supports the student in distinguishing between the cosmic reality and temporal reality and seeing the spark of God in oneself and all of creation. The Holistic Liberation Way recommends spending at least seven to ten days per year with one's spiritual teacher. This is the traditional Yogic teaching.

5. **Cultivating a quiet mind:** Creating a quiet mind helps one transcend the mind into the Truth of That. This is accomplished with meditation, mantra repetition, chanting the name of God, and prayer.

6. **Receive Shaktipat/Haniha:** Receive as much Shaktipat/Haniha as possible to awaken and support the flow of the Ruach Ha'Kodesh/Kundalini.

The Sevenfold Peace

1. **Peace with the body** – meaning good health and strengthening one's physical vessel to be able to hold the spiritual energy.

2. **Peace with the mind** – creating a quiet mind and transcending it with meditation.

3. **Peace with the family** – sacred relationship as a spiritual path; which includes love overcoming fear on the path of intimacy.

4. **Peace with the community** – doesn't mean you've necessarily signed a peace treaty, but that you're at peace or have developed a workable *détente* with the dynamics of the broader community, even if the community is a little socially chaotic.

5. **Peace with all cultures** – including all cultures beyond human cultures. In the Native American way, one includes the rock people (living planet), the sprouting ones (plant world); the

walking, swimming, and flying ones of the animal world, and finally the talking ones with history or human cultures. This is called Mitákuye Oyás'iŋ, which means "to all my relations", or understanding our Oneness with all of creation on all levels.

6. **Peace with the ecology** – also known as spiritual ecology or being at peace and in harmonious alignment with the network of life of the living planet.

7. **Peace with the Divine** – The Six Foundations and the Sevenfold Peace expand, balance, and upgrade the layers of the mind called the six koshas. The layers of the mind need to be balanced and transcended if we are to shatter the glass ceiling of the mind into the state of Self-Realization.

Speaking at the TOLF Essene gathering.

Chapter 16

RECONNECTING TO JEWISH ROOTS, EGYPT AND MYSTICAL EXPERIENCES

Teaching: Enlightenment awareness in Judaism is called deveikut/chey'rut (God merging/enlightenment).

Eventually, I was fortunate enough to meet Rabbi Gershon Winkler, who also admitted that he had no idea what I was talking about but said that he would try to understand and be supportive in helping me reconnect with my Jewish roots from the unique perspective of this soul-fire's spiritual state.

After twelve years of study, Rabbi Gershon Winkler would eventually ordain me as a rabbi in 2008 in the traditional biblical way. By this time, it became clear that there were a few spiritual teachers in

the Jewish world who indeed had some spiritual depth that I could
align with. In Petaluma, there was a wise Jewish elder, the late Herb
Newman, who was willing to train me for my bar mitzvah. Herb was
a great soul and a friend known for years. He prepared me for the bar
mitzvah at Temple Beth El in Petaluma by an old rabbi friend from
Mendocino, the late Rabbi Hanon Sills. I was forty-four, and this
mitzvah which usually happens at age thirteen was finally fulfilled. At
the bar mitzvah, my talk was about the "*Shema*"—one of the most,
if not the most core sacred prayer in Judaism reads: "Hear O Israel,
HaShem is our God; HaShem is the One and the Many." I spoke
about it from the liberation perspective of the dual and non-dual
awareness in a way that none had ever heard before. Herb was in
tears with feeling the depth of the ceremony and teaching and other
people in the Temple audience were moved by it as well. As a result of
this ceremony I began to understand that there was a gift that I had
to give to the Jewish world for those who were ready to hear. That
gift was a more profound spiritual understanding of our daily life
and prayers and also the Torah liberation teachings hidden in plain
sight. For example, when it says Moses engraved the Ten Speakings
in the Tablets, the word "engraved" also translates in Hebrew into
the word "liberty" (liberation) which implies that the Torah is a
guide to enlightenment. The exact quote from the *Talmud, Eruvin*
54a reads: "And the tablets – they were the Work of Elo'heem; and
the writing—it was the Writ of Elo'heem *ḥa'rut* [engraved] upon the
tablets" (Exodus 32:16). Said Rabbi Aha bar Ya'akov: "Do not read
it as *ḥa'rut* [engraved] but rather as *ḥey'rut* [liberty]."

***

My Jewish dharma resulted in the writing of my book: *Torah as
a Guide to Enlightenment*. Beginning in 2004, Shanti and I began to

teach in Israel leading spiritual fasting retreats, a few liberation seminars, as well as spiritual nutrition talks to vegan groups. Eventually I
started teaching at Reidman International College for Complementary
and Integrative Medicine, also known as Reidman College, which is
a private Israeli college founded in Tel Aviv by Sally Reidman.

I was surprised that Israel has one of the highest percentage of
vegans in the world by far – 8.6 percent in 2018. It also has the second
highest percentages of vegetarians in the world with 13.6 percent
(India being the first) according to the Israel State Health Department.
My teachings, in general, were met with moderate to positive success.
My liberation teaching and spiritual fasts comprised the first phase
of our mission in Am Israel. It was laying down the groundwork for
phase two, which was supporting Am Israel to become a light to the
world (Isaiah 49:6). We now live part time at Mevo Modi'im, a village
in central Israel, at the Carlebach Moshav, created by the famous holy
singing Rabbi Schlomo Carlebach. I had the pleasure of being his
holistic physician from 1979 until his death in 1993.

Teaching: Meditating on and singing for love
and peace helps to calm the global mind.

In 1985, as part of my service in these post-liberation times, I
created the Sonoma County Peace 21 movement, the purpose of
which was to meditate for Peace on each equinox and solstice around
the world. Peace 21 started in Toronto on December 21st, 1984
and we began our peace group on March 21st, 1985. It has reached
thousands of people in nearly sixty countries around the world.
We even meditated for Peace at the United Nations in the early

'90s, where we did it yearly, up until the United Nations drastically changed regarding its more overt commitment to the New World Order. So, by around 1996 we were prohibited from holding public peace meditations in its public meditation room in the United Nations lobby, even though sponsored by the UN employees who were the majority of the group. We are still continuing these Peace 21 meditations at 7 p.m. on the 21st of each equinox and solstice with many groups around the world. It has been scientifically proven in many studies that meditation for peace as a group helps to calm the global mind. These meditations for peace still remain a steady and enthusiastic part of my world service.

***

One of my most powerful set of spiritual occult adventures occurred in Egypt in early 2003 when Kevin Ryerson and I were leading people on a spiritual tour at holy sites in both Egypt and Israel. The first of these experiences occurred in the King's Chamber at the Great Pyramid. We had arranged that only our group be let in privately for a short time. I had the opportunity to get inside the sarcophagus in the King's chamber. Our group surrounded me, and we chanted the perfect note of C, which vibrated throughout the room. While meditating inside the sarcophagus during the chanting I experienced what would be described today as a wormhole or portal opening to other realities. Other multi-dimensions beyond third dimension planet earth and this solar system opened, as I ascended out of my body through a mystical blue-white light that was clearly an extra-dimensional opening through which my I-ness traveled. The Great Pyramid is certainly a powerful energetic inter-dimensional portal.

Other unexpected mystical experiences occurred at the Temple of Karnak in Egypt. While I was in meditation in an outer Karnak temple area, one participant described observing a mist gathering in an arch around my head and several people actually saw an image of a falcon perched on my right shoulder. The falcon symbol is connected to the Eye of Horus. During this particular mediation, I had both an inner experience of the Eye of Horus and an outer experience of the falcon as the energy of the Eye of Horus. This powerful energy felt quite familiar. I had planned to keep this to myself, except that people shared with me that they had actually seen the falcon image on my shoulder and a couple on the tour actually took a photograph of it where the image of Horus was visible. This photograph was an additional level of outer reality, which validated that it was not simply my imagination.

While Kevin Ryerson and I were exploring a few little temples in the area inside the greater space of the Karnak Temple, we entered a small unlit temple, where I could vaguely see a seven-foot statue of Sekhmet (a half cat and human) in black onyx. Just fooling around, but inspired by what I witnessed at the Ganeshpuri Ashram where Swami Muktananda activated the new Nityananda statue, I gave Sekhmet Shaktipat by touching this Sekhmet statue in the third eye. This unexpectedly activated the primordial energies within the statue. To our surprise, the whole small temple room lit up, and both Kevin and I could feel the energies of Sekhmet. Later, on the tour, we took people to this Sekhmet Temple, and when I touched the Sekhmet statue, the whole temple lit up again. People also felt the mysterious energies of Sekhmet at this time.

Obviously, some of these ancient mystical occult forces were somehow being activated by my presence. With these Egyptian occult, mystical energies revealing themselves, I was reminded of my past lives spent in Egypt actually working with these occult energies. It was as if old friends were calling me to reconnect with them. However, it was clear that my spiritual evolution and liberation consciousness was more important than being drawn back into these past life occult and powerful astral plane energies, no matter how seductive they were. The path of Holistic Liberation goes much beyond the astral plane.

Teaching: Although it is good to be aware of past lives and their karmas, there is no need to allow oneself to be drawn back into them, especially if they do not necessarily support the next steps of one's spiritual evolution.

Chapter 17

ILLUSION OF FREE WILL, RELEASING LOST SOULS AND MORE SPIRITUAL ADVENTURES

Teaching: On the higher planes of consciousness,
there is no illusion of free will; there is only
the Divine Will of God unfolding.

On the late '90s, (as I mentioned in Chapter 7), contact was made through a friend with a person from India whose family had been trained in the interpretation of the *Book of Bhrigu* (*Bhrigu Samhita*). The sage Maharishi Bhrigu, referred to in the *Mahabharata*, purportedly channeled the text an estimated 5,000-plus years ago. The power of the great sage Maharishi Bhrigu, one of the seven great sages created directly by Brahma according to the ancient teachings was the first compiler of what could be called a detailed prophetic reading of the akashic records. If one appears in the *Book of Bhrigu*, determined by a number of variables (including birth date, height, weight, length of shadow at a certain time of day, etc), the book's records reveal a person's whole history, from birth to death, with significant detail. The idea was fascinating, and I had the good fortune of meeting with this *Book of Bhrigu* reader. He found my life parameters in the book and began reading out the whole history including tuberculosis at the age of one and the exact month and year of my Self-Realization. Maharishi Bhrigu could read future lives, including those who will become enlightened. Anyone who is mentioned in the *Book of Bhrigu* will find their name even today. In the process, the Maharishi grew ecstatic with the revelation of my reading, extending our one-hour session to three hours, wherein he shared many subtle insights about my life. The true book is written in Sanskrit and held privately by two separate families—one in Mumbai and another in New Delhi. Family members are trained from generation to generation to read the patterns revealed in the book. This *Book of Bhrigu* reader became excited because he felt I had the same configuration as the avatar Rama, the king of dharma. He recommended that I find the cave in Rishikesh, India, where Yoga Vasishtha, the yogi sage, trained Rama. I now have actual knowledge of where this cave is and do plan to go. The Indian reader also warned me that if Nora could not more fully align with the direction of my life mission that we would divorce. He strongly advocated that she become clear about her life's path. This immediately reminded me of the Mango Man's prediction about the role my future consort would play. The reading confirmed the belief that the essence and

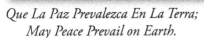

Que La Paz Prevalezca En La Terra;   *Temple at the Tree of Life*
May Peace Prevail on Earth.   *in Patagonia, Arizona.*

even the details of this soul's life were essentially predetermined, and the most important thing I could do was align with the unfolding Will of God. The metaphysical message from the *Book of Bhrigu* is not a fatalistic one but it does minimalize the egocentric delusion that we have 100 percent free will to create our historical reality. Although our destiny in the larger picture is laid out, we do have a limited free will choice to uplift our life expression to its highest octave. Contrary to the earth plane awareness, called *assiyah* in Kabbalistic terminology of the Tree of Life liberation paradigm, where we have the illusion of free will, on the higher plane of *atzilut* (Oneness awareness) and on the higher planes of *keter* (the pure Divine Will), there is no illusion of free will.

Teaching: We have some free will, such as how we choose to relate to our unfolding destiny; and at what octave of our spiral destiny we choose to live. In other words, we paradoxically are guided by our general destiny, but we also have the appearance of the play of free will on the physical plane.

To further clarify this paradoxical and somewhat difficult teaching, in the world of assiyah (the earth plane), our consciousness determines which octave our destiny plays out in that we do have some level of choice as we have possibilities to choose at what height we choose on the spiral of consciousness of our lives. An analogy for understanding this most important spiritual paradox is that our destiny, as the Will of God unfolding, provides us with a general level of fixed destiny. Metaphorically we can think of it for example as a movie theater, with a set of pre-selected movies designed for different levels of spiritual evolution. These metaphorical movies are God-designed for our spiritual evolution. We get to pick the movie in our movie theater "destiny" which is the expression of our "free will". As we naturally become more and more aligned as the unique expression of the Will of God unfolding at the highest spiritual level of our lives by being lived by the Six Foundations and Sevenfold Peace. On the physical plane, there is a need for the illusions of free will because having the power of evolutionary choice is part of our spiritual development.

Teaching: Our free will is the freedom of our consciousness to select the specific movie we get

to play out. Our destiny is the movie theater with
the selection of movies in the theater dependent
on our different levels of spiritual evolution.

***

During this integrative and explorative post-liberation time, around 1985, my body developed a hernia. It seemed to be an excellent time to test, in practical reality, my power of meditation by choosing to do the operation without the routine anesthesia for an abdominal hernia operation. The plan was to go into meditation and to reach a state of pratyahara, the fifth level of the Patanjali's Eightfold Path of Yoga, known as sense withdrawal from the body. The hardest part was getting the nurse and surgeon at Petaluma Valley Hospital to go along with the plan. We reached a compromise of absolutely no medications or anesthesia, but they could put in an IV, so they could feel comfortable in case an emergency occurred. It worked. I did not feel any pain during the operation. I was out of the hospital in one hour to return to my home in Petaluma, meditating nude on our sun porch in full lotus detoxing from the short stay in the hospital. I did, however, take the day off from work since I was a little stiff in the abdomen the next morning.

Teaching: It is possible to meditate so deeply
that there is a sense withdrawal from the body
and no pain is felt, even during a surgery.

In the late '90s while living in Patagonia, AZ the hernia repair did not hold, so the operation was done again without anesthesia in

Phoenix, AZ. This time I had to drive for three-hours back home to Patagonia after the operation. In my typical style, I was back at work the next day. In both situations, the hospital staff seemed amazed and fascinated by someone living in awakened normality not needing to be anesthetized. I applied this approach to dental surgery as well. I had some infected areas called cavitatations which needed to be scraped out of the jawbone. All five cavitations were done without any local or general anesthesia. The tendency for bone problems is part of my astrology but applying a high level of dental hygiene has been effective in minimizing any more dental problems. Defining these everyday challenges as spiritual tests refreshes and empowers my spiritual strength.

Teaching: Mundane challenges faced in a spiritual
way can renew spiritual resolve and strength.

***

In 1987, for the Harmonic Convergence, we brought together a group of approximately two thousand people to meditate and chant for twenty-four hours on Sonoma Mountain in Sonoma County to honor and energize the event. It was a testimonial to the power of group meditation to heal the world. After the fall of the wall between East and West Berlin, which some of us believed was a probable result of the Harmonic Convergence energetics, I led a group of people to do ceremony to help release the lost confused souls murdered by the Nazis in the in the concentration camps in Germany and Poland. Both Swami Muktananda and Nick Nocerino had prepared me to do this work of releasing trapped souls at several Nazi concentration camps and then later at Blood Island in 2016. It may be obvious, but this work is not for everyone. I would not be releasing trapped souls had it not been the directed Will of God.

We went to three of the concentration camps. One was a women's work camp called Ravensbruck, located about eighty kilometers north of Berlin. Our group was staying in Berlin where we were doing some workshops on peace and were having a good time. When it was time to take the train ride to Ravensbruck to do the process of releasing the dead souls back into heaven, everybody had their excuses why they couldn't go, so just another brother, Dan Minto, and I dared to go. We went on a seemingly long train ride wondering what was going to happen, having never done this particular ceremony before. We planned all our ceremonies for the Hebrew month of Elul, (August/September) which is the best time in the Hebrew yearly cycle, according to Kabbalistic teachings, for helping lost earth plane trapped souls to complete their journey back to heaven. Just after I began the ceremony, empowered and shielded in my tallit (a Jewish prayer shawl), unexpected things started to happen. Evil and mean looking demons emerged out of the earth, which both Dan and I were able to see; and these demons did not look very happy. However, I continued to do chanting, prayers, and psalms in front of our portable fire pit. Fortunately, demons are forced to retreat by the sound of the name of God.

Teaching: Demons do not like prayers or the name of God.

A shofar is a mystical ram's horn dating back to the time of Abraham, approximately 3,800 years ago. Blowing my *shofar*, I initiated the ascension process for the trapped souls who had died in this concentration work camp. We could see a column of energy rising to the heavens, and these poor, suffering, previously stuck souls, began to ascend to complete the next step of their journey. Meantime, Dan noticed a group of young Soviet soldiers who had gathered about twenty yards away looking at us in amazement and wondering what we were doing. Fortunately, they were watching in awe and bewilderment as the ceremony was going on and were wise enough not to interrupt us. We were not sure if they saw the demons coming out of the ground with their subtle howls, but they did keep their distance. I could see their soul shapes and counted 100,000 souls ascending. After the ceremony seemed to be complete, we visited the Ravensbruck Holocaust museum. I was surprised when the museum keeper, when questioned, said a hundred thousand had died at the Ravensbruck concentration labor camp. It validated the process that we had witnessed with our own eyes.

It was a great train ride back, as we were both relieved, joyous, and humbled by our success. We did share what happened with the other people. We encouraged everyone to be part of the next ceremony at the Buchenwald concentration camp near Weimar, Germany. On the tour of the Buchenwald museum, it was disgusting and nauseating as we looked at the human skin artifacts to see how humans had degenerated. Hate is a powerful satanic dark force that draws people into the way of evil. We successfully did a similar ceremony to release the murdered souls there as well.

Finally, we came to Krakow, Poland, near Auschwitz-Birkenau, the most famous of all the concentration camps. There we met with some wonderful Polish people to do some spiritual nutrition workshops and teach meditation. I had been communicating with key

Polish organizers to set up a whole series of events, live-food meals, and spiritual teachings. The room I was teaching in was so packed full of interested Polish people of all ages that I had to stand the whole time. People were so hungry for information and inspiration that they kept me there for twelve straight hours. The Polish people were wonderful to work with. For our two-day stay in Krakow, we worked very hard in advance to plan a live-food menu, which wasn't so easy in Poland at that time. In connection with this, a funny teaching occurred. One of our group held a popular New Age "I create my own reality" philosophy. When she came down for breakfast, which we had planned three months in advance, she said, "Oh my goodness, I manifested this breakfast." We explained to her that she did not create the breakfast, as we'd planned the menu three months before. Instead, she had aligned with the energy of the breakfast menu. It's a subtle teaching for the people who think they have the independent power to create their reality. If they are successful, it is because they're aligning with the reality of their destiny already unfolding and also sometimes having an indirect impact on their destiny as a co-creator.

Teaching: We do not create our own reality, but align
with the reality of our already unfolding destiny.

Auschwitz-Birkenau was a big, dark place. We set up crystal grids at the full length of the acreage. We began the ceremony with appropriate prayers to help create the pillar of light for the souls to ascend in. Indeed, in the pillar of light as the ceremony proceeded one could see the souls ascending. The ceremony went on for at least six hours and the souls ascending seemed in the millions. It was hard to count how many ascended, but we just kept the prayers up until the column of light seemed empty. This time we had many people joining us from all over Europe, so it was a much larger group. It just happened that one of the people who had joined us was an old friend from Santa Rosa, California, called Bernie, who had escaped from the Auschwitz-Birkenau concentration camp at the age of 13. He coincidentally happened to be back in Poland, trying to reconnect with the energy of his mother and his sister who had died in Auschwitz-Birkenau. Bernie had been entirely unsuccessful in making any sort of contact with them over the weeks he was there, but in the middle of the ceremony, he described seeing his mother and sister in full physical astral form as souls going up in the column of light into the heavens. For him, it was profoundly healing, and he was quite grateful for being part of the ceremony. We were all a little exhausted at the end of that process.

As previously described my father had emigrated from what is now Bialystok, Poland (once part of Russia) by walking across Europe in 1917 with his father, so I had some deeper connection with the Polish people on multiple levels. Briefly, we also visited Bialystok, which once had the largest concentration of Jewish people in any city in Europe, but there was not much to see and I was not able to make any historical connections.

Teaching: In aligning with God's Will, what one visualizes
and co-creates from the alignment is the fulfillment
of the Divine Will and not your ego creation, as there
is no I to create independently from the Divine.

This soul-releasing ceremony I performed three times in the concentration camps has been done one other time, in 2016, at a location called Blood Island near Upper Lake in Mendocino, California. A few months previously, as a contributor to the White Buffalo Caretaker Association, my son Rafael and his 11-year-old daughter, my granddaughter, Rhea, went to visit the white buffalo. Little Golden Bear and her husband Charles have been taking care of the white buffalo and slowly growing them into a small herd of more than thirteen adult buffalo over the years. Other people also came to visit, and the topic of Blood Island came up. In 1851, U.S. soldiers massacred 250 women and children for unprovoked reasons. This tribe was associated with the coastal Pomo Indians, with whom I also worked with when serving as the mental health director of Project Head Start in a 300-square mile area in this region in 1973 for three years, so there was already a connection. I was also adopted into the Lakota Sioux Horn Chip Clan, after completing the four-year Sundance commitment and given the name Ta Sunka Hinzi (Yellow Horse) and also appointed as the Yellow Horse clan leader. My adoption into the Lakota Sioux Horn Chip Clan was a further inspiration to do this ceremony to release the trapped Native American souls on Blood Island.

The ceremony started with an *inipi* (sweat lodge), which I guided as the sweat lodge leader for a variety of Native Americans, Pomo tribal elders, as well as other people committed to this ceremony. After this energetic purification and unity, we drove about twenty minutes to Blood Island where we completed the full ceremony. During the release ceremony two columns of light arose, which was unexpected, as usually there is only one. Many of the people participating saw the two hundred and fifty souls going up and then another one thousand five hundred Native American souls ascended from around the area, who also had been killed mostly by the American troops and settlers. The ceremony went on for about an hour and a half until all the souls ascended. It was a powerful healing of the land and for the people. During the ceremony, it was notable that two wild white horses came out of nowhere to watch. Blood Island was a harsh reminder of the profound cruelty that humans can do to each other in self-righteous, culturally empowered hate. There was a distinct feeling that this hate had been ameliorated after the ceremony.

Teaching: Until we upgrade the consciousness of the planet to live in harmony with the perennial cosmic moral, ethical, love- and God-inspired spiritual teachings, violent acts will continue to happen; and part of my planetary work, is to dissipate these demonic energies.

Visiting the White Buffalo.

Chapter 18

THE PARENT'S ROLE
IN EVOLUTION

Teaching: As a parent, it's good to share
your life mission with your children.

As a parent, no matter how busy life is, I still always make
an effort to bond with Rafael and Heather and to spend
individual time with them in the overall evolutionary process of
our lives. Heather, who was a teenager in 1989, came on the tour of
Germany and Poland with us. She was an actress in high school plays
and also a high school play director at the time. During the trip she
had the opportunity to plant some seeds of her stage production/
management career. While I was giving the teaching seminars,
my daughter worked with Polish high school students, and they

developed a peace play in the two days that we were there, which premiered for the entire group. Heather has since taught in the New York University theater department and has been the PSM (production stage manager) for the Broadway play called Spring Awakenings, which won a Tony award. It was a particular joy to do this tour with my teenage daughter and see how the experience matured her. In 2018 on Father's Day, Heather at age forty-five wrote a card to me saying she had "hit the jackpot" with her dad. Parenting is not so easy when one is as actively involved in a bigger service mission as I have been, but somehow on a regular basis I had made it happen for both my daughter and Rafael. It's nice to have my parental love acknowledged.

Teaching: The role of the parent never really ends; it is life dharma that takes different forms at different stages.

Even today with my 50-year-old son, Rafael, who has run a Kenpo karate school for about twenty-eight years, and my 47-year-old daughter, I make at least weekly contact, also with my grandchildren – Rhea, Katja, and Anaïs. The love we share gives a gentle sweetness to everyone. Nora (my former wife and their mother) and I still discuss their well-being as needed. Our family love and connection remain a strong support and bond for everyone... and a joy.

Teaching: As children age, the parent-child dynamic changes and graduates to more of a friendship, but one is still the parent in the background.

The importance and power of the ties of family blood needs to be acknowledged. This is important because people sometimes think it is spiritual to let go of their dharma with their family and children. This is not the case, and unfortunately some people learn this lesson too late. In my spiritual evolution, the tantric play of family life and sacred relationship has been and is an important part of the spiritual challenges that continue to add experiential spiritual wisdom. The spiritual teachings may appear in different ways such as when Shanti and I had the opportunity to take care of her mother from New Zealand. Emma was a natural mystic and wonderful person loved by the whole town of Patagonia. We cared for her for eleven years before she left her body at ninety-three. Near the end of her beautiful life, we were visiting and caretaking several times daily, so she could live and die, as per her request, peacefully at home. We did this while we were doing full-on programs at the Tree of Life Center U.S. and Tree of Life Foundation and around the world. And, yes, it does take some real thoughtful planning and extra effort, as well as love. During this time, I had some unusual mystical experiences with Emma.

Several years before Emma permanently left her body, her heart and breathing stopped, and her part-time attendant felt she had died. Having just walked into her home from my workplace, there was no detection of any chest movement or carotid pulse. There was no clarity of how long she had stopped breathing, but it was at least four to six minutes. Without hesitation or thinking, I put my hands over her silent heart and sent her an intense dose of spiritual energy. Moments later her heart began to beat, and she began to breathe. I was pleased to see her come alive, as it appeared she was indeed dead. It was this soul's first experience of actually "raising someone from the dead". Our souls had touched in this intimate process. We both were amazed and laughed. One usually does not have a tantric soul relationship experience with one's Jewish mother-in-law. The truth is that I had no preconceived idea that this could happen and was just as surprised as everyone else. After that experience Emma looked at me differently as we had entered into another stage of an already sweet and loving relationship.

Teaching: Love and commitment to the family
has the strong potential to elevate us spiritually.

About a year later, while we were out of town for several weeks, Emma began intense coughing, and when we returned, she was rapidly fading. Again, the same thing was done with sending direct energy to her heart and lungs; and, again, the downward death cycle was broken. It was clear that she and God had given her son-in-law, at least temporarily, the power of life or death regarding her. Although uncomfortable at having so much direct power and responsibility for another human being, I accepted this dharma. A loving heartfelt relationship with all members of the family in the right setting can become a subtle form of Tantric sacred relationship in the proper context.

When we all had a definite feeling, including Emma, that she was truly ready to leave her physical body, Shanti and I guided her through a beautiful death process. We had already purchased a kosher pinewood coffin and a plot at the cemetery. As per Jewish tradition, I stayed overnight with her body after she died, to protect her soul, which ascended during this time, from dark forces. We were able to avoid having her body sent to the funeral home, since as a doctor I was able to clear everything with the county health officials and the police whom we needed to notify of her death. This was also my first funeral service as a rabbi with quite a few people in our town of nine hundred attending. Dying is a complicated affair in our modern society, and we were fortunate to be able to create a natural, uninterrupted home death and burial on a high spiritual octave.

Teaching: The intimate process of sacred relations and family can be an intense and powerful transformative part of the spiritual path of the householder.

Chapter 19

CHALLENGES OF A
HOLISTIC PRACTICE

*O*n 1987, I began to be guided to activate the next step of the larger mission, which was to create an eco-spiritual, organic, live-food, veganic, holistic health, spiritual liberation focused community as a platform for reaching the world. It did not feel that California was the right energetic place for this, so I began looking for land in Arizona. Our decision was supported by knowledge that the medical board in California, at that time, was actively attempting to destroy the careers of holistic physicians and the holistic health movement in California. Many leading holistic doctors, who were friends, were leaving California. Doors opened in Arizona and Nevada where both states had created holistic medical boards to accommodate harassed holistic doctors from all over the country. Arizona became our choice. In 1987, I was the thirtieth person to become licensed by the Arizona Homeopathic and Integrated Medicine Examiners Board that year. It was perfect because it was and is a board run by holistically and homeopathic peers, who would promulgate the evolved holistic education and approaches of homeopathic and holistic medicine. It is also important to be judged by your peers. Although eligible to get an allopathic license in Arizona as well, I decided not to do so because it made me vulnerable to be judged by an often holistically uneducated, unsympathetic, politically motivated group of allopaths, who had little understanding or empathy for holistic physicians. It was a liberating decision in the world of illusion. However, I still keep my allopathic license in California, which I have had since 1972.

We searched for six years throughout the whole state of Arizona, and we were not able to find a place that was suitable. In the last month of searching, we decided that if we didn't locate our optimal location for our community, we were going to give up. On the very last day of that thirty days, after six years of searching, we did indeed find the perfect place in Patagonia, Arizona. In the big cosmic picture, astro-cartography charts suggested that Patagonia was my location of power expansion and safety in the USA. We purchased the Patagonia land for the Tree of Life Community in 1993. This relocation to Patagonia, AZ marked the beginning of a whole new astrological cycle of my journey.

Over the next few years we began developing a community on bare land, one step at a time using straw bale construction for all our buildings. I spent half of my time in California as a holistic physician for about a year in order to support the project financially. At the ending and beginning of our astrological cycles difficult karmas may arise. Indeed, after we'd already bought the land and set the plan to move within the year, there was a strange incident in which a Hare Krishna person came as a client. This individual was very much out of balance, I saw him as a favor for an acquaintance. His surgeon had put him on an enormous and actually illegal amount of pain medication following a failed back surgery, in which a piece of his intervertebral disc was left in him causing much pain. I was able to decrease his medication down to the legal limit according to the local pharmacist and the state laws, while he awaited a second back operation. He was also referred to a pain specialist because, as a holistic physician, I rarely give pain medications. I prescribed the correct amount of pain medication he could have within legal limits. Under my care, he was being maintained and was growing stronger and more spiritually awake.

His wife whom he was divorcing watched him become more functional and decided to undermine him by reporting me to the medical board for "over-prescribing". Coincidentally, he was coming off his pain medication at that time and was completely off all pain medications after his successful second back operation. However, unbeknownst to me, he was getting additional prescriptions from other doctors. Absurdly, the medical board literally decided that, as a holistic physician, I should have been checking every pharmacy within forty-mile radius to prevent this. Moreover, there was no double-check to ensure he was meeting with the pain specialist he had been referred to. For these "oversights", they placed me on the shortest allowable probation period. They did not choose to go after his previous physician for actually overprescribing, but instead his holistic physician, who had cut his medication down to the legal maximum. I was given a three-year probation, which however, did allow me to continue practicing medicine in California. Fortunately, it did not interfere with my medical license or right to practice medicine in California for even a day, but it meant that I had to reside in California at least half-time for three years. Because of my perfect record, as I rarely prescribed allopathic medicine, after two years, my lawyer, with the positive support of my probation officer doctor, convinced the presiding state judge in Sacramento to mitigate the probation from three years to two years so that I could move to Arizona. The next step was to get this okayed by the State Medical Board, which seemed more than a reasonable request. I warned the lawyer that it would not be easy because of the prejudicial attitude of the medical board toward holistic physicians in California. He was shocked that they actually denied mitigating the probation time and overruled the judge, thereby creating another year in which I had to stay in California half of the time.

Teaching: No matter if one is liberated or not, karma still happens. The liberated one is just less susceptible to being affected by negative karmic effects.

Chapter 20

CONSCIOUS DIVORCE

Teaching: Divorce, even if the correct
thing to do, is not easy.

From 1994 to 1996, as previously explained, I had to divide my time between Arizona and California. This created a strain on our marriage, but also highlighted the truth that Nora wasn't interested in living in a live-food, plant-source-only spiritual community in the middle of the desert, isolated from the city life and her friends. Thus, in one way, this was a blessing for us, as we were so tightly connected for close to twenty-eight years that being away from each other half the week helped create a little distance. In the big picture, maybe the California Board's actions were a blessing in disguise; in any case they have been completely forgiven and have also become much more open to holistic physicians in California. At some point, in 1995 we mutually decided that the move to Arizona wasn't going to work for Nora, no matter how thoughtful we were; and we mutually and lovingly decided to become divorced. It was just as the Mango Man and the *Book of Bhrigu* reader predicted. Nora was neither interested nor willing to be the prophesied female spiritual leader; and she had her own life she wanted to live. In the big picture, I truly believed it would be damaging to her if we acted against what we both knew was best for her. Our divorce was the right, but painful, decision. At this point, both our children had long since graduated college, and our dharma as parents in its primary phase had already completed itself. Today, after close to twenty-five years of divorce, we work in cooperative, aligned parenting roles with our children and grandchildren. After a year of continuing to live together, we departed amicably, lovingly, and respectfully in the state of sweet peace and sadness at the Big Island, Hawaii airport after we finished leading our last joint spiritual fasting retreat. It was very symbolic.

Teaching: Life is like an airport in which people come
and go in one's life. The art of "airport life" is both to
be fully loving and non-attached at the same time.

This is a not so subtle, yet paradoxically difficult, take-home teaching from this. There are also a variety of other teachings in this happening. One is that when we got married our marriage vows included being committed to being together as long as our relationship supported our total life unfoldment and spiritual evolution. Through a lot of effort on both our parts it appeared we could resolve how to do this in most of the situations we could foresee. At the time we got together we both were only marginally involved in spiritual life, so spirituality was not part of our contract. Unanticipated changes in life direction are not uncommon in people who marry young. When we wed, Nora was twenty-three and I was only twenty-four. Ten years later when I met Swami Muktananda, I made a significant change, shifting my primary focus toward my spiritual life. Although she did have some interest in spiritual life, the same degree of spiritual change and shift in life direction did not happen for Nora. This happens for many couples in that one member does not share the same spiritual direction, intensity, or lifestyle of another that either occurs later in the relationship or is already happening at the time they come together. It is worth trying as hard as possible to work it out. It is best if the member of the relationship that is not involved in spirituality at least be as supportive as possible. Couples usually do well with this. If one can't be supportive, then at least they can be neutral. This also often works well. If one of the partners chooses to undermine the spiritual life of the other, this can be a severe problem and may even cause a divorce. In our situation, none of this accurately applied to us, but an additional issue was occurring in that we both were going in different directions in our life path and lifestyle that did not seem to be logistically compatible. We were honest enough to acknowledge this.

People come together for different reasons. We were dharma mates, and not soulmates. It took the last ten years of our relationship to realize this. We shared a great deal of loving and joyful dharma, such as creating a family, creating spiritual centers and two communities, participating in political activism together, holding spiritual fasting retreats, and starting the spiritual nutrition teachings. It was clear that our marriage dharma had completed itself, and we had no healthy evolving choice but to move with the cosmic flow. Divorce should never be the first choice, and one should put every effort possible into making the dharma of a relationship or family work before stopping. Almost always there are essential psycho-emotional and spiritual lessons to be learned from relationship challenges.

Teaching: Dharma mates are not necessarily soulmates. They come together to perform an important life mission.

Chapter 21

SACRED RELATIONSHIP AS A PATH TO LIBERATION

Teaching: It is good to wait at least eleven months
after a divorce before entering another long-term
relationship. This is a time for soul-searching,
rebalancing, and reorganizing one's life.

After my divorce I spent a great deal of time engaged in intense
soul searching. I asked myself whether I should be a monk, or
if it was my destiny to engage in a sacred intimate relationship once
again. I contemplated my way of life and questioned which would
be most appropriate as part of my world teaching, and as the fulfillment of prophecy. After waiting for eleven months, post-divorce,
as part of the traditional mourning time, it became clear to me that
sacred relationship was in alignment with the Will of God, and was
the highest and most appropriate way for me to live and teach in

our Western culture. The Mango Man, the *Book of Bhrigu*, and the great Torah Way had confirmed this message to me, so I felt deeply that the way of sacred relationship was the most powerful spiritual evolutionary path, especially in the West. It is the full Tantric path, beyond sexuality, in which every aspect of the relationship becomes transformed into the holiness of everyday life.

Teaching: It is important to use our life transformations and challenges as situations and opportunities to refocus our life dharma. There are two aspects to dharma. One is the highest dharma, which is to know and merge with God in the process of becoming liberated. Another aspect of dharma is to become aligned with one's specific individualized life purpose or specific dharma which gives us the challenges, that if we are conscious enough, can be used to elevate us spiritually.

The death of my brother, father, and mother at relatively early ages, as well as my divorce after twenty-eight years of marriage created some fear of loss in intimate relationships that I also needed to face if I was to grow in this area and again enter into an intimate sacred relationship. For this reason, a significant challenge for me was to love fully, in an unreserved and unqualified way, regardless of possible loss.

Teaching: Sacred relationship is a heroic journey into the unknown, into the "risky" world of love and intimacy, where one has to face the fear and risk of losing all while loving all. It is a Tantric challenge that elevates one on the ever-evolving spiritual way of liberation.

Shanti and I fulfilling our dharma of teaching together.

In our western society, it seems that sacred relationships and the process of intimacy are the newest, yet oldest, frontier. Complicating it is an increasing level of gender and relationship confusion in our society. Additionally, it is easier for many people to relate to their pets, computer or cell phone rather than overcome their fear of intimacy in a human to human relationship. From a liberated perspective, we are neither our biological sexual identity nor our psychological gender identity. We are the soul essence prior to personality identifications associated with body and mind. For this discussion it seems more accurate to refer to male and female essences. In the process of sacred relationship, love is the power to overcome one's fear of intimacy.

Teaching: Everyone possesses both masculine
and feminine essences within themselves and
ultimately, we need to integrate these in the liberation
process and intimate sacred relationships.

Sacred relationships often activate our deepest level of intimacy thoughtforms, such as our issues with our family of origin, our personality patterns, who we are, our ability to express and receive love, and also the question: what is the essence of spiritual life?

Teaching: Intimacy takes us into the mystery of life; it is not about safety or security. It is about the alchemical process of transformation. It takes us to the frontiers of human existence and brings us face-to-face with our angels and demons.

From a liberated view, it is possible to be fully intimate, while burning all thought forms in the fire of sacred relationship. Sacred relationship asks one to be vulnerable and to face and overcome one's fear of intimacy.

Teaching: Ultimately, sacred relationship asks us to consider what it means to be a fully awakened human being.

Before going too deeply into the alchemical mystery of marriage as a spiritual path, it is useful to touch on a few definitions and distinctions between dharma mates (which Nora and I were), twin souls, and soulmates. Twin souls seem very familiar to each other and share personality features. They often learn life lessons together, because twin souls are usually part of a shared soul group. In general, twin souls do not do well getting sexually involved or getting married because they are too similar, but they can be very supportive of each other in a variety of ways as part of a spiritual evolutionary team.

There may be a variety of twin souls in one's life, such as those who deeply resonate with a shared mission.

Teaching: Twin souls are two people who are very similar and deeply resonate from many lifetimes together. They are part of the same root soul. They are not necessarily meant to be in an intimate relationship, but often are part of a shared spiritual team or collective meaningful mission.

Shanti & I demonstrate couple's yoga.

Soulmates may be one or a few people incarnated at the same time in the world for each other as spiritual and total life partners, if they are spiritually ready. Contrary to some popular beliefs, a person may have more than one potential soulmate; and in rare circumstances, a mate can even transform in the powerful context and love in a relationship into a soulmate. Although it did not happen, it is what I initially prayed for with Nora. In resolution, we both mutually recognized that after we completed our primary dharma of creating a family; of child raising, which is never really finished; and a shared dharma we continue as grandparents, as well as a variety of other dharma's we fulfilled like creating a block organization in Petaluma with a food co-op, joint family garden; full meditation group; and our community in Mendocino; and travelling with Swami Muktananda.

Teaching: Although many people pray for their soulmates, soulmates are earned through spiritual evolutionary work.

Soulmates may not even recognize each other as soulmates until they are ready. This is what happened with Shanti and I. Soulmates are not necessarily the same in personality, as are twin souls. Soulmates are not necessarily the same age and often come from different parts of the world.

Teaching: Soulmates energetically complement each other and support one another in their life dharmas; in the maturing of their spiritual evolution; and in the way of Holistic Liberation.

Divorce raised complex questions for me about the meaning of relationships, love, and intimacy. For the next five years following our divorce, I had time to reflect about the type of relationship I wanted or even if it was spiritually productive to be in a relationship at all. A few dating relationships helped me become clear about what type of woman I wished to spend the rest of my life with. It was not an easy process to find someone, since my soulmate had to be already living a committed spiritual life aimed at liberation and eating at least an 80 percent live-food, and 100 percent vegan diet. These were preconditions for me to even consider a relationship. I had no interest in trying to convert someone to live this way of life, which was already part of my teaching to the world. Additionally, my partner could not be only a student because of the natural distortions and imbalances that so often occur in the teacher-student relationship.

One of the interesting dynamics during this five-year search was that I became involved with my twin soul for the first four years in a distant on/off intimate relationship. What made the relationship even more complicated and yet more authentic was that we had an integrity pact and agreed that if we got involved with anyone else sexually, we had to tell each other and to forewarn whomever we got involved with that our distant twin soul relationship was active in the background so there would be no betrayal or "stealing of the mind". People who do not share that they are having other intimate relationships in the process of choosing a mate, are setting up betrayal situations because they are denying the other person the right of choosing whether to participate in such an evolving selection process. Without deception, the play of betrayal is avoided, or at least greatly minimized.

Teaching: If someone is involved with a variety
of women (or men) who all believe they're the
only one, which is common in this world of
deception, it's an energetic violation. It is called
"g'neyvay da'at" (subtle stealing of the mind).

Any woman who chose to get involved with me was explicitly informed of my distant relationship with a woman. I eventually realized and accepted this woman as my twin soul but my intimate relationship with her ended when I understood we were twin souls and not anything more. The marriage partner and soulmate I was looking for also needed to be a woman of courage, as my somewhat unconventional lifestyle and humanitarian work took me to a variety of dangerous places around the world. I have also lived in risky places or done service work even in places in the U.S. that had certain overt physical dangers connected to them.

My soul mate also needed the courage of the heart necessary for developing a sacred relationship and to be willing to merge into the Divine. There is an inspiring sacred relationship story of Crazy Horse's "half-side" (mate) riding into the line of fire against General Custer's men after Crazy Horse's horse was shot out from under him. She swooped him up onto the back of her horse and brought him to safety, so he could continue the battle on a fresh horse. This story hints at the courage needed to participate in my world lifestyle as a marriage partner and soulmate.

In reflection, these interim five years were not the time to be in a sacred intimate relationship, as those challenging explorative post-divorce years were needed for healing and moving to a new level of relationship consciousness after approximately twenty-eight years of marriage. After these five years I was actually ready to make the decision that sacred relationship was part of how I wanted to live on the physical plane in my spiritual world and as part of my living teaching.

Around the year 2000, my awaited soulmate emerged. It was Shanti who had been my TriYoga teacher since 1988 when she used to teach TriYoga with Kali Ray. Shanti also taught both at our center in Petaluma and also on our spiritual fasting retreats. There was not a soulmate recognition for either of us in 1988, although we knew we had some special level of energetic connection. She had her own spiritual teacher, came from the distant land of New Zealand, and we were not the same age. Interestingly enough, these are some of the outer pre-conditions often associated with soulmates in the Torah tradition. We had not communicated at all for close to five years after my divorce. I happened to be in the San Jose, California area giving a workshop and called to see if a TriYoga private with her would be possible. Since our lives had both changed, we were able to see each other with new eyes and the veil blocking our soulmate recognition lifted. A much different context developed for us, and we fell in love. Once the veil lifted, it was easy for me to see that Shanti, her live-food lifestyle and her dharma were already aligned with my dharma/mission as foretold in the prophecy of the Mango Man and the *Book of Bhrigu*.

Teaching: The spiritual adventure of sacred
relationship is a heroic journey into the unknown,
and one I was finally willing to embark on again.

What highlighted the soulmate relationship with Shanti for me was a tremendous sense of feeling entirely at home. As our relationship evolved, space opened for us at a level of heartfelt communication, love, and spirit that elevated both of us. All our inner experiences, as well as outer experiences and shared dharma experiences, came into a holistic body-mind-heart-soul synthesis. Aside from an almost total alignment on living a full multidimensional holistic lifestyle together, for me it meant a full alignment with my life's meaning and purpose. Perhaps most important for me, as one living the life of a magical, romantic, prophetic, spiritual liberated visionary was to be with a marriage partner who totally supported, agreed with, and was willing to accept the hardships and challenges of living this liberation based mystical visionary life. To this day, our soulmate connection continually provides me with a source of holistic support, spiritual evolution, joy, love, and aliveness.

Teaching: In a sacred relationship there is a constant endeavor to bring holiness, love, joy, and sanctification into every moment.

My sacred union with Shanti continually reminds me how important it is to pay meticulous attention to the language I use so that I am always communicating love. My interaction with Shanti and the intimate heartfelt life we share, in which we consciously endeavor to bring holiness, love, joy, and sanctification into every moment together, prompts me to understand and use words and subtle metacommunications on the physical plane as a medium for love filled communication, so that our exchange is continually that of love and spiritual upliftment.

Teaching: Love is not blind; it is like a microscope which helps us see and activate the spark of the Divine in the other.

A key ingredient to this process is starting every level of communication, verbal or physical, with the energy of love, peace, joy, oneness, and interconnective harmony. In this way, I have come to learn more and more how to make an opening for the light that radiates within every word of communication. Our relationship has created a space for Shanti and I to empower our words to shine with the light of the inner self in the silent smile of our communication.

Teaching: Conscious language is the means to infuse each thought with the meta-communication of meaning, love, and the spiritual glow of the Divine Light in each word, sentence, and gesture.

This type of conscious interaction has created an additional entrance to inner space, creating an external portal to experience the One. We also spend a lot of our time together in silence, and that silence forms an opening beyond words, culture, and the matrix. It's the space of peace, love, spirit, and revelation.

Teaching: Love is the perception that allows us to see the inner beauty of the other.

I later learned that Shanti also had an earlier prophecy about me. When she was twenty-one, upon leaving New Zealand, a palmist at her twenty-first birthday party told her she would marry a Taurus (my sun sign is Taurus), and we would do great work together. Shanti told the palmist that she did not want to marry a Taurus. About a year before we reconnected, a psychic, Ma Mata, told Shanti that she saw her husband standing next to her; he had blue eyes and was a doctor. Shanti thought at that time that the only doctor she knew was Dr Gabriel Cousens, but ruled that possibility out since she had not seen me since I went off to start the Tree of Life community in Arizona five years previously.

When we reconnected for the TriYoga session, Shanti knew what was going on by the first week. For our engagement, Kevin Ryerson a dear friend since 1982, best known as the psychic for Shirley MacLaine, gave us a special reading in a Kiva in New Mexico. He said we had been together thirty-two times before. There is a subtlety to this in that some of the Kabbalistic stories about soulmates infer past life connections; and the number thirty-two is the number of all the connecting pathways in the Tree of Life. Shanti also embodies rare romantic, spiritual, and courageous qualities needed by me for a soulmate.

Teaching: It is best to wait a year before committing
to marriage as we want to know our partner in
all four seasons and the seasons of our life.

After waiting for one year to make sure we had the correct understanding and to optimize our astrological flow, we were married on March 4th, 2001 in a three-day ceremony including Native American, Yogic, and a traditional Jewish rabbinical ceremony. Over one hundred people came from all different backgrounds. It was a wonderful, joyous, spiritual happening. On day one we did a Lakota Sioux ceremony led by my Sundance Chief, Kam Nightchase and supported by my Sundance brothers and sisters with separate inipis (sweat lodges) for men and women and the traditional jumping through a literal fire as part of the marriage ceremony. On day two we did a special sunrise Yogic chanting ceremony that Shanti and I designed. On day three we did a traditional Jewish ceremony under the hoopa with Rabbi Gershon Winkler. It was clear to me that Shanti was indeed the woman seen in the prophecy. The inner beauty of Shanti is continually inspiring my heart.

Teaching: To love someone is to see them in
the raw nakedness of their authenticity.

In true intimate relationships, one experiences enduring love, steady trust, and safety that increase our willingness to be vulnerable. Durable intimacy requires the continued courage and willingness to keep one's heart open under any circumstances. Intimacy is not about having a fixed and secure relationship. The desire and resistance of primal intimacy is an inherently spiritual struggle that people face, and it is ultimately about the power of giving us love and the courage to overcome our fear of intimacy and the Divine.

Teaching: Love coexists with fear in the process of intimacy.

On a more practical level, she also fulfilled my other criteria, as she wasn't my direct student and I find it amusing that I married my

TriYoga teacher. We have evolved since then; and Shanti has played a significant role in my dharma, which is also her lifelong dharma.

Teaching: Love is not blind; it is the only thing that
lets us see each other with the remotest accuracy.

Love only rises from the experience of being in the Eternal Presence, as love renders the critical mind powerless. In this process, love creates the space for us letting go of the illusion of perfectionism and purity.

Teaching: Intimacy also involves the process of
letting go of our ideal fantasy of relationship so that
the dream of relationship does not distract us from
the path of love in the reality of relationship.

As the poet Emerson wrote, "There is a crack in everything God has made." When we love enough, we feel ready to risk being vulnerable.

Teaching: Love means seeing the crack and not
creating a separation of intimacy over it.

The warrior spirit faces the fear of intimacy with an open, vulnerable heart. Love is not letting go of fear; it is embracing the fear as an aspect of our intimacy process. The path of love is the path for spiritual adventurers.

Teaching: Real intimacy requires a journey
into the unknown, mysteries of Self, couple, and
life. By relating to and accepting the unknown
in each other, we have gone further in the
discovery of the unknown within ourselves.

Shanti and I had consciously chosen each other as partners in this spiritual adventure of intimacy and marriage. Becoming more fully human means discovering and learning to live from our fullness, which yields the courage to bring forth more of ourselves.

Teaching: Love has the power to transform
each other into a higher octave of consciousness
according to our own uniqueness.

In this adventure, love has helped us overcome our limited thought forms of who we think we are. Love and consciousness inspire us to face our life issues with an open heart.

Teaching: Intimate relationships are so powerful
because they inspire our hearts to stay open while
simultaneously activating all the pain and confusion of
our present and family of origin karmic entanglements.
Love is powerful because it brings the expansive and
contractive sides of ourselves into direct contact.

The wakefulness of love gives us the strength and motivation to confront and heal our shadows that necessarily arise in the process of sacred intimacy. Our personality rigidities have melted and softened in the fire of our love. Intimacy takes courage. Courage in intimate relationships is the willingness to stay open to our fear and vulnerability without running away. Sacred intimacy can be a powerful spiritual way of life that supports the Holistic Liberation process.

The process of intimacy has allowed Shanti and I to unite heaven and earth so that we can live in the "Wow!!!" of love and the earthy aspects of experiencing the sacred in life's day-to-day play. Unconditional love connects us to the vastness of our Divine Self, and also to each other.

Teaching: In intimacy it is key to remember, love is not letting go of fear, but embracing our fear and then having the courage to love in spite of our fear.

My relationship with Shanti, like all levels of relationships, requires attention. Both of us have committed to approaching the outer levels of relationship as an organization of time, and space, and energy for the creation and sustaining of love, meaning, purpose, and continued enhancement of Divine Revelation. This understanding requires some organizing work to make the continual adjustments needed. We organize our day after the morning meditation as to what is needed. It is imperative to have clear individual work and service time, clear study time, clear writing time, clear teaching time, and clear lovemaking time as part of my manifest dharma in the world. Shanti also takes her space to take care of things that are particularly important to her. Aside from teaching TriYoga, Shanti runs the household and prepares our meals and puts her blessings and love into the food and, in that way, changes the food into healing potions.

Teaching: Not only is it important to love each other and to love the relationship, but it is also essential to make every detail of one's relationship be a message of love, light, appreciation, and increasing spiritual awareness.

In our sacred soulmate relationship, the details are important, and that includes our roles around the house. For example, one of my jobs is to do the dishes and make sure other things are happening like preparing and blessing our drinking water. One of my most important "jobs" is taking care of and helping Shanti manifest her life dharma and dreams, so that she has the space to create her life fulfillment, as well as directly and actively supporting her liberation process. It is a subtle dance to be both equal in our relationship and for this soul-fire to be her spiritual teacher. As it evolves, we're always adjusting to the needs of the internal relationship as well as to the external world. For some this daily routine consciousness may seem mundane, but the active communication of light, love, and sacredness in the mundaneness of our everyday routines transforms them into a holy sanctification of our lives. A soulmate relationship orients us toward the evolution of human consciousness and personal enlightenment beyond personal dharma. Soulmates naturally give a fuller multidimensional quality in their relationship. All relationships on some levels have all elements of these things. Soulmates can see and are more focused on bringing out the authentic self in each other.

One of the keyways Shanti and I continually enhance our love is by supporting each other's authenticity.

Teaching: A high level of intimacy manifests
when we support each other to become the fullest
authentic expression of that which we are meant
to be—the wild female and the wild male.

There are different models for soulmate relationships. For example, in the Torah, Rebecca committed to her soulmate relationship before she even met Isaac. Their soulmate connection was activated at first sight, as, upon seeing Isaac meditating in the fields, Rebecca nearly fell off her camel. He took her to the tent of his deceased mother Sarah, and the light of the sacred feminine was restored within the tent. They became married, and then they fell in love. Together a powerful light was created that exceeded the light of either of them individually. In this case, they played out the teaching that soulmates come from long distances and are of significantly different ages.

Teaching: Soulmates are not only motivated by
chemistry and emotions but also by a higher shared
life mission and emphasis on spiritual evolution.

Another biblical model of soulmates can be seen in Abraham and Sarah who came from the same region and family culture and were about the same age with only a ten-year difference. Sarah was also Abraham's niece. They knew each other over time and grew through love to express as soulmates with a great mission of awakening the world. They lived and taught a dynamic male and female equal oneness that was an entirely new paradigm for the Middle East 3,700 years ago. Soulmates have often done a significant amount of spiritual work to graduate to a place where they can vibrate on the same frequency. They know where they stand in their lives and thus align in a shared interpretation of life's meaning.

Shanti and I share a cuisine of a live-food, organic plant-source-only nutrition. It is clearly conducive overall increased vitality, longevity, life force, holistic health, and spiritual life as well as being supportive of our overall way of life and bonding. As previously mentioned, in 1975, a Divine Voice directed me to learn to eat and live to best support the Kundalini's unfolding. Sharing and teaching the live-food, plant-source-only, Genesis 1:29 diet worldwide is an active dharma and mission for me and Shanti. Of course, one can't eat their way to God, but the nature of one's diet can aid or detract from the flow of the Kundalini. An animal-based diet increases the amount of animal pain, misery, and fear, as well as animal ego energy invading one's consciousness. Animal flesh acts as a sludge to the Kundalini flow through the nadis (subtle energetic channels) and koshas (layers of the mind). My teachings and the detailed information in my other books, such as *Conscious Eating, Rainbow Green Live-Food Cuisine, Spiritual Nutrition and the Rainbow Diet, Spiritual Nutrition – Six Foundations for Spiritual Life and Awakening of Kundalini*, makes a point that plant-source-only, live-food cuisine is not just about its uplifting effect on spiritual life and overall holistic health, but also protects against animal cruelty, engenders compassion, creates oneness, protects the environment, and uplifts the whole network of sentient life on the planet. A lifestyle that includes a plant-source-only cuisine is implicit in the spiritual teachings of almost all the great traditions. After this strong and enthusiastic dietary proclamation, it should be clear why spiritual nutrition is such a major part of my world mission, which is to activate and support spiritual awakening and Holistic Liberation worldwide.

Teaching: What we eat affects consciousness, which affects the mind, which affects one's thoughts, and which affects one's actions.

Opening up to the risk of intimacy is part of the evolution of human consciousness. The challenge of intimacy is part of the frontier of human consciousness. We are challenged to maintain and grow within a live intimate relationship in a society that no longer significantly understands or supports the spiritual evolutionary transformative power of marriage and sacred relationship in general, and even less as a spiritual path of liberation.

Continually renewing, living love supports a couple trying to do something in our present society that few societies have attained. This rare feat is the joining of romantic love, sexual passion, reproduction, and spiritual path in a marriage of complementary equals in an enduring relationship, resonating on all physical, emotional, mental, and spiritual levels. It asks couples to develop a new depth and definition of intimacy by exploring and cultivating unrealized potentials and shining light on shadows supported by their love and intimate connection with their consort. In this process, trust develops in intimacy because of the commitment to work through everything, including that which is not trustworthy.

Teaching: Sacred Relationships may become a
vehicle for the evolution of human consciousness.

Intimate relations ask for a turned-on connection and love, which at the same time helps to free us from old patterns of pain. In the process, we also need to create space for the other to exist and to thrive. Sacred relationships also help us access the authentic original spiritual self we are meant to be. We have the choice and ability to create and give space for the other to become their full, original self. This is very different from the typical relationship, in which we try to tame the other person into our idea of who he or she should be for us. In the intimacy of sacred relationship, our role is to help the other reach their full holistic and spiritual potential as a human being. Sacred relationship, as I have defined it, is a spiritual path that involves invoking the presence of the Divine in the relationship. It is the alchemical merging into the One.

Having an open heart and expressing unconditional love does not mean there are no boundaries in a sacred relationship. Every enduring healthy sacred relationship has boundaries that should not be crossed. Agreed-upon boundaries help define and clarify the relationship as well as maintain its safety.

Teaching: Enduring intimacy requires a continual
space of safety, so we can manifest our authentic self.

A successful relationship means both partners love each other unconditionally and also love the relationship itself, along with its appropriate agreed upon boundaries. In this paradox, love and fear may rise together, which may create a dynamic tension between self and other as known and unknown. This is part of the fuel for the passion in an intimate relationship. Sacred relationship is on the razor's edge where heaven and earth connect and help create aliveness.

Teaching: A key to intimacy is to dance with our sacred other as the focus of our passion, but not to be dependent on them as the source of our passion. The source of passion and love comes from within us as an emanation of our Divine Self. The sacred other helps to activate our connection with the light and love of the Divine within ourselves.

Paradoxically, a living relationship is continually moving subtly in and out of balance as it dances on the razor's edge of intimacy. The effort to continually rebalance and renew passion are essential for sustaining an enduring, intimate relationship.

Teaching: Passion is the feeling of life wanting to connect more fully with life.

Passion's natural activity is to connect intensely. In this intimate dance, we become consorts. Consorts have a conscious raising and wakening role to play in each other's spiritual development.

Teaching: A consort is someone who initiates
us through intimate contact into mysteries we
could not readily penetrate on our own and thus
helps us awaken to the fullness of our being.

A mystery to this alchemical non-sexual Tantric Oneness is a balanced exchange of energy in which the masculine and feminine may even be free to reverse in polarity. In this ecstasy of temporary androgyny, a love-filled, egoless Oneness shatters our false identification with personality and gender. There is only the existence of the One. Erotic energy requires two separate poles, yet in the alchemical merging of sacred sexual relationship, there is no polarity left in the moment of full intimacy.

—⁓—

Holy Touch

We lay together in abject
Singular silent, holy ecstasy
Draped over and within each other
In subtle blazing love
Our skin succulent to the full body touch,
An erotic full light show
As our sensuous bodies
In quiet breath touch
Yoni to lingam
Belly to belly,
Breast to breast

Lips to lips
The light radiating from the magic of our touching skin
Melts us into a singular Divine wholeness
In our holy touch, all universes are healed
Creation smiles in its unity
And laughs with the play of the Radiant One.

—⁐—

A particular challenge in the intimacy process is developing the strength and maturity to maintain an open heart in love with the other over the duration of time. Intimacy is more than a special moment in time. Intimacy is a commitment to creating a continual flow of special moments over time. It is a commitment to be continually present as love for your sacred partner.

Teaching: The male and female essences are an expression
of the culture of liberation, in which the celebration of
the Divine is the center and primary expression of life.

In intimacy, we have two essences that must be balanced. The female essence, which can be in a male or a female biological body, is the Rainbow Radiance of who we are—the full flow and dance of Love. Shanti is the ultimate rainbow radiance in my life. The rainbow radiance naturally wants to shine and to be seen, and needs to be recognized and to be known. The female essence is the flower and the joy of fullness. The female essence is everything that changes: light, colors, sounds, aromas, feelings, and flow—the flow of the universe as the dance of the Shakti symbolizes the feminine essence in this paradigm. Shakti is the wild play of consciousness in the world.

I love you endlessly.

—⚏—

Love You Endlessly
(A Poem from Shanti)

My Rock,
With you always;
Something in me wants to love you endlessly.

—⚏—

The male essence, which can also be in a male or a female biological body, is to die into the unknown—a total focus on Oneness and dissolving into the Nothing. It is also important for the male to be seen and to be appreciated for his thoughts, ideas, actions, and willingness to disappear into the Nothing, and for the willingness to have a purpose and direction in life. The male essence is about emptiness and the female essence is about fullness. These two essences need to match and balance for a relationship to work. The male essence is an unchanging witness. In the Hindu paradigm, it is symbolized by Shiva as the endless existence of the non-dual nothing.

These characteristics help us to understand and experience the differences between these two archetypical essences. When the male and female essences connect in sacred relationships, there is a merging of sound, light, and consciousness. This alchemical energy merging is the essence of real intimacy, one of ecstatic love merging with God. It may be helpful to think of these two essences as a battery with sparks, a polarity that gives attraction power to the relationship. If a couple doesn't have the erotic polarized energy between the two poles, it is hard to have a deep ecstatic relationship on all four levels of physical, emotional, mental, and spiritual relationship. By understanding and honoring these essences, we give and receive in a way that activates the sacred in each other and allows space for us to be our full, authentic selves. For this to be possible, however, both people have to be operating from the same level of spiritual intention and awareness. This is an important part of why Shanti and I are continually attracted to each other.

Our level of intimate relationship is about the alchemical merging into God through the medium of relationship. Here, the goal is supporting each other, by both giving our holy gift to uplift the other spiritually. Shanti gives her holy gift simply to be the radiance of the Divine. Her gift is to inspire everyone into that radiance. Shanti's Rainbow Radiance inspires me to share the energetic gift of disappearing into the nothing. We inspire each other. Our sacred relationship is bigger in that we are continually inspiring each other into the Divine... merging into the alchemical Oneness. Yet, we have clear boundaries. These boundaries are not about political correctness, but are naturally part of being an evolved, unique, and spiritually mature person. We can dissolve our boundaries at appropriate times into the alchemical merging of the Oneness of the Divine. This is a key factor of the sacred relationship. We are lived by love and liberation, and the only thing that matters is God.

Teaching: The source of our first thought and word shapes our following thoughts, words and actions.

The love of God in the Tantric play of sacred relationships is an essential part of my life, which is why so much space is spent talking about, explaining it, and writing poetry about it. For me, merging with God through disappearing into the nothing is the complete center and goal of life. We go beyond the egocentric and ethnocentric into the mystical experience of the One as the core of our sacred relationship. Love and God-merging are living us, and that is a foundational essence of our sacred relationship.

Teaching: We ask ourselves, "How can our love and light shine most fully in every moment?"

Even if we give up our personal preferences, it is for the sake of a broader purpose—to be the expression of God. In our sacred relationship we use sexuality to liberate love and open ourselves to the Divine. It is where sexuality is used to inspire and share love with the world by merging the Heavens and the Earth. Being the dance of the Divine in every moment expresses love's most profound level, as we go beyond ego needs and our boundaries, to discover what would most serve our partner, the world, and God. Simultaneously, my masculine essence lives in emptiness, mystical death, dissolving into the nothing, meditation, and liberation. Shanti's liberated feminine essence is joyfully serving the fullness of life.

Teaching: Each soul essence needs a different "generalized" communication message. The female soul essence needs one thing… to know she is loved. If the male soul essence does not communicate to the female that she is loved, things don't work so well. The male essence needs to know that he is succeeding. The difference in needs causes the male and female essences to communicate on different levels. All sacred intimacy communication—in relationship, in lovemaking, and in everyday life—needs to carry at least these messages.

Spiritual Eros and Divine Ecstasy is also an essential component of our sacred relationship. In our sexual expression, the unity and dance of consciousness, sound, and light is our deep experience. It is experienced as the alchemical, merging expressed in my poems. Key to this process, the female essence is looking for a male who can feel her depth. The male essence shows the female essence love through intense presence and intention. The acknowledgement of me being present for Shanti by Shanti is the positive feedback needed by the male essence.

Teaching: Erotic living is taking part in the
subjective reality of the happening of each moment
of life; it is living in the direct knowing.

Sacred or not, all relationships need to be fed and nourished. When people do not honor the time, space, and energy needs of their relationship, it often weakens in all areas.

Teaching: Sacred relationships are a preparatory
microcosm to our macrocosmic relationship
with the Divine. To maintain and nurture them,
sacred relationships require a certain level of
soul effort, love, and willingness to risk.

Eros is the ability in a relationship to perceive and celebrate the inner beauty and Divine essence of the other. But Eros is bigger than this—Eros is celebrating the ecstasy of the Divine in all of creation. For me, the Shaktipat awakening in 1975 activated the Tantric sensitivity for experiencing the Divine Dance in all of creation. It is a merging of heaven and earth. It is at the level where sex between the male and female essences liberates the gifting of love. Erotic living only partially includes sexuality; and actually, erotic living does not even require sexuality. The profound secret of living in Eros is knowing how to live on the inside of all our life experiences. When one does not feel consciously engaged in the walk between the *B'limah* (Nothing) and the Mah (Something), they are not really on the inside of the experience of life.

Teaching: Dancing in the consciousness of Eros is a way of living in which we rejoice in the incredible blissful inner experience of the ecstasy and erotic love of merging with the Divine in every moment and in every situation.

Lovemaking with this consciousness merges the heavens and earth in the energetics of "as above so below". The full meaning of Eros is celebrating God in all of creation and experiencing the face of God in each other. Living in Eros heightens the Divinity experience of our everyday life. When we are making love in sacred relationship, it is making love with the whole universe and thus healing the entire universe.

Teaching: Sacred sexuality is not merely for sexual pleasure or even for the merging of two people… making love creates a healing reunion in which the He-Adam and She-Adam become essentially One Soul again.

When we go deep enough, even our separate faces disappear. We are healing the whole universe when we heal the male/female split. "Tikkun ha'nefesh" means healing yourself, and "tikkun ha'olam" means healing the world. In our lovemaking, inhaling sends love downwards and within, and exhaling sends love out to the whole universe. In this way we are healing on both the microcosmic and macrocosmic levels.

Teaching: To be inside of an experience is to be in a state of direct knowing of the experience. Not being on the inside, puts one in the world of what one knows about, but does not know directly.

In this walk between the B'limah and Mah, between the *Ayin* (Nothing) and *Yesh* (Something), we have the continual opportunity to rebirth ourselves into a new spiritual evolutionary awareness if we so choose. To live erotically is to be fully present on the inside of the experience. The opposite of Eros is alienation or being on the outside. Living on the inside of the experience of life means that I feel the aspects of God in all of life. This is a real challenge for the reader to consider. It appears to be a paradox in that the classical enlightenment spiritual teaching is to reside as the witness. The more advanced enlightenment teaching is to reside both inside the experience and feeling the presence of God within the experience and living simultaneously as the witness observing the play of consciousness of the experience.

Teaching: Eros, or living erotically, is seeing and experiencing the dance of God in all things and experiences. In this way, the experience of sacred relationships and intimacy becomes a path to the Divine.

I have always lived with a natural, sublime intensity, from playing football to meditating, and to sacred relationship. It is choosing to live in an erotic magical realism that seems to activate the Divine sound, light, and consciousness in all things. Sometimes people interpret it as being "too serious" but it is an erotic intensity as a way of engaging in life. It requires no props or drugs to feel alive. The subtle mystery here is that when I go deep enough into the emptiness within, there is continual access to the sound, light, ecstasy, and love of the Divine.

Teaching: Only when one can hold and penetrate the emptiness can one be filled with Eros and know the Divine Kiss.

Most people are uncomfortable with going deep into the emptiness to connect with their soul and therefore often choose to avoid it. Without the connection to our source, it is easy to be seduced to vainly try to have some experience of aliveness through addictions that we may follow to avoid the emptiness such as: food, partying, entertainment, public acclaim, cell phones, drugs, excess work, gambling, satanic activities, and even politics. All these ways are superficial and short-lived substitutes and can lead to psycho-spiritual addictions. This is called pseudo-Eros. All areas of my life are the antithesis of this. In helping people to wake up much effort is made to create ways for people to bridge into the experience of authentic Eros in their lives. Eros is experiencing the feeling of fullness in the other. In meditation, in the process of disappearing into the nothing, this soul-fire regularly penetrates into the subtle, ecstatic delights of non-causal love, peace, compassion, contentment, cosmic Oneness and natural Eros. It is experiencing the beauty and wonder of God in all of creation. Sexual union, in this context, is the great mystical act that can merge us into the experience of the nothing that heals all the worlds. In this way living erotically means to be and celebrate the Divine in all things and is the key to living erotically in the non-sexual areas of our lives.

Teaching: The erotic non-sexual and sexual life becomes the Living Kiss that powers our desire for God, and at the same time may be the cause and result of God-Merging. Out of the Divine Kiss comes even more yearning for God.

Once the yearning for God started, I was inspired to take it to higher and higher spiritual levels. In this process, I became more present. If I slipped out of being present, I could not truly experience Eros and the Divine Urge that comes from it. Presence is critical in relationship. To be present we have to let go of the past, all of our baggage, the goal-oriented present, and the anxiety and fear-filled future.

Teaching: To be fully present is to be in the Eternal Presence and to let go of all control and all ideas of how another person should be as well as letting go of perfectionist consciousness.

When we are present in ourselves, we also create space for the other to exist. This is a crucial aspect of my relationship with Shanti. If someone is narcissistic, there is no room for the sacred other to uniquely exist because the other is seen to merely exist as a projection of one's needs. At the narcissistic level of relationship, both are trying to get each other to act in a certain way to meet their egocentric needs, but neither is trying to help the other to be his or her full potential essence, or full original, authentic self.

Teaching: The inner state of presence is letting go of the illusion of control and of the idea of how things "should be."

In my lifestyle of liberated magical realism, the illusion of "individual control" and an "idea of how things should be" has long since faded for me. Life has become a wondrous alignment and unique, spontaneous expression of the Divine. This is the play of sacred Eros that connects me to the Divine. Being seen and seeing the other person comes from being in the direct knowingness of the relationship, which is part of what makes it sacred.

Teaching: Seeing the face of one's mate means connecting on a deep level. It means having that sense of presence to allow each other to be who they are and giving up our idea of how we believe they should be.

In *Tantra*, practiced in the East, as well as in the Tantric approach of the West, the merging of the male and female can enhance awareness of the presence and non-dual wholeness. Being in a relationship or not has nothing to do with the wholeness awareness of enlightenment or with waking up. However, being in a relationship, if understood and balanced, can support the path because each partner helps the other become their authentic self and helps give them feedback when they are not in the Divine Presence.

Teaching: The drive for wholeness through relationship
remains an illusionary and common trap.

In relationships, the desire/attraction between male and female essence, at its deepest spiritual level, correlates with the longing for wholeness. Although for a moment we can temporarily experience the end of duality in the alchemical merging especially in the sexual experience, it is only a temporary taste of the wholeness of liberation. So, a potential pitfall of relationships, not properly understood is that although they temporarily may create the experience of presence, wholeness, and non-dual reality, a relationship is no substitute for being in the Eternal Presence or wholeness within oneself.

Teaching: Presence and wholeness can be
tasted in a relationship, but the inner awareness
of our wholeness comes from within.

In our sacred, intimate relationship, Shanti and I continually subtly remind each other that we are the deeper essence of God expressing. Eros, intimacy, sacred sexuality, and sacred relationship express a consciousness that builds into time and space a holy radiant partnership. When we let go and allow erotic sacred intimacy to show us the way to sacred relationship, the awareness is expanded from the Self to the relationship, to the world, to the universe, and to the multiverse.

Teaching: The healing of all worlds is a result of living
a wholly erotic alive sacred life through celebrating the
Divine in all of creation. In that way, we create world peace
by being peace within ourselves and in our relationships.

Love renders the mind powerless. Authentic communication helps to create Divine communion and the realization of Oneness, which is an expression of that love. Brief glimpses of the experience of love happen, but deep, consistent love can't flourish unless one is primarily free of mind-ego identification and thus open to dancing in the Divine Eternal Presence. Love may dissolve the sense of lack of wholeness temporarily, but to fully receive or give love, one needs to be primarily free of the pain or misery body which keeps us in separation consciousness. The more we remember to witness, the more we have the power to change dysfunctional patterns within ourselves. For Shanti and I, all of these subtleties are held in our active awareness as part of our sacred relationship and spiritual life. This includes the readiness to address family of origin or personal ego patterns that are brought up in relationships that need to be healed.

Teaching: One powerful benefit of sacred
relationships is to bring up family-of-origin patterns
to be healed; it is a profound evolutionary gift.

We certainly can't transform our partners without their consent and participation, but we can at least create and protect the space for transformation to happen when the opportunity for growth arises. That is one of the tremendous, potential benefits of a sacred relationship. In the space of the Divine Presence, grace and love can enter and create the time, space, and motivation for healing. One still needs to love themselves enough to heal themselves for this to happen. Creating a space of love supports this healing process. The idea is to create a space which then allows peace, love, and joy to come in; and non-causal peace, joy, and love to become more permanently established in our consciousness over time is a great gift. The beauty of relationships is that every challenge is an opportunity to more fully wake up, and this occurs at every stage of the unfolding consciousness awakening process. A key healing process that may happen in sacred relationship is the creation of an open and protected space for healing transformation to happen. By being present we either drive our partner crazy, or, if they are ready to walk through the door that one has opened for them, we may bring them closer to love and liberation.

Teaching: Giving emotional, psychic, and
spiritual space to our consort and ourselves is
vital for relationship health and growth.

Shanti seems unbelievably ready for healing transformation at almost all times as I am as well. A significant evolutionary power in sacred relationship is presence and witness consciousness. This opens the thoughtfulness to create and protect the space for each other to heal and to allow one's co-participation in the psycho-spiritual healing process inherent in relationships. This is something Shanti and I actively create for each other as part of our vision of sacred relationship. Although not often mentioned in the general relationship dialogues, we feel that creating transformative space for each other is one of the most important gifts that may occur in a sacred relationship.

Teaching: One of the most important
awarenesses in relationship is for the consorts to
be consistently present for each other in a way that
creates a healing space for either or both.

Humanity is under pressure to evolve because our survival is at stake.

Teaching: Sanity and consciousness come into the
world through us living in Divine Awareness.

Sacred relationships are part of the evolution of consciousness happening in our world today. However, we don't need to wait for anybody else, including world leaders or even sacred relationship to wake up. Being in the Eternal Presence allows things to be as they are, and therefore provides the awareness for healthy relationships and ultimately liberation. It creates the space for the other person to be in that process and thus to generate aliveness and the awakening potential for the other person. Within the healing and loving space of a sacred relationship, it is naturally easier to give up judging ourselves, feeling sorry for ourselves, living in victim consciousness or pride, or not loving ourselves.

Teaching: Forgiveness allows the present moment to be as it is, uncontaminated by our past attachments or past experiences. Forgiveness becomes easy when we relinquish identity and attachment with the past. It then empowers us to release our resistance to presence in sacred relationship and actually all relationships.

Non-causal love, when we understand it from a liberation perspective, comes from residing in the awareness of the Eternal Presence within ourselves. This enlightenment-based love can never be lost. It emanates primarily from within ourselves. However, in our relationship, when we share the reflection back of our love and of our Eternal Presence to each other, our sacred relationship amplifies our experience of the love of the Divine Presence.

Teaching: Liberated love, in essence, is feeling the presence of God within and without. Feeling the Eternal Presence in all. In this way love renders the mind powerless.

To sustain consciousness prior to the mind requires several fundamental internal consciousness transformations as I have learned from my own internal transformation experiences. The mind is always seeking to entrap me and actually all of us in I Am-ness. When I transcended the I Am-ness of my mind into "I-ness", I experienced the natural non-causal love, ecstasy, compassion, joy, peace, passion, and contentment that emanates from the natural state of "I-ness". Prior even to the realm of consciousness of the "I-ness" consciousness is disappearing into the Nothing. Not even the "I-ness" consciousness is left at this level; only pure Eternal Presence, prior to existence, resides. The more I found myself in the state of the Eternal Presence, prior to the "I-ness" awareness, the less power the mind had over me, and the easier it was and is to dissolve the thoughts of my mind and become free from them. This is another way sacred relationship amplifies the experience of the Divine Presence.

Teaching: With enlightenment one no longer has identification with the body-mind-I Am complex, and what predominantly remains is only the "I-ness" awareness of "I Am That" shining through.

In the big picture, with enlightenment I ended my primary relationship with the ego-self. My identifications are not necessarily entirely gone but are significantly diminished. This also means the constant struggle between the witness state and my identification with the body-mind-I Am complex has dissipated over time. In this context, sacred relationship for me has become an increasingly timeless experience of the cosmic Truth.

Suffering, which almost everyone experiences in the awakening process of sacred relationships and life in general, can be used as an incentive to release resistance to life and liberation, if we so choose. The key understanding is that we have a choice. There is no suffering when we are not attached to the outcomes of our actions. There is no suffering for the Self. I gained this understanding at the age of sixteen after my older brother, with whom I was very close, died. I had a choice as to how to respond beyond the normal grief cycle. I chose to let go of suffering and began to spontaneously meditate and recreate life by building a heart-lung machine in his former bedroom living space. My parents chose to suffer and hang on to their expectations of what they thought the flow of life should be. This created a slight shift in our relationship as they began to depend on me as a source of strength and spiritual support. It took them five years to end their suffering for his death. As a result of this situation, from the age of 16, I began to see long-term suffering as a choice.

Teaching: When we let go of life expectations and let go of our attachments to outcomes, and can forgive, then we begin the first step in ending suffering.

At the time of this book publishing, Shanti and I have been happily married in a sacred relationship for twenty years. Every relationship has its own particular time, space, and energy needs that create the context for a loving, sacred relationship to continue to grow and blossom both romantically and spiritually. For us Shabbat is more specifically that time as a holy seed energy each week that energizes this holy love energy throughout the week. The word "romantic" may seem a little strange as part of a spiritual discussion but keeping the romance in a relationship over time is very important and a lot of fun. Eros, bhakti (dualistic devotion), deveikut (drive for God merging) and rasa (spiritual juice) are other overlapping words that may be useful in expanding the meaning of romantic. Experiencing sacred relationship as living romantic poetry adds a lot of "juice" to the relationship.

The Divine Kiss!

Shanti and I during a wedding ceremony.

Chapter 22

THIRTEEN POEMS
TO THE BELOVED

No Return

Jumping off the sacred mountain of love
Burning in my heart
Into the great mystical unknown
Of sacred love, intimacy, and relationship
Of passionate radiant enduring love
Cannot be reversed
It is forever.
That is what makes it sacred
At the deepest level.
As we passionately plummet
Into sacred intimacy and love
Beyond time and space
Into the cosmic oneness and love
Beyond understanding, logic and the mind
Into the eternal presence of the ONE

---ɯɯ---

Entering the Palace Gates

Before the Adamic race

Before we incarnated and became two

In our suckling I feel again

The bliss of the magical fluid of your breasts heals my soul

It enters every cell of my being

You permeate this soul with your holy gifts of love.

The experience of our Divinity

Of our merging

Is beyond belief

We become the awakened Shekhinah spirit of making love

Every cell of your skin radiates this truth onto my tongue

Proclaiming your eternal beauty

Sucking on your holy toes

My toes tingle with love for you

Who are you?

Who are we?

We have invoked the Divine

And it is in the alchemy of our relationship

Our love materializes the Shekhinah energy onto this planet

We are a planetary resurrection of the feminine face of the infinite one.

The ambrosia fluid begins to flow from your palace gates

You invite me to enter

Moving further into our merging

As our rivers of love become one ocean

Our hearts touch in a way that is new

The experience of you as infinite enlightened compassion

Opens a locked door in the heart of surrender
That no woman has known before.
I am completely yours
My heart opens in infinite compassion
The heart opening happens
Since becoming aware...
I weep with gratitude
An oceanic wave of your organism is released directly
From your womb into me
Your energy is so strong.
The power of it fills me with your essence
Every cell drinking you in
You penetrate
Every cell of this one's consciousness
My whole being absorbs it all.
The ecstasy of our union... could we not be here forever?
As we slowly separate
My soul cries as we pull apart
Feeling torn
Out of our natural and true state as One
And now we become two again.
The heartache of our separation begins again.
Yet you are always with me.
I have become the awakened feminine
Transmuted in the alchemy of our love
The Shekhinah energy has been resurrected within and in the world
Blessed by your infinite compassion
Your energy that is now in my energetic womb reverberates to my heart
Your love dances within

You are there in the core of every cell.
Your pain, rage, and sorrow
About the desecration of
All women the holy feminine throughout time
Your energy carries it all
And now so does this soul.
The heart, womb, and cells carry the pain of the oppression
Of the loss of spirit in all things
The raping of the planet
Of the animal and plant life
Of real womanhood and manhood
May you guide
And trust me
That in silent wisdom and love
You are always honored.

Awakened Love

I look into your eyes
And love you;
I hear the melody of your voice
And love you;
I hear the wisdom of your words
And love you;
I feel the coldness of your words
And love you;
I feel the touch of your cold body
And love you;
I feel the absence of your body
And love you;
I suckle from your magical breasts
And love you;
I enter you
And love you;
Your energy penetrates mine
And I love you;
We merge
And become love.
I experience the beauty of your mind
And love you;
I feel the joy in your heart
And love you;
I feel your clarity
And love you;

I feel your ambivalence and confusion
And love you;
I drink from your sweetness
And love you;
I burn in your fire
And love you;
The hills turn to ocean waves on the full moon
And I love you;
I wonder at the beauty of the stars
And love you;
I delight in the taste of your food
And love you;
Rejoicing in the ecstasy of body and mind
I love you;
Even if you turn away from me in your beautiful woman form
This soul-fire will still love you;
The only way love can stop flowing
Is for me to close my heart
Which cannot be done;
There is no room for love to stop flowing
You will always be loved.
Since my heart touched yours
I will always love
You are the Divine pulse in every moment;
The ecstasy in all of creation;
The brilliant light of sunrise
The rainbow dance of sunset,
And luminous moonlight dancing on my soul;
It is impossible to say no to you.

This soul-fire can only celebrate you in the naked
Cosmic dance of our lives
And become you,
And be as love.
In every moment there is only sweet and subtle love;
Pulsing with joyous love for you;
And when we know each other
There is no he or she,
There is only space of eternal and Divine love.

Holy Woman

An eternal smile of the light
Inner world
Smiling
Nurturing
Loving
Where did you come from?
Does it matter?
You are here
The kiss of our foreheads
Explodes the mind into freedom.
Our innocent flow
Tao unfolding silently
Without expectation
In total acceptance
And appreciation.
The illusion of struggle ends
And we become
Effortlessly
The joyous dance of Shiva and Shakti
In the glow of our eyes
Our hearts embrace.
As we enter each other
Merging into the One
Invoking the radiant presence of the Shekhinah
Love flows
A delicious nectar

We sip this holiness with every kiss.
You are a blessing.
Your loving, glowing eyes
Are a warm mikvah
Soothing life
Bathing in all accepting love
Safe... this soul enjoys the peace.
A timeless way we spontaneously connect
Easily becoming
One mind
Beyond mind
Our Love
A cosmic gift.
Your presence within is a lightning bolt teacher
Beyond words reveling in your ecstasy,
Cellular joy eternally dancing with the one
As your molecules celebrate within me.
Your wondrous mystery is celebrated
May we be blessed to dance always as one
In the blue lotus of liberation.
Your cosmic lover.

I Take No Vows

I take no vows
Except to always give you all
This one is
In Every moment
To be with you as the ecstatic,
Untamed love dance of Yah
In the subtle movement
Of every heartbeat and breath.
To let our celebration
Of the Devi's wild love party
Continue forever
In every blissful cell of my body.

On Our Nowness

In our nowness
There is the ecstatic nothing
Of who we are.
God splits me open
And there is only you.
Without expectation, past, future, dreams or projections
This one appears before you
Alone, empty of all concepts, pictures, projections, and hopes;
Resting blissfully in the power of the present
Giving this essence
Naked and raw
Not even a covering of skin, muscles or bones.
You have become this essence,
This one … yours.
In our merging
We reenact the mystery of the foundation of the world.
We become the Oneness of the original Adam and Eve.
Reuniting as one flame.

—〰—

Dancing

Dancing as one soul in the Garden of Eden.
Independent of externals,
Unconditionally, without expectations;
Free… wild… God essence… love.
That is where you find me;
Where we will always meet in every moment.
Our souls are filled with flowers
Giving birth to the spring of God's creation.
Asking nothing… wanting nothing.
We live in the searing fire and beauty of Yah's presence.
Like two falling stars
Alive in the intensity of the moment.
Our sublime beauty shines eternally
As we burn holding hands with God,
Arching through the sky in a sacred existence
That transcends all poetry of ecstasy and love.
Heart exploding in untamed love,
Beyond the slavery of common sense.
Choosing only freedom and love
Drawing forth the wild holiness and love in you.
Lie down naked with me next to God
And madly forget all
But the Truth of our Divine union
In every unrestrained mysterious moment of existence.

Being Love

We make love
Until every cell of our physical body
Alchemically changes to love;
Until our full sensuous lips and sensitive tongues
Become one embrace;
Until our breath becomes the one exhale of the universe;
Until we become the Divine subtle white nectar
I suckle from your incredible life-giving breasts;
Until our bellies merge
As one umbilical cord connected to the creator;
Until what I thought as my burning lingam
And the fire of your yoni
And it's delicious magical nectar
Forget their owners and become the cosmic Shiva Lingam.
We love until there's nothing left
But the Divine One laughing in holy joy.

—⚭—

Only Myself To Give

I give you all
That
There is
Nothing left
Do not be deluded or seduced by
Name fame power or money
Labels of realization
Sattvic lifestyles
Dharmas of what I can give.
In untamed childlike sweet innocence
I give you all
I Am That I Am
You are the chosen One
Because you can receive it all,
You can hold it all
And dance wildly with me
Until we become the ecstatic dance
And joy of the ONE
Beyond understanding
May the Devi's dance party in our hearts be eternal.

—⚭—

Tantric Sunrise

Awakening from the exquisite bliss of sleep
Gently massaging your breast in succulent vortexes
Feeling the subtle heat increase
As your nipples and this body pulse with blood
Our lips lusciously touch, giving birth to our tongues
Which mate like ovum and sperm, giving birth to life.
In that moment, the light of a thousand suns explode in my head
What an awesome sunrise, which goes all day long,
Forever keeping me awake!

—⚭—

Waves

The Shekhinah enters so strongly
Surrounded in the white light of her power
A wave hits me
And knocking me upside down
In the sand of the infinite universe
Out of control
Of senses and body
Enjoying the power of the Goddess wave
Humbled
Off balance
Crumpled on the sand
Like a fish needing to be in water
Entering the cosmic ocean again
Perhaps in time I will understand how to ride the wave.

—⚊—

Women

Wild reflection of the Shekhinah,
Dancing your dance
With abandon
Innocently
In devotional love
You are loved as the infinite One
May these actions and thoughts always glorify your dance.

—⚊—

Holy Nectar of Love

Your consciousness so soft
Body silken skin
Luscious to this skin
Our skins making love
As these arms rub lightly on yours and our thighs softly touch
Our feet embrace in arches.
Our hearts touch in silence
Lips feel full on your luscious neck
Tongue begins to taste the nectar of your skin
The sleeping Shekhinah slowly begins to respond to propitiations
Your breasts turn into fountains of Divine Essence
As the etheric milky nectar pours forth
In a holy stream into my mouth
Can such holy nectar be for real?
It is awesome to suckle this unbelievable cosmic energy
Blessed by the white sweetness that flows from your wondrous breasts
Transported back our one soulness joy-filled way to live.

Chapter 23

HOLISTIC LIBERATION

Teaching: A truly free person can move in any
direction and in any realm of consciousness.

Looking back over the course of my life, everything I ever learned
came from meditating, playing football, sacred relationship,
and parental love, supported by the way of life of the Six Foundations
and Sevenfold Peace. I left everything, including my first marriage,
as part of the endless non-causal desire to disappear into the Cosmic
Nothingness. *Non-causal* means that the source of love is coming
from within oneself emanating from the true Self and does not
depend on an outer cause to create the feeling of love, although an
outer cause such as one's marriage can activate that inner experience
but is not the primary the source of it.

Fortunately, my present marriage with Shanti consistently
supports this unending Self-Realization evolution into total

God-merging. The power and steadfastness of my parent's love gave me the basic trust to be able to open to sacred relationship, and also to the mysterious process of merging with the Divine. My parent's love had always been a constant and it has filled the life of my soul with a sense of steady, deep self-esteem. It was one layer below knowing God's love in my life, which came into consciousness after years of meditation. From 1982 to 1993, I began to comprehend a new layer of Self-Realization: At the beginning of this initial Self-Realization cycle, I was attached to remaining in the comfortable, but limited, "now" of the world of direct knowing. During this period of time however, I began to integrate the understanding that I live as a multidimensional being walking between all the worlds, while not being part of any.

The unfoldment was like being in a new world of awareness and sensitivity. For example, until I figured out how to handle certain energies in the at-One-ment state of non-dual consciousness, it was a little like walking around as a raw nerve. This meant feeling everything, including everyone's pain. Certain people were almost too much to be around because they were in so much pain. It took a while to become transparent in the Oneness, so I could still feel the pain of the world but let it pass through me in a way that did not disturb my energetic field and physical system. This was part of an important training for me in how to stay in the Oneness while not becoming vulnerable to what may come with the openness. Although not an easy task, once I slowly was able to master this challenge, my attention was naturally and paradoxically placed on how to stay both anchored in the Oneness and Nowness while walking in all five worlds simultaneously. The five worlds include the physical, astral, world of pure soul, world of the over soul connecting all souls, and soul world which is hard-wired into God. Over time I gradually morphed into a walker between the worlds.

This expanded awareness developed over my first ten post-liberation years. With the integration of all five worlds, there is a more consistent, illuminated, multidimensional world of deep sahaja samadhi (being active while still in samadhi) while appearing to be an ordinary person having ordinary experiences. This sahaja samadhi state is a world of continually being inspired and empowered by the Ruach Ha'Kodesh, Holy Spirit, Kundalini, Shekhinah, or activated energy of God. For me to drive a car in this state, it has been necessary to condense my consciousness more into the physical plane, so Shanti does almost all of the driving. Computers sometimes cause my consciousness to contract as well, but I can generally work with them. As I continued to integrate my liberation awareness, my ability to contract my consciousness down to the physical plane was key in entering my next phase of Divine service. My ability to condense consciousness has also been supported by the natural grounding of my spiritual warrior football background and doing some aerobic exercise, pranayama (breathing practices), and TriYoga six days per week. During this post-liberation period, my "coming and going walk" between the B'limah (Nothing) and the Mah (Something) has become a more natural alternating flow.

As previously mentioned, the major entryways to the Self and the Holistic Liberation Way for me included Shaktipat and the awakening of the Kundalini, meditation and sacred relationship. There are other portals that open us to the experience of the Divine and the Self, such as spending time in nature, body awareness, breath, silence, prayer, and repeating the Name of God that are primary for some people but were not so for me. Jnana Yoga, which spontaneously evolved out of my meditation experience, also known as the Yoga of the Mind or *Raja Yoga,* which utilizes the practice of self-inquiry to transcend the ego also became an important part of my spiritual worldview.

Teaching: Part of the Jnana Yoga entry way to the Self is consciously remembering we are not the mind or its thoughts but exist prior to the mind.

I so appreciated the awakening liberation power of Jnana Yoga that in the late 1980s, I and another person from the Muktananda Ashram created a westernized form of it. Since the early 1990s out of my own liberation inspiration I have morphed it into my Zero Point course which I presently teach. The Zero Point course is a powerful vehicle for awakening the Western mind to the understanding that the "personality is a case of mistaken identity".

Teaching: After repeated meditation Shaktipat experiences and grace, true knowledge of the real Self tends to spontaneously and naturally arise.

At another level of spiritual evolution, the awareness of the non-dual Nothing alternating with the appearance of the manifest in the three-dimensional world began to more fully develop. It means experiencing the spiritual potential of what is in the material plane. This non-dual awareness in the Great Torah Way tradition is called *koach mah.* Koach mah is a direct experience of the spark of God in all of material creation. By becoming aware of the illuminating (*berur*) empty consciousness space within, one becomes aware of the no mind of the silent, still inner space. In this context, nothing real can be threatened, and nothing unreal can exist.

Teaching: One of the secrets of the liberated life is
that when we know nothing real can be threatened,
and nothing unreal real can exist, we lose all fear.

From a practical perspective, life is always out of our control, except for our ability to control our response to our unfolding destiny. However, it is necessary for us to spend a certain amount of chronological time for things like scheduling airplane tickets and being on time for airplane flights. The physical world is important because it creates tests for the manifestation of the liberation of consciousness to be realized.

Teaching: Paradoxically, both death and our
identification with physical form are illusions. There
is death only for the physical body. We are not form,
but we live in a physical form. There is no death for
the Soul Self because the Soul Self is immortal.

Freedom is a fearless state. In liberation I became free of the past, free of the present, and free of the future, or any feeling that I needed to be something other than the ecstatic emptiness of the Divine Will manifesting. In liberation one remains steady in the deathless moment of the present, including the present, past, and future beyond time and unrelated to time.

Teaching: The desire for time-related liberation is
a subtle trap of a time/goal-oriented mentality.

In my own liberation process, neither time nor a goal of liberation was ever the focus. The power of the unfolding liberation was so overwhelming that my main effort was simply manifesting the energy to keep showing up.

Teaching: Nothing has ever happened and,
paradoxically, everything has already happened.

Dreamless sleep, in which all remains bliss throughout the night of sleep, began to happen spontaneously without any particular intention. The bliss is particularly strong in the moments between falling asleep and in the moments of awakening. My main sleep awareness was and is to go to sleep repeating the *Tetragrammaton* (sacred name of God as YHWH). I attempt to remain conscious of the sacred name in my lighter sleep cycles, and to wake repeating it. If I don't wake repeating it, then I close my eyes, and more consciously awaken again repeating the Name.

Teaching: Grace moves us into the Eternal Presence
the moment we realize that we don't need to seek the
Divine, but that we are That within ourselves.

Part of the result of an in-depth spiritual unfolding is that we naturally become open to all there is, like the sky is open to the birds, and the flowers, and the sun, and the clouds passing through. In any moment, by grace in the present, we can move into the Eternal Presence. We awaken to the Eternal Presence by realizing we are already there. Sometimes we are given a taste of this liberation truth to help us pay attention and inspire us. Many people have had temporary enlightenment experiences. The vast majority of us will not become permanently liberated without building and nourishing the awareness preconditions that transform us over time. The more we choose to enter into that Eternal Presence through the various levels of intensity of our steady spiritual life, the thinner the glass ceiling becomes. At some point, by an act of grace, the glass ceiling of the mind permanently shatters, and we enter into a consistent unbroken, conscious awareness of the Eternal Presence within us which is at least greater than 51 percent of the time. This is the beginning stage of Self Realization.

People often ask me if they are ready to start the liberation process. Based on my "starting" experience, the moment in one's life where one intuitively feels the door is opening is the place to start one's liberation process, not next week, not when your exams are over, or whatever postponement one can create. It is now that matters. Nothing in our history matters. Nothing we think will happen in the future matters.

Teaching: Life and liberation happen most easily
if we are willing to repeatedly disappear into the
Nothing and live in a way that continually opens
us up to the experience of the Divine Presence.

However, there is a psychic structure that will resist Divine Presence. It is known as the ego. Ego is the unobserved mind that runs our life when we are not in the witness state. The ego strategizes how to avoid being in the Eternal Divine Presence, which naturally would dissolve the ego into the formless and thus render it powerless over us. Most people love to hold onto their stories of the past, though these stories may hamper spiritual evolution in the present. Many individuals choose to live in a self-induced trance, believing they are their stories of past, present, and future. The general resistance to awakening often manifests in strategies of control, power, drama, war, hate and illness.

Teaching: The evolving spiritual path
demands awakening from our dream of the I
Am-ness of a separate self with its stories.

When two or more egos come together, as they do in relationships, we often get drama that if beneficially understood, supports our liberation process. From an awakened perspective, we all have the potential choice to end our dramas by releasing the past, discharging psychological time and pain, and shifting our consciousness into the spiritual time of the present moment, which exists without the past's psychodynamic contamination. Many people fear the end of the drama because they know either consciously or unconsciously that the toxic, often power-related, yet comfortable, aspects of ego would cease to exist.

Teaching: When one lives in complete acceptance of what is, there is no argument or drama. A fully conscious person is not in conflict but uses their mind in service to consciousness. Once, we are no longer identified with the mind, the drama ends and we can use the mind appropriately.

All suffering is ego-related due to resistance to the Eternal Presence. Liberation allows one to be in the eternal "I-ness" of I Am That which was, is, and will be. In form, we have birth, death, growth, and dissolution.

Teaching: Physical forms are not our life; they are only our life situations.

In the liberated/enlightened state of awareness, I began to realize that I (not any relationship, action, or addiction) was the source of their inner, ongoing spiritual experiences and state. As I previously explained, sacred relationship has the potential to create the liberation/enlightenment space and to enhance these spiritual awarenesses. In the context of my inner awarenesses, co-dependencies dissolve, and the highest level of sacred interdependent onenesses emerge. It's deliciously wild!!!

Teaching: In the Sacred Self, there is only the non-causal bliss, love, peace, joy, oneness, compassion, passion, eros, and contentment.

Chapter 24

BURNING KARMA

Teaching: Nothing in our life is "unfair".

---

*H*olistic physicians have been attacked over the years by the allopathic and pharmaceutical world throughout the U.S. and Europe. What I faced in 1993 with the California Board, was pretty minimal in the big picture compared to the many attacks against holistic physicians. Fortunately, my California license is still active today. It was never revoked and the holistic health practice I had in California was not interrupted for even one day. However, there was a powerful situation that consumed time and money as part of my karma burning; this situation has occasionally been deliberately misused by anti-holistic health elements to appear discrediting; which of course was the whole idea.

In 1999, in alignment with entering the nineteen-year Saturn cycle of my Vedic Astrology chart, increased "negative" karmic events started to happen. A person who had been on some of our tours to Israel in the past developed what the pathologist diagnosed as acute encephalitis (inflammation of the brain); and what later on after going through the literature was further diagnosed by me and my specialist consultant as part of a rarer disease called Fourniers. My research strongly indicated that the acute encephalitis was from a cell extract rejuvenation therapy he had procured illegally from Europe. It was illegal in the U.S. because there was a twenty-five percent rate of acute encephalitis associated with this European therapy. He had been taking this therapy on his own for at least a year and suddenly started to feel extremely unwell. After three weeks of seriously going downhill, he was referred to me for an evaluation and "panchakarma" (a week-long, non-invasive, Ayurvedic rejuvenation therapy). Over the four days he was with us this person continued to go downhill, and he was given a legal homeopathic dose of medicine to boost his adrenals, but he died the next day of the acute encephalitis and its side effects. This situation created a whole lot of legal difficulty for me as a holistic physician and also showed the subtle corruption of the legal system against holistic physicians at that time.

Fortuitously, the Arizona Homeopathic Medical Board sent a high-level member of the board, Dr. Garry Gordon down to investigate. He was also a world famous holistic medical expert. Dr Gordon was so convinced that there was no malpractice involved that he gave up his impartial investigative role on the board regarding my case to actively help me prepare a case to defend my innocence and reputation as a holistic physician. After two years of investigation and preparation, in 2000 we arrived in court with literally twenty-nine cubic feet of evidence, an obviously overwhelming amount of evidence, proving my innocence. Fortunately, once the judge overruled the opposing attorney's outrageous motion to throw out all the evidence that Dr. Gordon and I had compiled, the pre-hearing went positively. During this whole process, I sat in the wondrous witness state at the cosmic drama going on. I will be forever grateful to Dr. Garry Gordon for his enthusiastic and detailed research help in this situation. Although the case was not summarily dismissed by the court, in the pre-hearing, the opposing lawyer called for a settlement within the first hour of discussion. We never went to court and settled out of court for a minimal, symbolic settlement that basically covered lawyer's fees, pennies compared to a wrongful death settlement (often in the millions). The malpractice insurance paid this minimal settlement fee with no resistance.

When one has such a ridiculous but severe situation, it is a clear sign of burning karma. The perpetual question of "Why do bad things happen to good people?" is primarily asked by people who do not understand the multi-lifetime carrying out of actions of the laws of karma, or, as the Torah teaches, "measure for measure". Until we merge back into the one, the laws of karma, too mysterious to understand, will continue play a role refining and evolving us. That is why nothing in our life is "unfair". God never punishes us. It is the complexity of the laws of karma and karma burning playing out for our spiritual evolvement. This was a powerful spiritual test that expanded my awareness.

The second part of the irrefutable and basically positive ending was that this case was automatically referred to the Arizona Homeopathic Medical Board. I was completely exonerated after sharing the scientific evidence in response to the pathology reports, which showed the death was caused by acute encephalitis and Fournier's disease, an obscure deadly illness associated with the weakening of the immune system from the acute encephalitis, plus several other predisposing factors. It was good, however, to be exonerated of any wrongdoing by the board. As a holistic homeopathic physician, it was good to know I could get a fair, unbiased holistic and scientific hearing from the Arizona Board of Homeopathy and Integrated Medicine Association (AHIMA). This was is one of the major reasons I had decided back in 1987 when preparing to move to Arizona, not to get an allopathic medical license in Arizona. The Arizona Board of Homeopathy and Integrated Medicine license has the highest standard of practice, and gives me the same medical privileges of the allopathic medical license. This license allows me to legally carry on a high integrity holistic medical practice and offers me the freedom to research how to heal type-2 diabetes naturally without the use of allopathic medications. If possible, it is helpful to find a safe supportive setting to do one's life service/dharma. This karmic situation took place over twenty years ago. It is interesting to note that for the last two years I have been serving as the vice-president of AHIMA, which is my way to show my support for the board's avant-garde work in supporting holistic physicians.

Teaching: When life tests us, it helps to rest in the mystery and remember we are burning karma.

In 1998 I led a workshop at the Omega Center, a few hours north of New York City. As we were driving back after the workshop, I began to experience a funny feeling in my head and started to taste and smell blood. Over a progression of a few days, I began to lose touch with the right side of my body, especially in terms of spatial awareness, which was interesting in itself. It was actually scientifically fascinating to me that the mind and sensory system became disconnected from the right side of my physical body. It was a great experiential teaching as I actually couldn't tell where my right hand or right leg was. It was a direct experience of how we are not the body. In a paradoxical way it was enjoyably illuminating.

I stayed in New York City during this time with my daughter Heather, and decided to check the symptoms out at Columbia P&S where I had attended medical school. The Columbia P&S resident doctor became nervous when he was putting a cut down into my femoral artery of my right leg to insert the catheter to put the radioactive dye material into the brain, as they wanted to give me an anesthetic for the procedure, but I didn't want that. I gave them the clear message, "Just put it in already, and don't worry about it. " As the patient, I had to coach the resident to relax. "It is going to be fine. Do the cut down, and get the catheter into the femoral artery the correct way." It helped that he understood I was a graduate of Columbia P&S and was his senior, so he did listen.

The workup showed that I had an internal cranial bleed coming from a ruptured congenital defect called an AVM or arteriovenous malformation. This is a congenital defect in which the capillaries between the arteries and veins are missing in a certain area of the brain. It usually blows out in people in their thirties, potentially resulting in death so it wasn't the obvious thing to think of in a 58-year-old. Probably because of the holistic lifestyle and generally excellent health, my body was able to go another twenty years before the blowout happened. It was interesting to observe the strange way the doctors looked at me once they saw the results showing a massive bleed on the whole left side of the head. My skull and brain were full of blood pressing on the whole parietal area of the brain and partially in some other cerebral areas. Because of the massive extent of the internal bleed, they said they could not understand how my body was walking around and not hospitalized in critical condition. It was too deep to explain to them, as it was beyond their belief systems that there is more to life force and action than the physical nervous system and brain. It was hard enough for them to get that I had no need or intention to be hospitalized.

Teaching: There is more to life force and body function than the physical nervous system and brain.

In retrospect, this did explain, however, the clumsiness my body experienced even in grammar school. For example, in one particular football game as a young football player, I returned a kick-off, got through all the players, had a clear open field to score a touchdown and simply tripped and fell. Somehow the connection with the right foot simply failed in that moment. In college, taking music and language courses required a lot of work, as I was unable to easily memorize the sound or the patterns of the sounds. Apparently, this was all connected to the location of the AVM defect in the brain near the sound/memory center, which, from a reincarnation perspective, was most likely a past life karma carrying over into this lifetime as most congenital defects are.

Finally, after about three or four days, the bleeding stopped. The neurological specialist at Columbia P&S confirmed the AVM (arteriovenous malformation) diagnosis and made a recommendation to wait until clots from the brain bleed formed, and then the clots could be taken out with brain surgery. The ruptured vessels would be permanently tied off during surgery to prevent further bleeds. The other option was to wait until there was another bleed, which had a high percentage of creating serious damage or death. Surgery seemed the best choice, but I did not have the feeling that Columbia P&S was where I should undergo it because the Columbia P&S neurologist shared with me that there was between a two to six percent risk of fatality and a much higher risk of potential brain damage from the surgery. In the process of checking the best place for the surgery, I found, at St. Joseph's Hospital in Phoenix, Arizona, a real hotshot neurosurgeon that I liked right away. He claimed that he had no fatalities from this surgery and minimal to no brain damage. So, after waiting a few months for the clot to harden and begin absorption, he did the surgery. Also, I had a total of five radioactive brain scans pre- and post-surgically to track what was going on. The neurosurgeon was very particular, and he wanted to make sure there were no more AVM defects in the rest of my brain. Although uncomfortable with the radioactive dye, I was fine with this fastidious neurosurgeon. After all, one doesn't hire a neurosurgeon for being sloppy!

Getting one of these brain scans was interesting. They wanted to give me anesthetic for it, but I graciously explained to them that it wouldn't be happening. The brain angiogram did create a feeling of intense burning in my brain. In addition to having this done five times, an MRI was also performed. Again, they wanted to medicate me all the time, even for this, but I refused. There is a tendency in the medical world to overly avoid any potential pain by using anesthetics and tranquilizers, which is based on the assumption that people have no internal strength. The good news was that my neurosurgery operation was one hundred percent successful. The surgeon was kind enough to let me leave the hospital the next day and stay at my friend, the late Dr. Abe Ber's home in the Phoenix area to convalesce. Between the potential legal case and the AVM (arteriovenous malformation), there certainly was a lot of karma burning to start this nineteen-year Saturn cycle.

After about two years post-surgery, my body and brain seemed fully healed. Not only did it seem to be repaired but even seems to subtly function beyond where it was before the manifestation of the AVM brain hemorrhage. My personally designed self-healing post-surgery program involved a lot of sophisticated work such as acupuncture, neurological kinesiology (to reconnect all the circuits), brain exercises, and homeopathy. I also took nutritional supplements to decrease brain trauma inflammation, to remove the radioactive isotopes from the angiogram dyes, and to rebuild the brain. Today my brain is clear of all radioactive dye and other contaminants from the operation. Unbelievable as it may appear to neurologists and brain surgeons, because of God's grace and much sophisticated hard work, I have experienced an improvement in all brain parameters when compared before the AVM brain hemorrhage and the brain surgical procedure.

As a result of my direct experience, compassionately helping people repair their "broken" brains is almost a subspecialty in addition to helping people recover from post-concussion brain trauma, brain inflammation, and brain degeneration from car accidents, and athletic brain injury, which so many athletes have today, especially football players. It is amazing how many people suffer unaware from a previous brain trauma. As a result, in my Whole Person Health Evaluations, there is always screening for latent brain trauma. As of today, more than twenty-two years later, the AVM hemorrhage has minimal to no impact on my life. There have been a few times each year when I was working very hard that the sensory perception of the location of my right-hand is at a slight variance spatially. Also, for about ten years after the surgery, if I did not get enough sleep for a few days in a row, there would also be a unique headache in a specific location on arising that would last for thirty to sixty minutes. This is now one hundred percent gone. The only residue remaining is itchiness and dryness on the whole top of my head where the operation took place. They had to lift up the entire scalp to directly access my skull through which they had to cut a hole to reach the brain. Because of this I still have a need to oil my scalp every day to ameliorate this minor effect. The surgeon cut a two-and-a-half-inch circumference hole in the skull through which he operated and then replaced the bone back in with some bone chips to hold it in place until it grew back. They then put in forty staples to keep the scalp in place. My scalp remained puffy and with fluid for about a year before it seemed to reattach more permanently. I choose to go into my conscientious scientific detail side of my personality to help make the point of the reality of this overall adventure.

To add to the drama, around ten days post-operatively, Nora, my first wife called to say that she was bleeding from her intestines and they were thinking of doing surgery to resect part of her bowel, as they did not know what was going on. It was obvious to me after twenty-eight years of marriage one gets to know what is happening with your ex-mate and long-term friend. It was obvious that the stress of my brain surgery and the threat of my death set off a somatic process in her. I had the forty stitches taken out four days earlier than planned, so I could fly back to Petaluma, California where Nora was hospitalized. In an unorthodox medical move, I climbed into the hospital bed with her and simply held her for a long time. Her internal bleeding stopped and never returned. Her doctors declared she was okay and sent her home with no surgery. Although we were divorced, we were and still are close family and to this day we are still actively co-parenting with our grown children and grandchildren.

No one at the Tree of Life Center and Foundation even knew about my AVM brain hemorrhage and brain surgery. For me, it is always better to talk about these things afterwards. Although my gross motor skills were functional, it took about six weeks before I was able to relate to and work on a computer. Thank goodness my clinical skills came back so quickly, that no one even noticed. My total memory return took more than two years; and it initially took a lot of extra work to give a lecture, especially since I do not use notes.

Teaching: Most inherited congenital defects
are connected to past life karmas.

A few months after returning home from the brain surgery, there was a large live-food conference in the Bay Area where I gave a keynote address. Preparing for it was a challenge and giving it required a lot of focused mental strength that made me break out in a sweat due to the effort. At the end of the lecture, I had an unexpected and extended standing ovation. I have never been clear about what happened, as no one knew what I had been through in the previous two months with the brain surgery. Somehow, they seemed to know something significant had just happened. It was touching.

During my teen years, I had a sense of physical immortality, and never thought that I might undergo an operation. This, of course, was wishful teenage thinking. I have had a series of operations and injuries that in essence have possibly played a role in the opening and activating of my chakra system in some way, which is still mysterious to me. At 28 years old, as previously discussed, I had my first operation, which was a back surgery. It was performed to correct another congenital defect in my sacral spine. I sense this symbolized and was connected to the base chakra.

In 1986 at Petaluma Hospital also as previously mentioned, I underwent a hernia operation because of another congenital defect. During the operation, the doctor even lifted up my abdominal muscle wall to show me an additional hole in my abdomen, about the size of a half dollar, which was another congenital defect that showed up. It is amazing how much past life body karma I was born with.

Teaching: The fifth limb in the eight-limbed Patanjali Yoga Path is called pratyahara, or sense withdrawal. In this state there is no experience of pain or even body awareness.

The patterns of my surgeries and the childhood tuberculosis at the age of one were interesting because they related to all the chakras. The L-5/S-1 surgery covered my base chakra; the hernia operations were associated with my second and third chakras; the chronic scarring in the lungs from the miliary tuberculosis was associated with the heart chakra; the scarring on the larynx from miliary tuberculosis of the larynx covered the throat chakra; minor surgery in the third eye area to open up the blocked main tear duct for the third eye chakra; and the brain surgery at my crown, associated with the crown chakra. It is not clear what any of this means, but it appears that in my unique soul journey there needed to be some sort of physical initiation in some manner over the years at every chakra in the physical body.

The scarring from the TB of my larynx regularly manifested in India, especially in 1979, in a way that made it challenging for me to give lectures without coughing if my throat would dry out. This is something that still occasionally manifests today, primarily when my throat and larynx become dry. The specific karma of this larynx irritation and coughing has never been clear to me. A homeopathic remedy for TB of the larynx has been beneficial for this; and it's much less of an issue than in 1979. There is still some karma related to this as I may still cough when I lecture all day when giving workshops if my throat becomes dry, but it is minimal.

Teaching: Physical operations which appear to represent the so-called mundane happenings in our lives may cross into our spiritual evolution. It is worth looking at one's unique patterns, such as operations/diseases/scarring/chakra patterns. These unique details give us clues about what has happened throughout our spiritual, evolutionary process over lifetimes.

Chapter 25

ALIYAH

Teaching: Aliyah is the "stepping up"
to another level of consciousness.

Doing service in Israel seems to be part of my and also our mission. Shanti was raised in a spiritual context, not a religious one. As part of our pre-marriage agreement, although already biologically/genetically Jewish, she agreed to learn the appropriate, necessary prayers and understandings for a Jewish woman. Shanti even heroically went before the Jewish certification rabbis of the Bet Din in Jerusalem, Israel to officially affirm her Jewishness. She also made a technically important official "conversion" with Rabbi Gershon Winkler although it was "halachically" (traditional religious rules) unnecessary. As she is of Jewish lineage both on her mother's side and also on her father's side, it was not absolutely necessary to do the conversion, but it seemed important. Much of her close New Zealand family has reactivated their Jewish lineage, inspired by Shanti's awakening to this historical fact.

Giving a talk to a full house in Israel.

As we deepened our connection to Am Israel (the Torah based Jewish people), we made aliyah in 2008. With this we became Israeli citizens and received Israeli passports even though we were going back and forth, as dual citizens, between Israel and the U.S. As there is no formal spiritual initiation into taking aliyah, to fully fulfill the process at the highest octave, my spiritual shaman sense felt some ceremony needed to be created. This prophetic return to Israel is part of the fulfillment of the still small voice of the Divine, that directed me to return to my roots at the end of the forty-day fast in 1983. Following the Divine Will sometimes needs to be quite concrete to be fulfilled; it is not simply metaphorical. I created my own aliyah initiation by going out into the desert for seventy-two hours in a half cave, above the city of Arad, overlooking the Dead Sea, where the Qumran Essenes had lived. In this aliyah initiation I did a dry fast, meditating and praying in a half cave an archeologist friend knew of, where a Christian monk in the Middle Ages had lived for years. The half-cave was perfect, as it partially blocked the sunny part of the day. Friends and family were, however, a little concerned about this initiation because people have died of dehydration from being in the Negev Desert for even just one day without water. However, coming from a different level of awareness and dietary and fasting experience, it was rather easy to be without food and water for three days there in the desert. At night I had a little fire to keep myself warm. One of the nights I heard the unexpected sound of sheep and goats walking and their bells ringing in the area. This was curious as there were no longer sheep and goats in the desert at that time. Then a physical appearance of Abraham Avinu materialized. In the Kabbalistic teaching, as a test that it is not a demon, one should ask the apparition to identify itself, to repeat the name of God, and to show its feet. If it is a demon, it will vanish when a name of God is spoken. This figure identified himself as Abraham and did not vanish when the Tetragrammaton, as the name of God, was pronounced; and his feet were human feet. Abraham didn't say anything else but directly filled me with his ignited soul-fire, his full love, compassion, spiritual warrior essence, and the spiritual courage to walk before God as a blessing to humanity as he had done. It was an extraordinarily powerful transformative experience and blessing to become one with his spirit. This was an incredibly profound energetic initiation and explicit spiritual blessing into the land of Israel (Eretz Israel). It remains experientially engraved in my consciousness. This was not so much an enlightenment initiation, although Abraham was an enlightened spiritual warrior and great spiritual leader, as it was an initiation and empowerment to the love-based spiritual warrior, enlightened way of Abraham. It also implanted a deeper seed energy of the great Torah Way. Around this time in 2008, after twelve years of studies, I also received the traditional *S'micha* initiation as a rabbi.

Satsang in Israel.

Teaching: Historically Abraham's tent of hospitality and love was always open in all four directions, receiving people of all levels and being an inspiration to the world. It is a powerful way to live.

In 2013, empowered by Abraham Avinu's blessing, my own direct experience, and the background my Rabbinical Ordainment, I continued with my work of establishing diabetes prevention centers and organic veganic farming in five African countries. One of those

*A regional talk to 900 people on diabetes prevention
in the city of Ho, Ghana, West Africa, including
the key tribal leaders shown in this picture*

*A grammar school where we introduced kids to vegan food and vegan
farming in the capital of Owerri (Biafra) in the Imo State of Nigeria.
These kids are no longer starving.*

areas was a city, the capital of Owerri in the Imo State in the southeast region of Nigeria. In 1967, Biafra succeeded from Nigeria, resulting in brutal war and a deliberate government food shortage. After several years Biafra was starved into submission. I had heard about the "starving people of Biafra" and it seemed this was an obvious place to share my work. Once on location we began to work with their regional King His Royal Highness Dr. Clement Eronini. He had already visited me in my home in Arizona where he, myself, and John Arnold my humanitarian service partner from PPEP (Portable Practical Educational Preparation, a 501c3 educational program) developed our plan for our work in Biafra. What I did not expect on arrival in Biafra was most everywhere I looked there were painted stars of David.

As I was staying in the King's home and sharing meals with him, my curiosity got the best of me and I asked him what this was about. He explained that his tribe, the Igbo Tribe was one of the lost tribes that had migrated to Nigeria, most likely from some of the twelve tribes that was originally sent by King Solomon to Ethiopia. The whole Igbo tribe knew that they were originally Jewish although they had been forced to convert to Christianity by the missionaries, but they were determined to stay true to their origins. I suggested that perhaps as a rabbi and with the King's help, we could reconnect his Igbo tribe to their Jewish origins with a shamanic shabbat. He loved the idea and we gathered his thirteen subtribes in the region for a shabbat. I guided the different leading families from his tribe in a huge outdoor setting through a wonderful shabbat including giving the Haniha / Ruach Ha'Kodesh initiation by touch to all the family members including the children and babies. It was extraordinarily powerful, and the tribal members experienced it as a great blessing to be energetically reconnected to their original tradition. An incredible amount of spiritual energy was activated; almost the whole group had the Ruach Ha'Kodesh activated and even as we said goodbye three days later, the King's father (the former King, who was 111 years old) shared that he was still flying high from the shabbat Ruach Ha'Kodesh initiation and feeling fully connected to his source. It was humbling to be given the grace to be part of this service. As a Levite with thirty-seven Levite genes there was also a mind-blowing recognition that I was sharing part of the same tribal DNA which made our oneness connection even stronger.

It was also unique to be the only white person as well as a genetic relative. Having every single person look at me when taking a walk down the dirt streets was fascinating. This also happened in Ethiopia in a slightly different way where many had the awareness of our Jewish blood connection as they were actively aware of 1,000 people from each tribe sent down to Ethiopia by King Solomon. Nevertheless, in one home where I was staying overnight the hostess began to get faint and dizzy as we were eating dinner with her extended family. As a doctor I asked what was going on and she replied that she had become overwhelmed by the thought that a white person would ever be eating and sleeping in her house. We all had a good laugh and she immediately recovered. Even though I was aware of our literal genetic connection, it was still a little challenging for everyone to grasp the oneness. The truth was that I would not have been sitting at the table if we had not started with a heart connection that brought me to her family's home.

With my Native American brothers and sisters, the same genetic connection also exists, particularly with the *Cherokee* and *Choctaw* tribes who have well-documented Jewish genes. One Native American

Cherokee grandmother I spoke to about this remembers her grandparents actually speaking Hebrew. The Hopi Elders I spoke to were also aware of this as well as the Lakota Elders. In these particular situations the oneness is clearly there, but as I feel this unity with all people, I also feel this oneness with all people as we are far more connected as human beings than our minds and hearts which are so comfortable feeling division. This is also true with my Arab friends as the overt genetic connection is also there as a foundation for the heart and mind connection. For myself, because I travel in so many different worlds, the only thing I have learned to trust in terms of my survival is my sense of a heart connection but having the genetic connection does also help. Although I may be seen as naïve because of my direct experience of this Truth, it is my heartfelt and soul-felt belief that in time the whole world will wake up to the heart-mind experience of our oneness as children of God.

Chapter 26

ASTROLOGICAL LIFE CYCLES HELP CLARIFY ONE'S DHARMA

Teaching: Astrology is an additional aid to reflect and confirm our intuition of Divine Will unfolding in our lives.

People frequently ask me, "How do I find my dharma and know the Divine Will for myself?" It helps to be aware that we all have cycles in our lives. My primary tools to finding these answers are prayer, meditation, intuition, and a willingness to listen to the still small voice of God as part of my living faith in the ultimate truth of God. It is also important to be able to ask the advice of one's spiritual teacher or of those close to you like one's spouse while observing the external messages and symbols in one's life is another way. I wrote this chapter to answer the many people who ask me about the use of astrology as an additional aid to reflect on and confirm one's intuition of Divine Will unfolding in our lives. There is no one way to do this, but a sincere focus and intent to be aligned with God's Will plays a key role.

Mahadasha is a Vedic astrological term referring to significant astrological cycles in a person's life. A mahadasha cycle or time of life occurs when a person is affected most heavily by certain cosmic energies of a particular planet. My nineteen-year Saturn mahadasha cycle began on August 8th, 1999 and ended on August 8th, 2018. At that point, I began a new seventeen-year cycle called the Mercury mahadasha cycle. The Saturn cycle was a challenging and difficult time, and it also was a time of creating a strong foundation for my next cycle of expanding worldwide communication especially in the areas of spiritual life, liberation, spiritual nutrition, and holistic health. My seventeen-year Mercury mahadasha cycle, has given me more spiritual energy and incentive, and a greatly increased ability to communicate and share my spiritual energy teachings with the world. My key approach was and is to be aware of the cyclic forces unfolding and align myself with these flows as part of the Divine Will unfolding. This is a key dharma teaching.

My Saturn cycle was an incredible time of spiritual wisdom expansion, intense karma burning, trial by fire, and foundation building that has been profoundly, spiritually strengthening and elevating, for which I am humbly grateful. The internalized message is "*dristi shirsti*": the world is how you see it and how you believe it to be. Part of the service and structural organization developed during my nineteen-year Saturn cycle was the creation of our non-profit 501c3 religious corporation called the Tree of Life Foundation (TOLF). In the Foundation there are more than 100 international

*Feeding the people at the orphanage called El Reino de Los Ninos
(The Kid's Kingdom) in Imuris, Sonora, Mexico*

*El Reino de Los Ninos (The Kid's Kingdom) offered a celebratory dance
for the Tree of Life Foundation.*

*Opening a diabetes center in Benjamin Hill
located in the Mexican state of Sonora.*

humanitarian diabetes prevention programs; successful organic, veganic enterprises in some countries; orphanages in some nations; seeing clients and workshop attendees who have come from over 128 countries; the writing of thirteen books; the diabetes recovery movie, *Simply Raw*; and our new fifty-two-episode diabetes prevention video program, as well as an Essene Priesthood program. In this Saturn cycle over three hundred informative and spiritual teaching YouTube videos and podcasts have also been created.

Through the Tree of Life Foundation outreach, I have also created a vehicle for sharing a basic non-sectarian spiritual way of life for people of all paths to be able to follow called the Six Foundations and Sevenfold Peace. Also, under the Tree of Life Foundation is Congregation Etz Chaim in Patagonia, which holds all the Jewish holidays and Shabbat ceremonies for those in the immediate area

Lightning symbolizing the Shaktipat/Kundalini awakening
before meditation starts at the Tree of Life in Patagonia, AZ

from Nogales to Phoenix. The Tree of Life Foundation has sponsored an educational and spiritual base in Israel and spiritual fasting retreats in different locations such as by the Dead Sea when possible, as well as internet spiritual fasting programs, which we started in 2020. I also offer the Zero Point course; a western Jnana Yoga three day intensive in person as well as through the internet; and the complete Diabetes Recovery Program in Israel which has now become the only place in the world where this is being offered in person. It is also offered on an individual basis at the Tree of Life in Patagonia, AZ. The Tree of Life Foundation is also the platform for sharing my articulated concepts and teachings of the Holistic Liberation Way and the ever-expanding Sacred Relationship teachings. More recently a more protected and uncensored expression has emerged as a new online platformed community called Tree of Life Community and can be found at this link: *treeoflife.mn.co.*

In this nineteen-year, Saturn mahadasha cycle the Tree of Life Foundation (TOLF) educational, humanitarian, and spiritual services have extended into over forty-two different countries in which I have taught and sponsored workshops. Locations have included: Sao Paulo, Rio de Janerio, Goiania, and Brasilia in Brazil, Buenos Aires and Cordova in Argentina, Central America, Israel, Canada, Mexico, almost all the countries in Europe, as well as Australia, New Zealand, Papua New Guinea, Bali, Hong Kong, Taiwan, and China. Our Tree of Life Foundation website and Tree of Life Community website is now shared in four languages: English, some Hebrew, Spanish, and Portuguese. In Africa, the Tree of Life Foundation, in partnership with PPEP (Portable Practical Educational Preparation) and representatives from five other African nations, has started WARES (West African Resource Empowerment Society) to guide our activities in these areas. In Mexico, we have started the Aliza de Corazon with three other humanitarian organizations. As already stated, my major life emphasis from 2018 to 2020 is toward a significant focus on expanding our humanitarian diabetes prevention work, as well as expanding the worldwide spiritual and liberation teachings, spiritual nutrition education, and holistic veganism teachings.

As part of a bold move to enhance the expression of my Mercury mahadasha cycle, I have decreased many of our Tree of Life Foundation public programs at the center in Arizona. People are still coming from all over the world for holistic Whole Person Health Evaluations and individual spiritual retreats, as well as for individual spiritual fasting retreats, and even a personalized healing type-2 diabetes programs. We have also started a new two-day online meditation retreat with Shaktipat meditation three times daily called the Holistic Liberation Meditation Retreat Intensive. There is also an online three day Zero Point course offered several times per year following the meditation intensive as well as online spiritual fasting retreats. Essene Priesthood training certification is still available on an individual basis, but in a new energetic way and format.

Teaching: A teaching in both the Vedic and Kabbalistic traditions, and a cosmic teaching for all of us looking at our lives, is that one's overall destiny patterns are generally set, but the story, perception, and how we relate to and use these patterns is up to us as to what octave of spiritual awareness we choose to play on.

Since the Divine directed me at the end of my forty-day fast in 1983 to return to my roots, I have written and shared the *Torah As a Guide to Enlightenment* liberation teachings and weekly Torah commentaries (*parshas*) from the perspective of liberation.

Teaching: All religions are holy lies and the only true religion is the return to God as I Am That, or "ein zulato" (there is only God) both within and without and "ein od mi-l'vado" (there is nothing else besides God).

Torah as a Guide to Enlightenment was partly written to help refocus attention on the ultimate upper *sod*, or highest, Torah teaching of liberation *deveikut/chey'rut* (God-merging and enlightenment) while still honoring the Torah, Ten Speakings, Talmud and 620 mitzvot (good deeds) as a foundation, as well as love and joy of God.

Teaching: The presence of the Divine is revealed in the art, eros, and subtlety of experiencing God in the details. Without this living spiritual understanding, it has a tendency to degenerate into rote ritual or stays at a theoretical level. Living a spiritual life fully helps people become transformed by the experiential power of going into a higher spiritual octave.

After my 1983 directive to go to my roots, beyond the *bar mitzvah* training, God sent the support of several well-educated rabbis who in their own ways gave their deep gifts to me. One was Rabbi Gershon Winkler, who helped me with the translation of the liberation and Kundalini understanding into the Torah Way of Life. He also shared his profound shamanic, Talmudic, Kabbalistic teachings, and eventually ordained me as a rabbi. Rabbi Winkler is also familiar with the Native American Way. At a gathering at Gershon's previous home in New Mexico, he introduced me to the late Kam Night Chase, who became my Sundance Chief. Kam was Chief of the High Horse Family Sundance Clan of the Lakota Sioux in Wamblee, South Dakota. Kam was also from the Native Medicine Lineage of the Horn Chip family which descends from the chief medicine man for Sitting Bull. Another orthodox rabbi gave me some deep occult Kabbalistic and orthodox training.

The third rabbinical influence was the world-famous singing Rabbi Shlomo Carlebach, who also was a great Torah scholar, sharing the deep yet practical heart-opening aspects of the Torah through his everyday actions, teachings, and holy song. We met in 1979 in India and immediately hit it off. As I became his holistic doctor, we spent many hours by ourselves when he would just come to visit for the day for his "medical appointment" in Petaluma, California. Rav Shlomo was a wonderful, unique, and loving character, and his Abrahamic, open-hearted love for everyone was impressively inspirational. In 2017, Shanti and I began living, part time, in the late Shlomo Carlebach's Moshav at Mevo Modi'im, a Rav Shlomo style celebratory orthodox community in Israel. His most inspirational and greatest teaching was his power of song and the tremendous amount of Abrahamic love that Rav Shlomo shared. To offer these profound Torah gifts he didn't need to be a great, enlightened being. However, I was concerned that he only partially followed the holistic medical and nutritional advice I gave him. The supplements and diet I prescribed to him may have prevented or postponed his eventual heart attack, from which he died in 1994. Dying didn't concern him, and his health, too, was of minor concern. Shlomo's way was Torah and love, and that was the secret of his spiritual greatness. One of his most important inspirational teachings was: "Until the heart of Heaven" which alludes to the Torah being given on Mt. Sinai, "which was burning on fire and in the heart of heaven." This level of spiritual connection inspired me to let go enough to become a soul on fire, burning with spiritual passion as a way of living life.

Shlomo's primordial and most powerful teaching was the power of love to transform and uplift in all earth plane situations. It had a great positive influence on me. He was pure *chesed* (loving kindness) and being in his presence was the greatest practical experiential teaching of this transformative power of love. He was an extraordinary unique expression of the heart-based, universal, and cosmic-based love.

In Judaism, a person who observes Shabbat and the associated laws, is known as a *shomer shabbat*. In Yiddish a pious religious person is referred to as *frum*. Becoming shomer shabbat and frum in the late 1990s, which translates as upholding the great Torah Way of Life, especially on the Shabbat, completed the following of my explicit spiritual direction from the transmission of the "still small voice" of God at the end of the forty-day fast in 1983. It also is aligned with the advice of Swami Prakashananda, who had explained very clearly, that "wherever you go you need to hold the dharma." Of course, these were not the only reason, as becoming frum and shomer shabbat has been a powerful way for me to understand the meaning of the Torah teachings on a deeper level. It has also allowed me to experience the positive effect of actually living by those teachings with an attitude of sacred consciousness for each action. Living frum in our home setting, however, is the easy part. Sometimes it requires a little more effort to live this frum lifestyle. For example, at the Tree of Life Foundation, we had built a little temple and a kosher outdoor rain-filled and well-filled *mikvah* (ritual water purification pool space) in the shape of a womb because the waters of the mikvah are to be like the cleansing waters of the womb. In taking a mikvah, we become symbolically cleansed and reborn, which is part of the pre-Shabbat ritual that Shanti and I perform each week.

Outside of the Tree of Life setting, in our travels, it is often a challenge on Shabbat to find a mikvah and to keep frum. On Shabbat, if one is frum, one does not drive; instead we walk. Once during a Native American clan gathering in New Mexico for Sundance preparation, as we were walking on Shabbat to the meeting place, there was such a huge snowstorm that Shanti and I couldn't see more than two feet in front of us. Shanti courageously agreed to set out on this walk with me in this storm. However, we got lost walking in the raging snowstorm. In getting temporarily lost we went about three miles out of our way until we found the main road to the meeting place. As we were about to arrive, a search party of our Sundance friends also found us. Although holding the dharma to our shomer shabbat lifestyle may have been a little dangerous, it is often an adventure with positive consequences. It became a special bonding experience for us as a couple, because it created a situation in which we were "snowed in" with each other. The love of HaShem (God) was enhanced by the sacrifice of our keeping shomer shabbat under these challenging circumstances. Although this may seem small, it's a teaching of part of the bigger picture of holding the highest octave of God-merging *(deveikut)* and enlightenment *(chey'rut)*. In other words, within the details of this way of life, if one is open to experiencing God-merging, it is hidden in the experience of *Ayn Zulato* (there is only God) in every moment.

Teaching: Knowing that there is only God is one of the great mystical secrets of how to live a joyful, sacred energetic life in every moment that also simultaneously uplifts the web of life of the living planet. The secret is to start every action with the intent to create sacredness, sanctification, love, and God-merging.

Jokingly, this may be called sacred fastidiousness. However, being fastidious has major positive implications for longevity, as well as elevating consciousness. In one major eighty-year study on longevity, being fastidious was ranked as one of the top five qualities associated with longevity. Fastidious means paying attention to the details of one's life such as health, diet, environmental habits and concerns, as well as the details of our spiritual flow.

Teaching: The challenge is for us to recognize that God is in the details, while paradoxically not getting trapped in the obsessive materialism of the details. This is a relevant spiritual paradox that I, and actually all of us, are challenged to master.

Chapter 27

FOUR-YEAR SUNDANCE CYCLE

*A*n important part of my spiritual evolution is my deep heart-felt connection with the general consciousness of the Native American Way, especially the Lakota. The Native American Way completes the third aspect of my in-depth experiential training and dharma in these three great traditions. When I was 8 years old a significant vision was given to me, and then again at the last EST (Erhard Seminars Training) program given in person by Weiner Erhard in the early 1970s as previously mentioned there was a vision of Abraham, Sai Baba of Shirdi/Essene energy, and the third was the Native American Sioux warrior, who identified himself as Crazy Horse. This prophetic vision highlighted the three streams that created the flow and teachings of the lineage rivers of my life. The three streams are 1) Yoga, Vedas, Kashmir Shaivism, and Ayurveda;

2) the Great Torah Way/ upper-sod (mystical liberation Kabbalah teachings) 3) Native American Way, in general, and specifically the Lakota-Sioux Sundance and Spirit Dance (Ghost Dance) traditions.

My initial connection to the Native American Way was with the Pomo Tribes in 1973, when heading the Head Start mental health program, as a community psychiatrist. We covered a 300-square-mile region and the Pomo Tribes in northern Sonoma county were part of our area. The Pomos shared their ceremonies with me at the Strawberry Festival in Northern California and their form of sweat lodge. Later in the mid to late nineties, my latent Native American energetics, were brought to fruition by tutelage under Kam Lau Night Chase. Kam and I made a fascinating connection. He did not speak much, and so I talked a lot to receive as much information as possible from him. It was so classical that it was humorous.

At that time, I was not clear what my interest in the Native American Way was but had a certain faith that it needed to be explored. Later, a dear friend, Kevin Ryerson, made contact with me to communicate that according to his pictorial and psychic-biographical research, I not only had the physical appearance of Dr. Charles Eastman (the very first Native American Western-trained doctor), but that I was probably a reincarnation of him. Doctor Eastman was Lakota and according to the historical accounts, met Crazy Horse as a pre-teen warrior at the time of Crazy Horse's victory over General Custer. Dr. Eastman also had lived in the town of Amherst, Massachusetts, the location of Amherst College where I went to college. He was also the doctor on the reservation at the time of the massacre at Wounded Knee.

Sundance, which I actively participated in under Kam's guidance, is an important religious ceremony to many Native Americans. It lasts for eight days, and signifies the dance between life and death. Sharing a little context may help the reader appreciate this general, yet specific Lakota ceremony, which includes four days of preparation consisting in part with inipis (sweat lodges) at least once per day and often twice and four days of the actual dance with more inipis. In the actual dance, the dancers wear their ceremonial Sundance skirts (no tops for men) and a variety of objects that have meaning to them, including sacred bands for the legs and wrists. I was involved in Sundance over a four-year cycle which is the traditional number needed to complete the four year cycle of each cardinal direction – North, South, East, and West. Each direction had its own unique teaching and subtle energetic effect; all of them made a positive impact on me. According to tradition, one is not called a Sundancer until they have completed the four years of Sundance.

The first Sundance I participated in began under the hot Nevada desert sun with temperatures ranging from 100 to 110 degrees. Fifty-two of us danced from sunrise to sunset with a few inipis per day and other breaks. The tradition is to go without food and water for four days. However, by the end of two days in the hot Nevada sun, I was the only one out of the original fifty-two Sundancers still fasting. I was able to fast for the full four-day ceremony, and thus uphold the energy of the Sundance. Kam was very pleased that I was upholding the energy of the whole Sundance group. Actually, Kam did not have to worry because when I enter any ceremony, I would rather die than not complete it fully. Although this may seem extreme to some, the Baal Shem Tov, a Jewish mystical rabbi and shamanic healer taught that one should do all ceremonies and prayers as if one is about to die. This approach certainly amplifies the intensity which is obviously my style. In the Lakota way, all the dancers are essentially one, so if even only one person goes without food and water for the four days it is as if all have gone without food and water. This honoring of the tradition in this way went on for all four years. The rest of the ceremony included the four-day preparation time and dancing in patterns and ways according to the tradition and Kam's direction. For the rest of the year the Sundancers gathered a few times and did some inipis together as well as committed to the "Great Red Way" which is a virtuous and honorable Native American Way of life according to our Lakota tradition.

Teaching: A life of upholding ceremonial dharma in extreme conditions is both a joy and spiritually worth it, and, as the Lakota say, "We do these things so the people may live."

In the first Sundance I became so dehydrated that my urine on the fourth day turned black, suggesting severe dehydration, and the possibility of some level of kidney dysfunction. Being so close to the end of the dance there was no way that I would take some water and of course did not mention this to anyone. I did do some lab test to check out my kidneys about a month after the ceremony, and they were fine and still are fine at the present time. The Sundance ceremonies also require cutting four small holes, two each on both sides of one's chest where pegs about the size of one's baby finger are put through. As part of the ceremony, ropes are connected to the Sundance tree and are attached to the pegs in one's chest. This part of the ceremony is usually done on either the third or fourth day of the dance. Once attached, during one of the last dance rounds, one sharply pulls back to break the flesh of the chest with the pegs, freeing them from the tree. Not knowing any better, I had chosen the fourth day to do this part of the ceremony in the first dance. Since I was exhausted and dehydrated by the fourth day from the hot Nevada sun, some Sundance brothers kindly pulled me back to help break out the pegs in my chest. The holes in my chest looked to be the size of forty-five caliber bullet holes, and they certainly bled a lot. However, that's part of the Native American Way of bravery and courage and in this context, it was no big deal. It was an interesting scene with blood streaming down from both sides of my chest. I looked shrunken and dehydrated but was grateful to have held the energy for our Sundance Clan by having no food or water for the full four days of the ceremony. For the Sundance women in the group, the pegs were put on the outer shoulders rather on the chest/breast area. For some it may be hard to understand, but to dharmically complete this spiritual warrior challenge was a subtle joy for me. I love facing challenges like this. The Great Native American Way, which I fully enjoy, has a strong emphasis on courage, determination, honor, and spiritual strength as a spiritual warrior, which is actually a powerful teaching for all spiritual aspirants, as well as for what is needed for liberation and to rebuild our society. It is important to not think of these as simply rituals, but rather as a direct experiential way to build character qualities especially of courage, determination, honor, and internal strength.

During all four Sundances there was another sub-issue, which was holding the energy of the plant-based, live-food movement, as this appeared to be the other Sundancers' first experience with a solely live-food plant-based diet Sundancer. They spared no amount of time questioning and jesting about why the traditional pre-dance buffalo stew soup was not accepted by me and defending their carnivorous way of life. Their openness to a plant-based diet changed over the four years because all Sundancers respect courage. It was no accident that the pre- and post-feasts had more pure plant-based selections as the years went on.

Teaching: Teaching by example is a powerful
way to share a spiritual message.

In the first hours after ending the first dance, my body tissues became hydrated too quickly and my body went into full-body cramping and spasm. People thought it was some type of medical emergency but since I am a doctor, it was clear to me what was happening. People were told to "cool it" and let the process complete itself, which it did in about thirty minutes. After the dance there was a traditional big feast, but just about the only thing I could eat was watermelon, which of course was hydrating. Mastering the details of the Sundance requires some functional wisdom which developed as the four-year cycle continued. In the second and third dances, I "broke" without help of my Sundance brothers in the third round, and then for the fourth dance I did an Eagle Dance. For me as a spiritual warrior, Sundances were a lot of fun, although they appear hard. All four dances were powerful, unique internal experiences.

Teaching: Spiritual courage (ometz) is a necessary virtue
to develop for evolution on the path of liberation.

I was fifty-nine when I entered the fourth year of Sundance and, on the spur of the moment, I choose to do the Eagle Dance, where I was connected by my chest to the Sundance tree with ropes and pegs nonstop for the full four days, including standing from sunrise to sunset each day. The Eagle Dance was done six months after my brain surgery for the repair of the AVM (arteriovenous malformation). Of course, no one knew about the brain surgery or I may not have been allowed to dance. By the end of the four years, the tribal brothers actually moved away from making fun of me for being a live-food vegan to being respectful. But to be honest, what they thought did not matter, as the dance was a way for me to reconnect back into the Native American Way of multiple past lives that I had lived. As an Eagle Dancer after sunset, I was still connected to the tree by the ropes and pegs in my chest, but I was able to lie down and go to sleep. During the Eagle Dance, there was one Sundance brother, a person who had shared the previous three Sundances with me, who was one of Kam's five Sundance clan chiefs and an assistant at the dance who jokingly said to me, as a clan brother: "You know you're in your element, aren't you?" And it was true... as an Eagle Dancer I was clearly in my element. The ceremony and the spiritual energy generated was awesome.

Multiple past-life experiences were being played out during this Eagle Dance, which made the ceremony a holy joy. For most, the Eagle Dance was an ordeal, and actually I was the oldest and the only one out of eighteen Eagle Dancers who started to complete the Eagle Dance without breaking the connection to the Tree or leaving the Sundance circle for the full four days; and also to remain standing from sunrise to sunset each day. Something very primordially deep inside me ecstatically loved it; I felt it was a special returning home. For those who are wondering about bathroom breaks which everyone left the circle to take, I pre-solved the bathroom issue by doing an enema right before beginning the dance, and so without any further water or food, there was no need to leave the circle to have a bowel movement. For urination I used a bottle done modestly under my Sundance skirt. Jokingly, I call this a sophisticated level of spiritual fastidiousness.

Teaching: Forethought and fastidious attention to the details do make a difference in spiritual life.

One interesting quality of the Lakota Native American Way, is the respect for uniqueness and individuality within the larger unified ceremony. In a heartfelt faith guided way there was no question that this four-year cycle had to be done. It was another completion for me of a spiritual coming home to a vital spiritual warrior aspect of my life and my deep Native American connection over many lifetimes.

Teaching: It may not be true for everyone, but part of the spiritual path often involves reconnecting and completing some aspects with past-life spiritual paths and dharmas. Spirituality can be a way that recreates and continues to build the spiritual web we have spun for ourselves over lifetimes and in this way empowers our path in this lifetime.

On day 3 of the Eagle Dance and Sundance, as a sub-part of the overall Sundance event, everyone, at high noon in the blazing sun, chose to leave the field and seek shade and do an inipi. My soul was on fire, and I remained the only one holding space on the field for all the close to seventy Sun and Eagle Dancers. Kam upped the energy by asking one of the Native American drummers and chief singers from the reservation to start drumming and singing, and Kam motioned for me to start actively dancing. As the drummer got going, the drumbeat seemed to be dancing through my heart, whole body, and soul in a wild dance sustained by the drum's rhythm. As a soul on fire, I became the rhythmic dancing drumbeat that went on until the drummer got tired. Not only was I in full experience of dancing ecstatic Eros including many lifetimes of shamanic dancing simultaneously, but the whole cosmos seemed to download its cosmic fire power into me expanding my consciousness into the multi-dimensions beyond this world. I have no idea of where the "I-amness" travelled, but it was gone and only the overwhelming cosmic fire of God was left dancing into the nothing beyond my comprehension. It was an incredible fifteen to twenty minutes in which there was a physically empowering and longevity energization shift that occurred within me that is still happening; as if there was some sort of incredibly empowering epigenetic upgrade. The feedback I received from the group was that the power of this small wild sacrifice shifted and upgraded the total Sundance and Eagle Dance energy for everyone.

As the Eagle Dance continued into the fourth day, instead of getting weaker I got progressively stronger and stronger. It did not make logical sense, as normally one usually becomes weaker. It was as if my whole organism had gone into an energetic rejuvenation in those wild minutes dancing to the drummer on day three. As I mentioned before, at the end of the first dance, I was so exhausted and dehydrated that on day four, Sundance brothers had to pull me backward to break the ties from my chest to the tree. By contrast, at the end of the fourth day of Eagle Dance, so much energy was flowing that when my body jerked back on its own to break the ties to the Sundance tree, a perfect backward somersault occurred, and I landed on my feet! Some observers say I did a backflip, but this is doubtful. But since that time, with more times around the sun, my body-mind vitality is getting stronger and stronger. One year later, at sixty times around the sun, age 60, my body did 601 consecutive push-ups on the sixth day of a green juice fast. At age 77, I can perform 80 pull-ups and 1,000 pushups. By contrast, at twenty sun cycles of life, as captain of an undefeated Amherst College football team, I could only do 70 pushups and 7 pull-ups. It is puzzling and wild, but since that special third day of the Eagle Dance, my vitality is getting stronger each year. This increase in inner power and outer strength is a little mysterious, but, at this time in my life, all these paradoxes associated with a life of liberation are beginning to seem normal. Anyway, this inner and outer empowerment is not exactly something to complain about.

Another striking paradox was that, even though my body is light and fair-skinned I literally did not sunburn while most everyone else did. This is in comparison to Native Americans and some African American Sundancers who did get sunburnt, some seriously. I theorize that it was a live-food benefit in which my body had already learned to eat the sunlight directly.

Teaching: When one is on a ninety-nine percent live-food, plant-based cuisine for an extended period, one is no longer in resistance to sunlight. If one has been eating uncooked plants, one becomes, in a certain way, like a plant in the ability to absorb the sunlight and use it as direct nutrition. I jokingly call it... eating the sun.

After the end of the fourth year and Eagle Dance, Kam Lau Night Chase officially and unexpectedly adopted me as his *Hunka* Brother. The Hunka is the making of a relationship that is a bond that never breaks. With this ceremony, I was (without asking for it) given the name of Yellow Horse (Ta Sunka Hinzi) and made the Yellow Horse Clan Chief. The horse symbolism is curious, especially since I was given the name of Rohita (Red Horse) by Swami Muktananda, again without me even asking for a name. So, the horse totem has some symbolic meaning for me to look at and "ride on"; and even "horse around" with. In the Native American tradition, the horse is a symbol of power and freedom without restraint. The horse totem invites in qualities of vitality and power, physically, emotionally, and spiritually. Horse also symbolizes transcendental freedom. As a medicine animal in the Native American teachings, the horse is known to bring adventure, power, friends, and good family. While a horse gallops in the herd, he does not lose his individuality. The horse totem is also associated with service to self and others and is symbolically seen as a messenger to and from the angelic realms. In a subtle way, the Torah, in Genesis 1:22, suggests that all the totem animal energies are within us. The horse totem as power, vitality, and as transcendental freedom flying to the heavens, is a very empowering totem energy to be inspired by.

The shamanic shifts that came from the four Sundances created a not so subtle, non-drug shamanic awareness. In Kam's ceremonies, no drugs were even allowed thirty days before the Sundance. This was no problem for me as I had not taken any psychedelics for over forty years and even then, it was a limited one-time experimentation. This Native American shamanic awareness also opened my eyes to the shamanic levels of the understanding of the Great Torah Way and lifestyle. In the Native American Way, the animal totems for each of the four gates of the Sundance circle (North, West, South, and East) may vary according to the ceremony, so dancing from the four different directions during each of the four dances created a subtle energetic experiential difference. In honoring the traditional Lakota four directions and starting in the South, the totem energy is of the wolf, coyote, and thunder beings. It gives the empowerment of sacrifice for the preservation of the wolf pack, i.e. humanity. In my life this was expressed as humanitarian efforts to heal the world and in sanctifying the Tree of Life Foundation by choosing to give up the comfortable private holistic medical practice in Petaluma, California where the income was literally four times higher with minimal outer challenges as compared to Arizona.

Teaching: To the Lakota, the totem energy of the South has to do with thunder beings, coyote trickster medicine, the wolf, leadership, and the preservation of the pack.

The wolf energy gave me the enhanced power of leadership and teaching, as well as the ability to be a good follower and pack member working collectively for the good of the pack (world). These were all qualities I needed for various leadership roles in the multiple organizations that I both led and worked in collectively around the planet. The coyote or trickster energy has improved my sense of humor and the subtlety of my work in the world. Shanti regularly reminds me however, about being too serious. In connecting with the animal totems in each direction, it was helpful to remember that the vibration of all the animal totems is already within. Dancing in each of these directions for each year of the Sundance with this awareness awakened the latent energies and teaching gifts of these totems. These totems or archetypal energies are not who we are, as we exist prior to time, space, energy and " I-ness", but they can be used as a powerful horse to ride on, as needed, in the world to empower our dharmas and service in the world.

Teaching: All totem animals already reside within us. If we choose to discover and choose to use them as vibrational energies, they are there to empower us.

In the East is the energy of the eagle, as well as the rising sun of new beginnings. The sunrise is symbolized as a rising soul energy. By dancing from the East, I took in the power of the eagle, who witnesses all and sees the non-dual oneness of all things and the understanding that there is no birth or death for the soul. The totem energy of the eagle in this way has enhanced my understanding of the power of the non-dual awareness and single vision intensity, so essential for living a peaceful, spiritualized internal life. Being in the non-dual witness mode means to be experiencing the oneness of the dancers and the whole world, yet paradoxically observing myself dancing in this oneness. I became aware of how the power of the rising sun in the East, experiencing it as the rising light of the Divine in my life, empowered my soul and strengthened my soul connection to the Divine.

Teaching: To the Lakota, the energy of the East is related to the eagle, to the intensity of single vision, and the light of the rising sun.

In the North, the mystical power of the white buffalo was empowering me to humbly walk the Great Red Way with full spiritual awareness, spiritual power, and presence. The energy of the white buffalo was further inspiring me to walk with the balance of all "four legs" on the earth with consciousness simultaneously walking in the heavens. It gave me the gift of a shamanic consciousness that empowered the walk between the B'limah (Nothing) and the Mah (Something) as the essence of the everyday walk in the world. In addition, this experience of the North inspired me to become a close supporter of the White Bison Association, which has a no-kill breeding program.

In the West I discovered the mystery of the setting sun whose gift is the enhanced awareness of myself as a walker between the worlds. It also revealed the consciousness of the bear totem who walks between the physical and dream worlds and the world of the ancestors. The West activated an awareness to see and experience myself as a multidimensional being, simultaneously part of all the worlds yet belonging to none. With the ending of my four-year Sundance cycle, our Sundance group and others began what Kam called the Spirit Dance, which had evolved from the original Ghost Dance. After a few years of this with the total group, we started our own Spirit Dance at Tree of Life Foundation in Patagonia which lasted for eleven years.

Teaching: To the Lakota, the energy of the North
is connected to the white buffalo and living with
spiritual awareness. The energy of the setting
sun is found in the West, and the bear totem,
the one who can walk between the worlds.

The four-year Sundance experiences were poetry in themselves:

—∿—

The Eagle Soars
(Sundance, 1998)

Dancing from the East
Looking beyond the Tree of Life
This soul-fire becomes
Tree of Life Consciousness
Irrevocably.

Shanti and I in the Inipi Pipe Ceremony at the sweat lodge
at the Tree of Life in Patagonia, Arizona.

—ɷ—

Soaring Eagle Spirit of the East

Cosmic overview
Empowered by spiritual courage
The eagle flies close to Yah.
Standing in joyous silence
Four days of Divine awe
Transcending all pain and conditions
Exploding silently into unbroken
Cosmic Tree of Life Consciousness
Complete surrender
The deep peace of surrender
Total surrender
Holding onto nothing
Without separation
Devoid of past, present, future
Beyond time and space
Laughing surrender to life
Without a blink
Opening to all of creation
Subtly beyond duality
Pure, ecstatic grace and blessing
The mystery of surrender
Incredibly freeing.

Completeness
Fullness
Blessing endless big smile in every cell
Soaking in a spiritual bath
Of this Eagle-Sundance
Cleansed of impurities
A deep knowing
Grounded in a sweet non-causal peace
The Eagle Soars

And i Smile

The mystic dances in the sun of the East
Seeing what others do not see
Experiencing beyond belief.
The talons of Yah
Rip into my chest
And i smile.

Smiling from a place so deep
Beyond comprehension
The Deer of the East
Carries my soul beyond Understanding
Beyond the rising sun
Into the cosmic light
Of Illumination
And i smile.

It appears the mystic
Is attached to a Tree of Life
In the center of the Dance Circle
Standing for four days.
That external reality
Marginally connects to the Truth
Transported inward
To the Deep Light
And i smile.

The Sundance tree disappears
Dissolving into the cosmic Tree of Life
Beyond duality, chaos, materialism, and mortality
The subtle I-ness emerges
The Tree is a brilliant flaming light in the Garden of Eden
And i smile.

The Tree engulfs me in its light
Into a formless chamber
A curtain between the worlds dissolves
Complete Unity
Seven within Seven
Merging with the Oversoul
And i smile.

The subtle i is still aware
It is smiling
Radiating light from the face
Dancing in every cell
Every twist of DNA smiling with Light
And i smile.

This light is beyond the grasp of awareness
Felt in the mind
Beyond the grasp of the mind
And i smile.

An unrevealed rising sunlight of the East
Shining in the mind
All levels filled with Light
A dancing wholeness
A subtle Tree of Life reemerges
And i smile.

Let there be light
And there was light...
This light is prior to existence
It can be experienced but not grasped
And i smile.

All is lit in perfection
The seven chambers above and below
Are one blazing light
Above, below, and within
Immortality
And i smile.

In Kodesh HaKodashim
The mystic dances
Naked in the Holy of Holies.
All five levels
Of soul awareness
Revealed Illuminated
Exploding with the unrevealed light
Whatever you Love you Are
And i smile.

The official dance ends after four days
Yah's claws attaching my body to the Tree
Are ripped out of my chest
Yet the cosmic Tree remains
Its cosmic seed grows in my heart
Dancing ecstatically from the East
In the I-ness of this body.
And i smile.

The concealed door to the Seventh chamber
Kodesh HaKodashim
Remains open
Every morning
And often at night
And sometimes
At the most interesting moments
It just pulls me in
And i smile.

—m—

This Bear Dances in the West
(Sundance from the West, July 1999)

This bear dances from the West
Merging and emerging out of the void
Fearlessly facing life and death.
The past explodes into the Nothing.
Clumsily yet gracefully
Bondages of the past dissolves.
Past illusion of I Am-ness
Disintegrates in the truth of the void.
Past and present relationships lose their grip on me.
All projections for the future become a hollow note
In the immensity of the void.
Remaining dreams, concepts, hopes burn in the watery lava of the West.
No need to understand stories of the past or future.
The past like the wake of a motorboat,
Loses its form in the ocean of the void.
All stories end.
Past life programs have no hold
And all history dissolve in the liberating waters of the West.
Continual birth and death in the void
Time ceases to exist for me
The illusion of I Am-ness
Dissipates
Without hope or expectation.
This bear dances in the West

And all illusion of dharma or dharma partners ends.
This bear dances in the West
Alone… connected to all;
Silent… talking from the heart;
Singing from the eyes;
Alert, innocent, harmless, sweet, at peace
Glowing with a light of Self and Truth.
Every cell radiating love
Inner being filled with flowers,
Blooming the energy of Spring.
Free to move in any direction
Inward-Outward
The non-causal joy cannot be touched
By externals or by time.
Piercing for the world.
Sacrificing and committing to the healing transformation of the world
Liberation is deepened.
Letting go of the belief that life is hard and a struggle,
Free to flow with ideas of easy or hard in life.

—m—

Liberating Power of All Four Directions

Soaring with courage and ease of the Eagle of the East;
Red blood oozes from the chest
Walking the earth with the four legs of the White Buffalo of the North;
The hibernating Bear of the West
Guided by the Wolf spirit of leadership, sacrifice, and teaching
Of the South
A new beginning of power and sweetness
of the rising Sun, Deer, and Eagle of the East.
The inner being filled with a white rose of innocence,
purity, and sweetness of the South.
The Bear pierces from the West,
And give itself to the timeless void,
Without past present or future.
Dancing in the freedom
Of dying into the Nothing of the West
Heart ripped open, dripping blood of compassion for the world
Caring not for death or life
There is only dying into the Nothing
Reborn again and again out of the void.
Free of the bondage of past, future, or even present;
Time loses its hold on me.
Birthed into the unknown
All remains unknown
Open to unlimited movement,
Dancing free.

—✿—

Flames

Flames surround the Spirit Dance grounds
Sitting up in my tent
The crackling of the fire is heard
Surprise -
There is no fire outside
Except a single remaining Shabbat candle
Flickering in the moonlight.
Returning to the tent
The mind illuminated by
The supernal light of Tree of Life consciousness
Exploding in the brain
Awake all night
Experiencing the Awesome white light
Of the Infinite Tree
Burning in all hearts.

—·m·—

The Last Dance:
Sundance Turned Eagle Dance

Umbilically tied to the Tree nonstop for four days
A standing vision quest,
A play of wind, cold, and burning sun
Beyond opposites
I smile in the radiance of the One
Total Grace
Total Blessing
Fullness and joy beyond causality
Living in the Tree of Life non-dual awareness
Being the big smile
The Divine radiance smiling beyond the Tree
Transcending the hot and cold duality of life
Crazy Horse appears on the first day
Laughing at me.
A real warrior needs not a Sundance.
They are living the Dance in every moment.

Day two brings Divine Lakshmi
Making love to me on the spiritual plane
And again, on days three and four
Others are here suffering, and I am making love
What a ridiculous paradox
Merging in ecstasy with the sacred feminine
Wrapped in spiritual and material wealth
Unexpectedly Cosmic Shiva moves through

I am a soul-fire dancing
In constant Tree of Life unbroken consciousness
Carrying me into the big smile
Shiva plays through my consciousness
Filling my soul-fire with the power of the infinite
Dance of Shiva
Dancing Wildly to the cosmic drum
As the Eagle dance
Becomes my life force.
On day four
In the midst of Shiva,
As the ecstatic expression in the world
Appears the trinity of Dattatreya
Old friends
Revisiting after many years
Becoming the Truth of perfect balance,
justice, beauty, love
Whole person enlightenment
Twenty-year cycle defeating the powers of darkness.
Nearing the twenty-first year
Awake
Fructifying this awakening in the world
Gabriel ben Ram
Expressing the birthright of Ram
In this austerity

All that remained is burnt up.
All is unleashed.
In the Tree of Life consciousness
In one dance only
Native American, Yogic, Tao, or Hebrew archetypes and energy
Appear
The holy messengers of the Radiant One
The big smile

Dr. Gabriel Cousens and Dennis Banks
2011 Native American Diabetes Conference, Washington DC

Chapter 28

SHAMANIC HEALING AND HEALING TYPE-2 DIABETES

I was later involved with the Native American energy after Sundance and Ghost Dance with my work in healing diabetes naturally. Type-2 diabetes is a huge problem in the Native American communities. The late Dennis Banks, one of the main American Indian Movement AIM leaders, who became a personal friend, healed his type-2 diabetes at the Tree of Life Center U.S. in three weeks. He then led a march across America for curing diabetes, during which he stopped at almost every reservation. When we met in Washington D.C., at the culmination of the journey, we both gave public talks. He shared in his talk on healing diabetes naturally that about ninety percent of the Native Americans have type-2 diabetes. At the Tree of Life during his twenty-one-day healing cycle, Dennis graciously let me, as Yellow Horse, lead our usual New Moon inipi in his presence and afterwards he gave his approval of me as an inipi leader which was a special recognition.

When I led a shamanic ceremony for the release of the bound and stuck souls from the Blood Island massacre back up into the "heavens" to recontinue their cycles of reincarnation, a variety of Pomo Elders, some of whom had relatives who had actually died in this specific historical massacre, attended our pre-ceremony inipi as part of our preparation for the "releasing the dead souls ceremony". They also empowered me to lead the inipi before the ceremony to be done later that same day at Blood Island. I do not share this to validate myself as an inipi leader but, rather, to make the point that Native Americans honor their brothers in spirit by their soul actions not just by their skin color. In the fire of the inipi ceremony near Blood Island, the light and heat of the inipi burned away over 150 years of European oppression. In some subtle way, they were able to see past the white skin of my body and perhaps understood that my tribal background was from the Middle East, as a genetic Levite, and not European, as well as being adopted into the Native American Medicine Lineage of the Horn Chip Family of the Lakota Sioux, after four years of Sundancing.

Teaching: The historical blood connection of the Ten Lost Hebrew Tribes with the Native Americans is well documented especially with the Cherokee and Choctaws.

These subtle healings between tribes can happen on a very personal level, and this was particularly true for the Pomo tribe in this situation. We emerged from our pre-Blood Island inipi as blood brothers and sisters in the process of the inipi. Immediately following this inipi, I then went on to Blood Island with the support of my new brothers to elevate the earthbound massacred Native American souls lost and stuck on Blood Island. The ceremony was successful in that several participants, including myself, could see not only the ascension of the 250 souls massacred on Blood Island but also approximately 1,500 more Native Americans who had been massacred in the local areas. Mysteriously two wild horses, my totems, appeared about fifty yards away as if to give their blessings to support the ceremony and then left after twenty to thirty minutes.

Healing Native Americans of type-2 diabetes was another way I, as a Sundancer and Eagle Dancer, have been able to support my Native American brothers and sisters. Although the data shows Native Americans have a genetic tendency to develop type-2 diabetes, it seems they also have an unusual, innate power to reverse it naturally. The most famous Native American to participate and be healed in my healing diabetes naturally program, as previously mentioned, was Dennis Banks. So far, every single Native American that has fully participated in my diabetes program at the Tree of Life Center has healed their type-2 diabetes. I am grateful and humbled for the opportunity to do this work with my blood brothers and sisters.

* * *

Since 2007, I have been recognized as a world expert in healing type-2 diabetes naturally with what appears to be the most effective healing diabetes naturally recovery program on the planet. With my relatively unconventional bystander and out of the box approach, a successful holistic healing approach emerged for me that eventually cracked the code on healing type-2 diabetes naturally without allo-pathic medications. Because of my humanitarian proclivity, it has also evolved into a complete type-2 diabetes prevention and positive, healthy lifestyle being shared through more than 100 programs in twenty-six different nations, as well as sharing this approach with the Russian congress, the prime minister and cabinet of Papua New Guinea, and the governor of Bali who were all interested.

This was not particularly planned as a life goal, but when the door of destiny opens it's important to walk through and fulfill one's dharma. This unexpected dharma started when a person associated with the Tree came to see me with a request to do a movie on live-food. I suggested that he make a movie about live-foods as a natural cure for type-2 diabetes. Healing type-2 diabetes with a vegan plant based live-food cuisine is not a totally new idea. In the 1920s, Dr. Max Gerson reported his healing of Dr. Albert Schweitzer of type-2 diabetes primarily with vegan live-foods. My work has been to systemize it for a wide variety of people.

The movie, *Simply Raw*, was artfully done and follows a four-week journey of six diabetics in our diabetes healing program. It was a big hit with over two million viewers around the world watching the healing process of these six people. Unexpectedly, two of these diabetics turned out to be type 1 diabetics. Since that time one of the type 1 diabetics has remained healed for over thirteen years and the other was able to reduce his insulin needs by ninety-five percent during the actual four-week treatment program and has continued to hold his improvement over the years.

Inspired by these results, I designed a much more powerful live-food 21-Day Diabetes Recovery Program. The results have been published in my book *There Is a Cure for Diabetes* which documents

Meeting the Governor of Bali to discuss a diabetes prevention.

*Meeting with the Prime Minister of Papua New
Guinea to discuss a diabetes prevention.*

a sixty-one percent "cure" rate for non-insulin dependent type-2 diabetes and twenty-four percent cure rate for insulin dependent type-2 diabetes in three weeks; as well as healing twenty-one percent of people with type-1 diabetes; and helping thirty-one percent of people with type-1 diabetes to come off insulin entirely. We did not have the resources to see how many more were cured after the three weeks. "Curing" means a fasting blood sugar less than one hundred without taking diabetic medication. Presently I only work with type-2 diabetics.

One important spiritual lesson for me has been learning to establish boundaries so that I stay aligned with my overall life purpose. I have compassion and desire to help everyone, including type-1 diabetics, but too much of a focus in this one area would significantly limit my bigger mission. As hoped, other medical doctors since our movie and my book have begun to do similar programs with good results. Even so these surprising and inspiring results with type-2 diabetes meant that I was unexpectedly traveling all over the world discussing this natural cure approach.

Teaching: Establishing boundaries helps one
stay aligned with one's life purpose.

As part of the larger unfolding of this work, I had the good fortune to meet Dr. John Arnold who also has a home in Patagonia. He is the originator of PPEP (Portable Practical Educational Preparation, a 501c3 educational program). John and I have become partners in our humanitarian projects particularly in Mexico and Africa. All these projects have a diabetes prevention and education diabetes prevention educator, and some have included organic, veganic farming programs, often financially started with the help of micro-business programs that John sets up. This way we can feed the people healthy plant-based food that they have created so as to maintain their diabetes-free state and prevent additional type-2 diabetes from happening. The programs are indirectly promoting a vegan live-food cuisine worldwide which is also part of my dharma. This holistic sustainability approach is practical in that it provides jobs, feeds the people, supports healthy agricultural employment via vegan farming; creates an indigenous preventative health model; originates an inspirational model for people to become connected with; and generates the subtle space for uplifting the soul energy of humanity back to God. It's no accident that many of the people in the diabetes program, by the end of the program, feel that they have reconnected with their soul, which is part of the whole holistic healing process.

Teaching: Reconnecting with the soul is part
of the whole holistic healing process.

We have also created jobs and training for our diabetes prevention paraprofessionals working for us in these more than one hundred programs. When the proper amount of funding arrives, we hope to expand these programs on a nationwide basis in more countries as well as to the Native American community where we have already begun to work with some of the 238 tribes in the U.S. The diabetes prevention and education work has become the foundation of my humanitarian programs around the world. This development has been a curious surprise guidance of the Will of God in my life.

Chapter 29

SHARING TEACHINGS BY BEING THE TEACHING

Teaching: To know the Truth is to
know the Divine Nothing.

Since my ashram years in India, my ability to communicate the liberation teachings has expressed in many ways. My liberation teachings include spiritual fasting retreats and Shaktipat meditation retreats, as well as Zero Point, a liberation course which empowers people to gain power over their mind and realize that the personality is a case of mistaken identity and thus awaken to the deeper truth of who they are. This level of awareness can't be labeled, bottled, or commercialized. Of course, if a person wants to awaken, they need to ultimately consider that they're asleep, and everything that the body-mind-I am complex takes for reality is a hypnotic dream.

Teaching: The truth of the central ecstatic awareness
of the One is articulated with silence, which is
the hum behind every thought or action.

At this time in history, not everyone ready to walk through the doorway to freedom. Yet people paradoxically seem more ready to go on this journey in the midst of the social chaos we are living in. From the liberation perspective, we are not our bodies, gender identities, religious beliefs, race identities, or whatever else people egoically use to separate themselves from the Oneness. Of course, not everyone is willing to interact at this level, but, amazingly, a vast majority are willing to be such a blessing to themselves and the world during these transformational programs. They are the pioneers and the heroes in our society because they're willing to go beyond the culture of death lifestyle and separation into a whole new way of being, become an original again, and walk through the doorway to freedom in unity awareness.

My dharma in this area is to provide this much-needed support for the small but growing group of people who are ready and brave enough for this transformative liberation process which overtly bridges them into the Culture of Life and Liberation as an ongoing way of living. I delight in taking people as far as they are ready and willing to go. It is a joy to see the deep soul smile people emanate as they get more in touch with their radiant inner Truth. Over time, my teaching style has become gently focused on the direct experience of accessing one's inner Truth and not on simply filling people with intellectual information about spirituality or nutrition. However, the process of waking up to the Truth and breaking out of our hypnotic trance does require some intentional effort and spiritual guidance. Paradoxically, no phenomena can capture the Truth because realization is not tied to phenomena. However, when we fly above the clouds of the mind, the sky becomes clear.

Teaching: It's essential to be the Truth and not
just speak it. One can't look for the Truth; one
can't lose the Truth; and also, one can't find the
Truth because all the time we are the Truth.

It is a wild task and a challenging piece of my life's mission to help people overcome their fear of stepping into the unknown and out of their comfort zone into the World of Grace and God. It is enjoyably paradoxical to play in a holy field in which the Divine doesn't play by the rules of the mind. Making it more complicated is that we're like a person in the desert, so dehydrated, from the lack of Divine nectar that we begin to see things that are not there. This is the hypnotic state of self-delusion of the post-truth reality that the power of the Six Foundations and Sevenfold Peace way of life help us to awaken from.

Teaching: The beauty of liberation is that one can't steal,
capture, or earn the radiant fire of liberation. Eventually, we
are consumed by the fire of liberation, ultimately eliminating
the illusion of a separate "I am" and a separate mind.

Of course, becoming liberated is not so easy. The work as a spiritual teacher/master and friend is to help people begin to be willing to taste the nectar of the Divine Self and not settle for stagnant, polluted waters of the matrix programmed mind. When the inner voice speaks, as a soft whisper and light of God, there is neither a leading nor a following but only That. The non-causal source of our joy emerges when we live fearlessly in the Nothing and free ourselves of the prison of our beliefs maintained by the prison-keeper, which is our ego. In this context, looking to make politically correct "good" or "right" decisions is not the goal, but to make decisions that express and develop our deep spiritual Truth and more deeply connect us to the One until we merge into the One. This is the secret of living a life of meaning without necessarily having a purpose. Some people are given very directed purposes or life dharmas like I have been given; and others are gifted primarily with the big dharma of knowing and merging with God in every moment.

Teaching: Meaning is about experiencing the presence of God in every moment. Purpose requires being aware of a certain dharmic role or function to be played in the cosmic orchestra.

In today's world, people are so culturally hypnotized and indoctrinated in post-truth emotional beliefs that they mistake their mindless, matrix-programmed ego expressing itself as emotional "truth" for the deeper spiritual Truth of who we really are. When a person is cut off from their soul-source and operating from the emotional programmed matrix mind, any matrix directive can be followed as the "truth" because they are not grounded in the deeper soul Truth of the Divine.

Teaching: The protective antidote to not being led astray by our subjective post truth "deluded realities", is to anchor oneself in the basic perennial cosmic truths and universal teachings of all traditions; the validation of one's spiritual perceptions by one's spiritual teacher or spiritual collective as a counterbalance to being deluded; and to feel an alignment with one's inner Truth. All three need to be in alignment before any action is taken.

Without the feeling of a connection to our soul, which connects us to all beings as one soul and helps us feel alive, people may easily move into hate, which may give a temporary illusion of aliveness and is an expression of separation consciousness. Unfortunately, this is happening in an uncontrolled chaotic way all over the world today. One of my roles is to help people reconnect with their own soul, so we can reconnect to all souls and thus create a world at peace. Hate is biblically defined as feeling disconnected. Hate disconnects us from others and from our own soul. We can see this in suicide bombers, who are so hate-filled they are willing to destroy themselves and others because they are so disconnected from the energy of the soul and of God. There is an obvious epidemic of hatefulness emerging all over the world. It seduces people to self-righteously act out their intensely felt transient sentiments as if they are the deeper truth.

Teaching: Hate disconnects us from others and
from our own soul. This separation consciousness,
unfortunately, creates an angry, intolerant, fascist
social environment, which works against our spiritual
evolution which is one of oneness and unity.

Any dissent becomes interpreted as a personal attack because
people are so emotionally identified with their temporary matrix
beliefs, rather than with the factual science or the historical facts or
perennial spiritual teachings.

Teaching: Without the ability to experience the spark
of the Divine within ourselves and in the other we are
potentially left with alienation and hate. When we
experience even a glimmer of the light of our own soul, *we*
potentially can create the space for a soul-to-soul connection
to take place and feel our human connection again.

As a person who has and is continually interfacing with many
levels of culture in many nations, it is painful for me to witness this
pandemic of human disconnection, especially because an endemic
spiritual disconnection from one's own soul and that of the other, is a
sign of a degenerating society. From my lifelong experience, all social
and most business interactions at their primal level are always about
the soul connections. For example, it is enjoyable to go shopping
with Shanti in the Arab markets in different Middle Eastern countries
because people remember these social business interactions are still

primarily about making the soul connection over tea before making a sale. This is the essence of spiritual business and social-spiritual life. The Tree of Life Foundation, through our humanitarian projects, is naturally a full spectrum spiritual humanitarian effort in this way. If we are not making that heart to heart connection, charity and service are not necessarily happening.

Many people don't understand the extent to which their minds are shaped by the worldwide, subtle and not so subtle, media/governmental matrix and mind-control realities that are more overtly affecting their general consciousness. For at least the last sixty years, and possibly since the 1920s, and actually since Cain in the Garden of Eden, there have been attempts to craft the reality framework of the planet into that of a "soulless technocracy" in different forms, in which some humans think we are the creators and the ultimate designers of the world other than God.

Teaching: Since Nimrod and the Tower of Babel approximately 3800 B.C. there has been a subtle yet sinister and persistent globalist goal to enslave humanity which directly and/or indirectly blocks the spiritual evolution and ultimate Holistic Liberation of humanity.

One of the most famous of these globalists was Nimrod, of the Tower of Babel infamy, who saw himself as capturer of "men's souls" in his conscious effort to create the first one world government since the time of Noah and the flood. This six-thousand-year trend is not for the evolutionary or spiritual benefit of the human race. It is contrary to the God-decreed liberation process for all of humanity because it creates the paradoxically voluntary and willing enslavement of the human race.

Teaching: Enslavement begins when people become disconnected from the inner truths of their souls. It is the experience of God-merging that links people to the perennial, cosmic, love experience and truths of all the great teachings.

It is wonderful to see so many people in the active process of breaking away from the illusionary, media-created, subtle seduction of the matrix in all these areas so that they can reconnect to the deeper reality of their souls and begin to dance free. On a materialistic level this insight may seem like more of a political discussion. However, that would be a trivialization of the greater spiritual meaning and cosmic struggle between light and dark that has been happening since creation, the Garden of Eden, post-Noahide times and is again becoming more obvious today. We all are consciously or unconsciously playing our roles in it. The assassination of John F. Kennedy in 1963 was the alarm bell that went off for me to simply know that it was time to participate in the bigger picture to elevate humanity and uplift the planetary web of life. The role of the spiritual teacher in this context, as in every generation, has always been to support people in their total awakening and freedom process.

Teaching: In a world attempting to actively create hateful and blatantly egoic divisions of race, religion, nationality, gender, and skin color in order to divide and enslave us, it is simply amazing how quickly those illusory divisions disappear in a soul to soul, heart centered spiritually supportive setting. This awakening transition may happen so rapidly that it symbolically gives hope to all of humanity that we humans are able to reconnect with the experience of our soul and humanity and in this process know our collective Oneness.

Chapter 30

THE JOURNEY OF HOLISTIC LIBERATION BENEFITS FROM THE SUPPORT OF A SPIRITUAL FRIEND/TEACHER

Teaching: The awakening of the Kundalini or Ruach Ha'Kodesh activates and turns on the spiritual switch for the final phase of the liberation path.

---

*M*any people throughout the world have begun to call me their spiritual teacher, spiritual guide, or spiritual friend. The clarity of my role as a liberated spiritual teacher continues to evolve over time as its own unique expression without being limited by a specific role model. My primary function and gift as a spiritual teacher includes awakening the Kundalini/Ruach Ha'Kodesh with Shaktipat/Haniha, which I have now offered in over forty-two countries and to greater than tens of thousands of people. The awakening of the Kundalini or Ruach Ha'Kodesh turns on the spiritual switch needed to be activated for the last phase of the liberation path to Self-Realization. These awakened energies upgrade the subtle internal anatomy of the chakras, nadis, and koshas (layers of the mind), and prepare all levels of the human vehicle to hold the increased spiritual cosmic energy and awareness of enlightenment.

The energetic field of the spiritual master through Shaktipat/ Haniha also helps to burn up the student's karma in their actual process of receiving the Shaktipat/Ruach Ha'Kodesh. The more times people receive Shaktipat/Haniha, the more burning up of their negative forces and karmas happens.

People often ask what it is like to give Shaktipat. My inner experience in being a transmitter of Shaktipat/Haniha is one of a deep soul connection with the person in the sharing of this energy and a non-causal joy and love in being part of the activation and support of their spiritual evolution.

Shaktipat/Haniha is also a subtle form of soul sacrifice in that a part of my soul spark goes into the student. Although part of my unique soul energy is added to the soul of the recipient, the Divine is more than abundantly refilling and expanding the force of this Shaktipat soul energy within me. To the best of my knowledge Swami Muktananda was among the first to share this energy with masses of people rather than the traditional guru transmission to one successor disciple. This in itself was heroic; and I sense intuitively that he paid a subtle spiritual and energetic price for it. While I was at the ashram, I observed that in his transmissions to thousands his aura would become subtly clouded with all the karmas he was burning up for his students. When I asked the people who were physically close to him about this,

I was told that he often had to meditate for an extended period after the Shaktipat session to burn up the negative karmas. Unfortunately, sometimes, if the karma can't be fully burnt off, one takes it on. For example, when Swami Muktananda visited the Native Americans in Oklahoma to fulfill part of their prophecy, he heroically was willing to take on their karma and later actually had a stroke associated with his visit. With this as a concern, I asked two different psychics with the ability to see auras to check my aura before, during, and after giving Shaktipat to a large group of people. They both agreed that the fire of my field was fully burning up people's karmas wholly and naturally during the process. It is my fastidious style to examine these questions, and also to learn from both Swami Muktananda and Swami Prakashananda by observing their lives and actions.

Teaching: One of the unique roles and a major responsibility of the liberated spiritual master is to be able to recognize when someone becomes liberated.

Working as a spiritual teacher/friend has its challenges and it always raises some questions for me, such as: how does functioning and being acknowledged as a spiritual teacher impact my evolution? I also often ask myself what it means to have a proper and spiritually healthy relationship with my students so that I can truly support their liberation process. Being married helps to clarify firm boundaries as well as supplying a model of marriage as a spiritual path.

One of the most essential parts of being a spiritual master, teacher or friend to a spiritual aspirant is the ability to inspire, and to resonate the certainty of the deeper spiritual truth of who we are.

Teaching: To know that one has a spiritual teacher/
friend who truly loves them and is committed to
their liberation is a powerful gift. Spiritual support
is needed, especially in these chaotic times.

The fulfillment of my two lineage dharmic directives is also part of my role. The continuation of the lineage energy from Sri Bhagawan Nityananda, given to me by Swami Muktananda to wake up and elevate the consciousness of the world through the power of Shaktipat and the associated liberation teachings, is a clear dharmic responsibility. However, the specific Siddha-tradition is the responsibility of other people. The transmission of spiritual energy is also part of the biblical prophetic tradition lineage I am also part of. This lineage transmission is more clearly described in in Deuteronomy 34:9 where it says: "Now Joshua son of Nun was filled with the spirit of wisdom because Moses had laid his hands on him." It also occurs in other sections of the Torah. As explained earlier, this is called *S'micha m'shefa/ Haniha* in Hebrew. There is no "doership" in being a Shaktipat vehicle as the cosmic Kundalini/Ruach Ha'Kodesh energy is just pouring through to fulfill this cosmic assignment. After giving Shaktipat/Haniha, I am blessed to consistently have a feeling of energization and expansion rather than any type of depletion.

Teaching: There is no "doership" in being a
vehicle for Shaktipat at the Guru's command.

Another area of service as a spiritual teacher, also initiated by the direction of Swami Muktanada, but clearly a shamanic part of the

Torah tradition, is the power to remove demons and entities from people. This was activated following my story I shared of his direction to remove a demon from a field next to the ashram to protect my 5-year-old daughter. Fortunately, as I learned from this experience and of giving Shaktipat, my energetic field is like a Sherman tank when dealing with entity and demonic dispossessions.

A liberated spiritual master also bears witness that indeed it is possible to wake up from the dream illusion of I Am-ness and to disappear into the Nothing. In inspiring others by example, I act as an awareness tuning fork for students.

Teaching: Self-Realization is the first major enlightenment step toward final God-merging of moksha.

Another role of the spiritual teacher is to encourage students to live in the awareness of vairagya/histalvut (the vision of seeing the light of the soul in everyone equally), as well as developing the ability to discriminate (*viveka*) between the cosmic truth and the temporal reality. In today's world with so many distractions and post-truth illusionary realities continually attempting to capture or confuse people's minds, just clarifying vairagya and viveka for students is a great service.

Teaching: It is important to develop spiritual discrimination and moral clarity, because both are profoundly missing in today's public spiritual dialogue.

Kavod, or living in the awareness of spiritual honor and truth, is another quality for the spiritual master to model especially in our current society in which the value of honor and truth have been overtly disregarded. In one's daily action, developing a sense of both community responsibility for uplifting as many people who are ready, as well as service and charity is also part of my role and function.

For a spiritual teacher, there is also a responsibility to create finances to support one's spiritual life. Rather than depending on donations of spiritual students for a personal income, as a holistic physician I am financially independent from my students. This has the benefit of allowing me to consistently give the most appropriate and spiritually uplifting advice without being compromised because of needing donations.

Teaching: A spiritual teacher must
not be bribable on any level.

Another role of the spiritual teacher is also to inspire spiritual discipline, including maintaining the morals and ethics it takes to live this way as well as spiritual perseverance by the presence of their own consistent actions over time. In today's objective outer world, as compared to the mental health statistics of sixty years ago, people are subjected to significantly greater negative energetic frequencies of an increasingly corrupt, chaotic, stressful, and degenerate culture. It is a major service to be an example of clear boundaries and a spiritual way of life that maintains one's physical, emotional, mental, and spiritual health. I have become clearly aware of the importance of being a living example of holding the dharma to inspire others in these chaotic times which is exactly what Swami Prakashananda directed me to do.

Teaching: It is critical to protect one's mind from the
spiritually and mentally corrupting matrix media, and actually
be and radiate happiness and joy in a world where anxiety,
depression, drug abuse, and suicide are skyrocketing.

Helping people maintain their soul connection, so they are
not negatively engulfed by these things, is one of the most crucial
functions. In other times, these were less essential functions of
the spiritual teacher, but in today's chaotic, politically correct
(a.k.a. perversion of consciousness or pollution of consciousness),
distorted, dysfunctional world, it has become a crucial role of the
spiritual teacher. The activation and enhancement of the Divine
Urge is always fundamental to the spiritual master's primal service.
Giving Shaktipat/Ruach Ha'Kodesh, and being a living example
of a pure and natural way of living that leads one to liberation, is
perhaps the most powerful way to support the Divine Urge and
spiritual life in general.

Teaching: Ultimately, spiritual teachers are milestones
along the way, as the final step in the liberation process
requires grace so that each person has the courage
to step into the Promised Land on their own.

In a subtle and explicitly non-sexual way, the spiritual relationship between the teacher and student may act as a support and
inspiration. This relationship may be considered a non-physical
mystical form of spiritual marriage. Many people are not spiritually

mature enough to be ready to have this level of relationship or even any serious relationship with a spiritual teacher on any level. The spiritual marriage is a non-gender specific spiritual contract that is explicitly articulated with people if they are interested in such a commitment. It is not a sexual relationship, but it represents the activation of the alchemy of the Eros of Liberation in the spiritual relationship between student and teacher.

Teaching: Clear boundaries are important in a student's evolution and God merging. A mystical marriage with a true spiritual teacher as a mature non-gender spiritual commitment, is helpful as a support and inspiration on the path to awakening. The Eros of Liberation driving force energy toward liberation may be enhanced by a non-sexual spiritual relationship between student and teacher.

This intimate work is supported by Shanti who is very much part of my interactions with most all students. Shanti, as was prophesized, works closely and particularly more with the women than with the men, although she's very supportive of the men as well. The relationship's clear boundaries create a sustainable energy that supports the long haul of the ups and downs of the student's spiritual evolution in relating to serving and merging with God in love and joy. This spiritual marriage model holds the paradox of the impersonal and personal, while sharing the spiritual joy, work, trials, and tribulations of thousands of spiritual marriages. Each student's struggle becomes the spiritual teacher's struggle in a way that allows an energetic personal connection to each person's process. As a spiritual teacher/friend, an important question is knowing how and when to inspire and awaken people to the different levels of their existence and how to help them walk the mysterious paradox without becoming confused or egoic. The subtle teaching with this approach is to see myself as a multidimensional being living as a fully integrated human being on the planet. This includes paradoxically living in a way that encourages individual aliveness and uniqueness in the expression of the Divine Will and yet living in collective harmony with the planetary network of life. For people to share this mystical walk between the B'limah and the Mah with a real alive human being and for me to witness my evolution in this process as a multidimensional liberated being in all my roles and functions, generates a whole new level of spiritual maturity.

The non-dual, paradoxical awareness of the Great Torah Way, Kabbalistic mysticism, Advaita Vedanta, Kashmir Shaivism, Lakota Native American Way, and seeing the dance of the Divine in all creation are all vital parts of my liberation teachings and awareness development. These teachings are explicitly and experientially imparted in all my daily interactions as they come from my heartfelt direct experiences. The practical teaching applications of these deep understandings to the mundane events of the world, such as politics, sacred relationships, family life and raising children, and everyday life in the chaos and multiple levels of societal confusion of everyday events and people's lives, gives significant support and insight to the idea of choosing to live one's life as a spiritual path.

Teaching: This approach that I have taken for myself has evolved into a model I have named the Holistic Liberation Way. It means being open to liberation on all levels of one's life and being free to move in any direction that supports this holistic organic evolution along the whole path in every aspect and cycle of one's life.

In 1973, I was given an unexpected direct opportunity to face my desire and resistance to and fear, of the unknown of God. It happened quite dramatically. I was listening to, my now long-term friend, J.J. Hurtak describing his direct energetic and intellectual experiences and teachings from the Enochian energies. It was in a class I had organized for him to teach in Cotati, California over a period of six weeks from 8 p.m. to 2 a.m. each night. One night there was a tremendous amount of energy illuminating the room and almost everyone had fallen asleep from the intensity of the energy, but I was still awake. Suddenly, illuminated heads formed of at least six light beings at J.J.'s right side, which I interpreted as angels. While watching them in relative surprise and shock, I thought: "Am I the only one seeing them? Am I hallucinating?" J.J. unexpectedly turned to them and addressed them by their angelic names. It was mind-blowing and awe-creating, and another concrete step into the relative unknown. At that moment I was actively struggling with my desire and resistance to encounter this level of the unknown of God. This intense struggle went on for at least an hour. I did not know if I was going to run out of the room in dread or if I was going to have the courage to overcome this fear of the unknown aspect of God's world. I felt like a deer in a set of car headlights... frozen. Fortunately, I faced and overcame the awe and fear in a "long hour"; and ultimately also overcame the dread of dying into the unknown.

Teaching: Feeling awe and fear of the unknown is normal
and is usually a temporary part of the spiritual path.

I share this about the awe and fear, because so many people are embarrassed to talk about their fears of dissolving into the unknown. Sharing this story has helped many spiritual aspirants overcome this common fear on the spiritual path. Once we have minimized the fear of the unknown of God, it usually stays minimal.

Teaching: As the resistance to God diminishes,
the desire and urge for God grows stronger.

I observed that this fear of the unknown of God usually appears in most people's spiritual evolution once they have chosen to pop out of the comfort zone of the matrix box of "normality" as was the case for myself. By acknowledging its existence, I could actively and consciously face and dissolve this fear of God and of the unknown. Part of my Zero Point course is designed to help people overcome and dissolve this fear of the unknown as it is such a critical challenge to master in spiritual life.

Teaching: Having courage doesn't mean there is no
fear. Spiritual courage is a crucial quality for enduring
and sustaining the walk of the spiritual path as it
bestows the endurance to surrender to the Divine.

Surrendering to the Divine became my primary spiritual effort for many years. The whole idea of liberation was secondary to allowing and supporting this cosmic force of Kundalini unfolding within this self/soul-fire. The most important good news perspective to this regular and intense experience, especially during meditation, was that the "mystery of God" was the pilot of the rocket and thus, confidence in a safe landing emerged.

Disappearing into the Nothing has been an extraordinary part of the paradoxical Self-Realization Holistic Liberation Way that I have had the grace to disappear into. The paradox is that in my consciousness there is no longer an "I" to refer to a self; there is only "That" playing through the emptiness of the *bitul hayesh,* the great emptiness inside. There is only the Will of God emanating through this *ahamkara* (a technical Vedic term for the boundary between one's full egoic functioning body, emotional, mind, and spiritual beingness and the boundaryless nothing). To be one's dharma in the world we need a fully clear, well-boundaried yet egoless ahamkara through which to express in the world.

Teaching: On this path of Holistic Liberation,
eventually even the "I-ness" disappears and only
the Divine Nothing of the Eternal Divine Presence,
prior to dual/non-dual existence, remains.

This is not something I could initially willfully do. It comes as an act of grace. Over time, I naturally, spontaneously and regularly began to go into that Nothingness prior to time and space even when being physically active.

The Torah teaches that we cannot see God and live. This is true because as long as the "I-ness" exists, we continue to exist separate from the Divine and, therefore, can't experience the full Truth of the Divine. As we disappear into the Eternal Divine Nothing, prior to existence, all illusion of a separate existence from God evaporates.

Teaching: When the "I-ness" disappears,
one literally "cannot live and see God".

This awareness is not an intellectual, theoretical construct. It is based on hardcore, internal, subjective, experiential and sustainable reality. This awareness did not come in one cosmic flash for me. It was a repeated experiential absorption into the illuminated Divine Nothingness over several years until it became self-evident that the "I Am-ness" and even the "I-ness" were a complete illusion, obscuring the unbroken cosmic truth in which "I-ness", or any other apparition or separation of the material or subtle plane, does not exist separate from the One.

Many people have both a desire and resistance to awakening. In addressing the usually unspoken desire and resistance to the Divine, different religions, at the beginning stages, may appear to protect us from the fear of the unknown of God, because they keep us in the safety zone of the known. By staying in our comfort zone, it is easy to miss the opportunity to walk through the door of liberation.

Teaching: Liberation requires the willingness
to disappear fearlessly into the ecstatic
emptiness of the unknown of the Divine.

In time, I was eventually willing and ready to truly surrender to the Will of God, which meant surrendering my ahamkara to the Divine Will. It is challenging for the rational mind (including my own) to understand. Often poetry can help us let go of our fear of the cosmic unknown and joyously slip into the mystery of the cosmic void, which is why I have placed poetry throughout this book. Poetry helps to free our left brained and often fear based linear thinking and inspires us into the Holistic Liberation Way of direct knowing. The Holistic Liberation Way helps us to dance fearlessly in the subtle bliss of the Cosmic Truth of the Eternal Presence.

An advanced part of the path of liberation is known as "histalkut" which is a Kabbalistic term for disappearing into the Nothing. For many, this is an unusual teaching. When one disappears into the Nothing, even the subtle "I-ness" disappears and one is able by grace to experience the Eternal Divine Presence prior to consciousness. On a subtle level I began to experience two levels of Nothing. One is the non-dual Nothing, or Oneness, which is part of the dual/non-dual dance. I experienced this at the level of a continual alteration of consciousness of the Something continually emerging out of the Nothing and back into the Something in every instant. It feels like one continuous paradoxical experience. At a deeper level, there is the also the awareness of the cosmic Nothing that exists prior to consciousness and prior to the Something/Nothing, dual/non-dual paradigm. This level of the Nothing prior to consciousness is what I am referring to when mentioning disappearing into the Nothing. Simultaneously it includes the continual subliminal awareness of the Eternal Divine Presence. Paradoxically, at this level there is no one there to actually experience God, as only the great Eternal Nothing Divine Presence exists. This is the primal core of my experiential liberation awareness and teachings beyond intellectual insights. Through continually experiencing this level of disappearing into the Nothing at this cosmic level enough times, this liberation awareness has gradually become my natural state. What more is there to say?

Teaching: In the Holistic Liberation Way, physical creation becomes one big, laughable, illusory reality, which does not exist, yet, paradoxically exists for our evolutionary benefit.

This God activated illumined illusory reality provides (depending on how conscious we are) situational experiences that serve the purpose of helping us to expand our spiritual consciousness. In the Holistic Liberation Way, we begin to understand that the path of liberation is a continual walk between the B'limah (Nothing) and the Mah (Something).

These refinements which I have gone through in the past, and continuously go through in the present, make the process of pre-liberation and liberation an endless wondrous unfolding. I am continually starting over. There is an enjoyable freshness and innocence to this. Awakened spiritual teachers come in a variety of forms, roles and functions. All roles, dharmas, and functions, although they may serve a temporary purpose are illusionary realities.

Teaching: The essential existence of the liberated spiritual teacher is to be a Zero.

—ᴟ—

Subtle Kiss of Disappearing into the Nothing

The subtle kiss of liberation
Has no lips
But you taste it in every cell;
An ecstatic wild pulsing in every DNA oscillation
Dancing freely in every chakra,
Coursing through the shushumna and all 72,000 nadi channels
In all four worlds
Once kissed
The One becomes alive
And there is nothing else worth living for
Except the ecstatic, naked wild dance of Yah.
Yah's kiss is the cosmic death
And cosmic rebirth into immortality.
Once kissed one becomes the breath of Yah as the play of the world.
Be careful who one yearns to kiss
Because there may be no return.

—⟋w⟍—

Disappearing into the Nothing

Existence disappeared into the great silent cosmic laugh,
And, in returning from the Nothing,
The belief in the illusory "I" had ceased.
All effort, however subtle, had ceased.
The overwhelming, aching, flaming desire to
merge with the One gently subsided.
Kundalini laughed,
And there was no one left to hear the laughter.
A sublime luminescent silence appeared as the emerging of existence,
Emanating as existence,
As the complete non-causal peace, as the DNA of existence;
An extraordinary glowing aliveness of the Absolute;
An Illumination so real that all else appeared unreal.
In the reality of this awakening, all previous reality appeared as unreal.
Appearing as the illusion of the transient three-dimensional world,
A new appearance,
As all of immanent existence now glowed with the radiance of That,
As the indescribable expression of God as, in, and prior to this world.
The illuminating radiance of God, shown as
the underlying Truth of all existence,
As the Eternal Divine Presence prior to dual/non-dual existence.

—∿—

Surrender to the One

The "I-ness" that existed
Burst into the flame of Kundalini
Continually fired up by meditation.
In a cycle of seven incendiary years
All was destroyed
Burnt by the Divine raging fire of God.
There was no choice
But to cooperate with the burning.
It demanded total innocent surrender
Beyond the ignorance of the body-mind- I Am complex.
Out of the flames danced
The most sublime, passionate
Non-causal love, peace, joy, contentment,
passion, oneness, and compassion
More powerful than any worldly attachment
Like a coyote
It laughed
At all the illusory I's
Thought to be real.
Biting through attachments
It challenged:
"Fool…you cannot lose what was never yours"
Killing the illusion of the body-mind-I Am consciousness
That had once been mine
Nothing was left
Except the untamed That

Expressing and manifesting
As service to all Life
In all forms
And all ways
Existing only to serve the Divine Will
The awakening and enlightenment of human awareness.

Chapter 31

BEYOND THE MIND

I began my spiritual journey with Swami Muktananda with roughly enough resources to sustain our family of four. It was used up entirely in the seven-year guru cycle from age thirty-three to forty which just also happened to be my exact guru cycle in my Vedic Astrology. Although all our monetary savings were used up in the seven-year time, at the end of this seven-year cycle what remained was a vast ecstatic, illuminating emptiness that allowed me as a soul-fire to live in the truth. It was a good deal!!! It was so inexpensive, and the grace of liberation has made me the wealthiest among the wealthiest in the world. Of course, we're not talking about money here, not physical gold and silver, but the gold of liberation.

—ᚓᚓ—

Throw It Away

Throw away all your arguments
About or with God
And join in the Divine Dance
On the empty and full field prior to consciousness

—ᚓᚓ—

For many people, the readiness to start the spiritual path in earnest comes from seeking the answers to the traditionally burning questions such as: Who am I? Who are we? What is life's purpose? Waking up from what? How do I wake up? What is the mystery of death? People often want to know what it's going to cost to wake up. Often, they're thinking money as well as other things when asking that question. And, yes, spiritual life in both the Biblical and Vedic traditions require some minimal financial strength according to our needs to support us on the spiritual path. Wealth or lack of it can be used as an excuse not to focus on spiritual life.

—ᚓᚓ—

Divine Urge

The seed of Truth
Eternally planted
Within the body-mind I am complex
Is awakened by your touch.
This seed of cosmic fire
Ignites the Eternal Divine Urge
Into a roaring flame

I am like a stallion after a mare in heat
Seeking to unite with the One
Crashing through the illusion of all barriers
Beyond imaginary physical and mental limitation
Charging into the endless subtle bliss of meditation
Whose experiences mystically deprogram
The body, mind, I am complex
From the illusion of the world;
A form of Divine behavior modification
Guiding me into the emptiness
Of Divine Stillness;
A wild crazed moth
Willing to be burnt up in the Divine Fire.
All one has to do is to show up
And be willing to die
In the endless flame of Divine Love
The "I-ness" is burnt to ashes,
And Yah's breath blows away the ashes.
Empty and full
As I Am That;
Complete peace;
The urge completes its mission.
Nothing is left;
Nowhere to stand;
No one standing;
No seeker
And nothing to seek.
The end of all process;
Nothing to do, be or become.

Free to move in any direction
As one becomes
The wild Divine Dance of Yah.

—ɯ—

For those starting on the path powered by Divine Urge carrying us back to our original, authentic God-merged Self, it's important to understand as I strongly state from my direct experience that: there is only God happening no matter what!

Teaching: Liberation is not a gamble. In
reality, it is the only game in town.

I discovered that all that's needed for the process to proceed was to cash in all the chips of my belief systems, my ideas, my concepts, my dreams, my pain, my projections, and my sadness that I had created through attachment to the unawake world of the matrix. In this liberating walk, less and less of a "ego-self" remained and more of a "wild one" who could be free to move in any direction emerged. I saw I had built a whole way of life based on the amnesia of Truth and a serious identification with my personality, birthed from the belief in and identification with my I Am-ness.

Teaching: The mind, as I Am-ness, is what is born and
is not the essential Self and is not the awakened Truth.

After years of meditation, my mind began to be perceived by the inner witness as an unreal egoic noose around my neck blocking me from awakening to the illuminated Truth of the Real Self. A vital understanding and insight given to me, in awakening from the spiritual nightmare of unawake normality, was the liberating insight that the personality is a case of mistaken identity. Until I apperceived this truth, I realized I was living in a false reality of separation from God and all levels of creation and was doomed to a limiting mental prison of unawake dualistic and materialistic consciousness. Being freed from this, it has become a passion and a joy to help students apperceive this as well and become free.

Teaching: The personality is indeed
a case of mistaken identity.

I saw that my perception of duality came from being rooted in my belief in and identification with my I Am-ness. Actual duality, at the level of cosmic truth, has never existed. Once I realized this beyond duality consciousness, I began to experience the disappearing into the nothing quite frequently. In this spiritual awakening process, my illusory belief in the three-dimensional dream world of everyday life slowly disappeared. With this understanding I began to engage in the illuminating process of ceasing to identify with the body-mind-I Am complex. This Self that emerged into consciousness naturally no longer experiences a significant separation from all humans, animals, plants, the living planet, and God. In a more sophisticated way of articulating it, the personality-identified objective world became experienced by me as a superimposition on my true nature. It became more and more clear that my true nature exists prior to consciousness.

Teaching: It is useless to renounce the world, as
the only true renunciation is our attachment to
our ego and "I'ness", as only "That" exists.

—ɯ—

It Finds You

Non-causal joy
Is never found;
It finds you
When one lives fearlessly in the Nothing
Free of the prison of our beliefs.

—ɯ—

Teaching: In liberation there is no attainment…
It is the recognition of who we are not, and the
experiential awakening to the Truth of who we are.

In the beginning of my spiritual path, I mistakenly thought the
mind was important because I had not yet created an empty enough
mind to go beyond it. What a blessing to directly apperceive the
Truth beyond the mind.

Teaching: Our egoic minds maintain the media matrix
mythical belief that our I Am-ness is the foundation on
which we should build our lives, but in reality, it is that
which keeps us in the ignorance of our True Self.

As the power of meditation took me deeper and deeper into the Truth prior to the mind, it became more and more obvious that liberation consciousness exists beyond and prior to time, space, and the mind.

Teaching: Paradoxically, nothing has ever happened, nothing will ever happen, and everything has already happened.

The wild paradox of the world of liberation is actually quite humorous. It starts with being born into the illusion of I Am-ness. Along with this unawakened initial birth experience also came the illusion of birth and death.

Teaching: Our minds are the foundation stone of the matrix which deludes us into thinking we were born and will die.

For myself, even at a young age I also felt subtly challenged to awaken to the immensely freeing awareness that ultimately there is no death.

Teaching: There is no death for the soul...

The deeper I went into the liberation process it became clearer that the essence of who I was and am is eternal. By stilling and quieting the activities of my mind, I had begun to transcend my mind. It happened naturally, spontaneously, and gradually after years of meditation.

Chapter 32

TRUTH OF THE DIVINE

Teaching: The mind / I Am-ness identity is like
a log burning in a fire of expanded consciousness
until it decomposes into ash, and the wind of God
comes along as grace and blows the ash away.

As my post-liberation spiritual journey continues to unfold, I am continually amazed and humbled by the direct experiential liberation insights and transformations that keep unfolding within my consciousness taking me ever deeper into a fuller liberation awareness. From a witness position, this expansion of consciousness has been both relentless and awesome. My crude body-mind-I am complex was sometimes gently and sometimes not so gently being permanently morphed into the illuminated subtle Body-Mind-I-ness and beyond an ever-expanding capacity to hold the ever-increasing

Divine influx to ever fuller and deeper levels of stabilized liberation. It helped me remain more permanently free from the I Am-ness dream/illusion that I was my pre-liberation stories of the past, present, and future. It naturally helped me create a way of holiness and sanctification for myself as a conscious part of the web of life on the planet.

Teaching: The Truth of who we are can't be known by the mind, because the Truth exists beyond the mind.

Sometimes the smallest event would catapult me into a new level of stabilized awareness. For example, on one windy day in 1996, outdoors at the Tree of Life café in Arizona, the wind blew over and shattered a glass top table. In that extraordinary mundane outer moment, the remaining thin "glass ceiling" of my mind broke, and all the remaining identifications with my mind disappeared. This one returned to the eternal home and realized that this soul-fire had never left. With no glass ceiling filter left there was a tremendous surge of subtle post-liberation non-causal love, joy, peace, oneness and ecstatic energy becoming a new baseline of this one's consciousness.

Teaching: In the spiritual evolutionary process, after the remaining thin glass ceiling of the mind broke, I naturally let go of the delusion of trying to find the heart of God as I realized that this wild soul-fire was indeed the pulsing heart of the Divine.

The Kundalini, Ruach Ha'Kodesh or Shekhinah energy is the hand of God that took me to the heart of God. It naturally and spontaneously tremendously overcame what was left of the ego or jail keeper as the planetary parasite that created a wall of separation and alienation built with the false identification with time, space, and I Am-ness, while using the drug of comfort to maintain amnesia of the Truth. The subtle ego forces that kept me imprisoned, designed the material universe for the care, comfort, and feeding of the impure ego which needed to constantly be fed and activated by keeping me focusing on the body, mind, past, present, and future, materialism, sex, and other forms of survival and pleasure to exist.

Teaching: There is never enough busy activity
to satisfy the hungry mind and never enough food
to feed a hungry soul. The soul will always be
hungry until it tastes the nectar of the Self.

Paradoxically, the Six Foundations and Sevenfold Peace are a pathless path and natural way of living that both supports shattering the delusion of the identification with the body-mind-I Am complex, as well as creating the pre-conditions to awaken to cosmic awareness and liberation. I understood that pure knowledge cannot be imparted by another; instead it came unasked when I was ready through direct apperception of these Divine experiences. The process for me was and is a cumulative understanding through repeated disappearing into the Nothing experiences in meditation until there was nobody left. My realization was not a one-time classical "Ah Ha!!!" experience. Poetry is one way to share the right brained sustained experience of the Truth. In the end there is no enlightened one. There is only enlightenment.

***

—·ɯ·—

Glass Ceiling of the Mind Shatters

One day the windy Grace of Yah
Blew so hard
The glass table of the mind
Turned over and shattered
Into thousands of useless fragments.
It happened so suddenly
So effortlessly
After so many years and lifetimes
Of thinning this glass ceiling of illusion
So suddenly
The mind just shattered
Just exploded into the eternal motionless, timeless presence.
The scintillating sublime
Absolute burst through
Uninterrupted
Alone
Disconnected from past, present, and future
And the illusion of "I Am-ness" was not
even there to claim it as my own.
There was no place to stand
And no one to be standing.
The Great Way
Which has no gate
Opened
And there was no "I Am-ness" there to walk through.

—·ɯ·—

Upon awakening from the illusory dream of reality of the "I Am-ness" of who I thought I was, I stopped merely playing at spirituality. I was then able to put the contents of my mind on the table and surrender them to God simply by no longer identifying with the contents of my mind.

Teaching: We can't lose what we never had, and
we can't attain the Truth of who we already are as
it is already attained. We never were the mind, the
body, or the imaginary figment of I Am-ness.

Participating in the path to liberation is no gamble. All we're doing is turning the fragmented chips of what was our mind over to God. But here is the catch... the ego wants us to think of it as a gamble, so it can stay in control and continue to dominate our consciousness so that we fearfully run from the Truth of who we are. As pointed out earlier, it is common that at some point the impure ego creates a lot of fear and resistance to spiritual life. When we let the Divine into our lives in a way that connects our outer awareness to our inner soul, that soul connection meta-communicates to us that there's no gamble here.

Teaching: The real risk in life comes from our
belief in the mind-body-I Am complex as reality.

—ɷ—

Fragrance of Liberation

Light chased this one
Until it burned him up.
It is only when we are burnt like incense,
That we have the fragrance of liberation?

—ɷ—

Chapter 33

THE LIBERATED
SPIRITUAL WARRIOR

Teaching: A free person lives and dies as an original.

*O*n my path of liberation, part of my work has been to clear the clouds of the mind in order to open up the doors of consciousness to the light of the soul. This journey led to the end of the perception of myself as a differentiated ego separate from God. In this context, I have becoming a window for students to look through, not at, as I am always pointing toward what's on the other side of the window. As a spiritual teacher and friend, one becomes, in essence, a space of silence through which one can view the world beyond the blinders of our conceptual mind. Through this empty window of silence, the delicious illumination of the Divine is seen and experienced.

Teaching: Our body-mind-I am complex is like the
moon; our soul is like the light of the sun, and our
mind, until free of thoughts, creates a cloud of ignorance
around us that obscures the light of our soul and God.

My hesitations about giving up my routine and work in the world seemed to naturally fade away as I immersed myself in the most meaningful thing in my life, the path of Holistic Liberation. Of course, in my liberation process it became easier and easier to see through the mind control efforts of those who have designed a political correctness system in a futile effort to control everyone's thoughts, including my own. The good news is by the power of the liberation awareness I had the clarity to choose whether or not to play. Without being bound by the limitations of politically correct concepts, I found myself free to be a spiritual warrior on all levels, to meditate for hours, raise my family with great love and joy, and walk my world in the most appropriate and authentic ways. In the process of breaking free from the PC (politically correct) matrix, I realized that all people are born originals, but most people die as copies. In this awareness context, part of my creative spiritual work is supporting people into reconnecting with their authentic Self and become an original again. In this way, I have come to playfully see myself as an artistic culinary chef of the Self.

Teaching: Existing in a liberated state is so much fun
because it's a constant romantic, humorous, sacred,
lovingly joyful, peaceful relationship with all creation in

its Oneness. One becomes free to move in any direction beyond limiting belief systems, behaviors, and concepts.

As a liberated spiritual warrior I found myself free to move in any direction, yet, only act in ways guided by God instead of the unfortunately impure ego-programming dictated by my traditional religious beliefs and customs, my political beliefs, post-truth reality belief systems or imagined stories that obstruct living in the authentic truth. Authentically following the Will of God requires much meditation and a deep connection with my soul self. My feedback system to keep myself aligned with the Divine Will and not egoic will is to consistently inquire if my inner direction is aligned with the perennial, cosmic, spiritual teaching, morals, and ethics of all the great traditions; as well as my alignment with my inner self; and also with the guidance of my personal spiritual teachers; as well as with the teachings of the recognized spiritual scriptures such as the Vedas and the Bible.

Teaching: All religious structures, whether holy, uplifting, and sanctifying, or the opposite, may become potential snares to the liberation process. Paradoxically, however, religious paths and traditions may be used to create a powerful context and base gateway to leap into the unknown and become liberated.

Living in the culture of life and liberation, it becomes clear that there are ultimately no external religious systems that offer direct access to liberation. And in this context one cannot technique their way to God. It is evident now as I write these words that how I live my life today has much more meaning. My life finally shifted when I experientially fully apperceived that I am made in the living image of God. I now choose to live in that illuminated, ecstatic emptiness, as the expression of the One as my ongoing Truth.

—⟶⟵—

Beliefs

People are willing to die
Or kill others to validate their beliefs or concepts
Whether it be for money, power, the "greater good" or religion;
Paradoxically, their concepts have already
murdered them and the Cosmic Truth.

—⟶⟵—

Chapter 34

BECOMING ONE'S PRAYER

Teaching: Meditation and prayer, no matter one's level of awareness, are continually empowering and expanding.

Prayer is another potent source of transformation. The deeper meaning of prayer in Hebrew is *l'hitpallel*, which means to become your prayer. When one is at peace, we can create an energetic of prayer that one becomes. The key to becoming one's prayer is to transform oneself into the result of the prayer. When we're praying, we are, in essence, creating a space for the experience and the transformation that allows us to become our prayer. By our holy actions we become a blessing for the whole world.

Teaching: Our prayers have power to heal ourselvesand others, transform and expand our consciousness, and uplift the world.

Swami Muktananda used to teach that one should repeat the name of God until it comes out of one's shoes. That may seem hard to believe, but when living in our small community in Mendocino, California, Dr. Lee Sannella and I used to chant the Name and meditate on the Name of God very intensely in the early mornings. One day some other community members, skeptical of what we were doing, came by the teepee where we typically did this. Neither Dr. Sannella nor I were on the land, but these people heard the name of God coming out of the empty physical structure. They were significantly amazed and had no negative comments after that.

Even today, an important part of my spiritual way of daily life is repeating the name of God, which further activates my love and joy of God. In 1995, at the end of a twenty-one-day water fast, during an extended ten-hour meditation, I was spontaneously Divinely given a particular way to repeat the Tetragrammaton (הוהי). It came on powerfully with a particular way of breathing the name of God. I was instructed to inhale the *Yod* energy up from below the base chakra to the heart and exhale energy out through the heart with a silent *Hey* sound going out to the world. The second inhalation is a *Wah* sound that goes from below the base chakra to the third eye (or *da'at* area), and then another *Hey* sound exhaled through the heart out to the world. The silent whisper of God directed me to repeat the name while awake, going to bed, while sleeping, and waking up; in other words, all the time. The Tetragrammaton (הוהי) is the name of God as grace that elevates us above the physical plane. It activates the merging of the inner male and inner female as well as the outer male and outer female into the Oneness. The use of the Tetragrammaton is appropriate for this time in history to help us stay God-focused in the midst of the world's chaos. It is also the numerology/gematria of most of the nucleotides of the DNA and RNA. Torah teaches that where one repeats the name of the Divine, Divine energy is activated and we more intensely draw the energy of the Divine to us. In repeating this particular name of God, I began to experience actually invoking the energetics of the name of God into my DNA and RNA.

Repeating the Name is an essential action I do as much as possible in all life situations. It's significant that such well-known Advaita Vedanta teachers as Sri Nisargadatta and Ramana Maharshi, as well as Swami Muktananda and Swami Prakashananda, involved themselves daily in devotional dualistic practices and love of God as well as repeating the name of God. These dualistic bhakti/love practices create, activate and add rasa or "spiritual juice" to my love of God. In the Great Torah Way this devotional merging with the spark of God in all things is called "Yechudim" and is called Tantra in Kashmir Shaivism. It's a scintillating, erotic ecstatic way to live one's life while still remembering there is only the non-dual existing. The spiritually romantic love of the Divine becomes a wonderful way of continually immersing oneself in the Eros of the Divine on a second-to-second basis.

Teaching: Doing good deeds and actions (mitzvot) and repeating the Name of the Divine with love and devotion are two ways of life that can lead to liberation. A third level which may result from the previous two, is the pathless path of direct apperception of knowing beyond the confines of the mind – and ultimately, the ecstatic Truth of God.

In the Torah Way, this third pathless path of direct knowing is called "achdut" and in Yoga it is called *anupaya*. The direct apperception of achdut or anupaya began to spontaneously emerge in a variety of ways near the end of my guru cycle years. In the first part of my post-liberation years from 1983 on, I began to experience all three levels synchronously co-existing more and more frequently. My relationship to time evolved into three perceptions of time: 1) finite time, which includes the distinct past, present, and future; (2) Infinite time; and (3) experience of time as the Prior to the Nothing awareness which is timeless. This third perception of time includes the awareness of the Eternal Presence, which includes: finite historical time, infinity of no time, and most importantly an "Expanded Nowness", which paradoxically includes and transcends all dimensions of time into the Eternal Presence. This level of Eternal Presence awareness originally spontaneously began to manifest in meditation near the end of my guru cycle, and now has expanded to encompass all aspects of my life. There is only God happening in every moment.

Teaching: The spiritual path and teachings of holistic enlightenment are fueled by living nonstop and simultaneously on all multidimensional levels of time and consciousness in our relationship with the Divine.

Chapter 35

SPIRITUAL WORK
IS NEVER DONE

Teaching: Be careful what you ask for. There is no end
to the purification and evolution of spiritual life.

In early 2017, I made an audacious and sincere prayer to HaShem (God) that I was willing to accelerate the burning of all karmas no matter what. The next day a burning rash appeared on both of my arms, spreading to both of my legs and all over my body, except for my feet and head and face. Over the next two and a half years, it soon became uncomfortably apparent that the burning itchy bumps seemed to follow the meridian lines corresponding with different organs undergoing purification. When it appeared on a particular organ meridian line, that organ also tested weak. After it finished in a specific area, that particular organ would test strong, as if it had undergone purification and strengthening. When it hit my heart meridian, my lower legs and feet swelled, and my heart tested weak. The lymphatic system in my legs was also severely affected. Near the end of the cycle, the rash eventually reached my lungs and throat, making me aware of my history of life-threatening miliary tuberculosis, as well as TB of the larynx, which, as I have already written, I experienced when I was a 1-year-old child. After a complete cycle including all the meridians, the rash seemed to move back and forth over several meridian lines, both weakening and then strengthening, suggesting my body was having several waves of detoxification. It was hard to do anything about this, as nothing seemed to affect it, including fasting. It was obviously an answer to my bold prayer. It was a living experience of the adage: "Be careful what you ask for." And suddenly about two years and one half since it began, over a seven-day period, it disappeared.

Teaching: The more we create the inner emptiness, the easier it is to be an expression of the Divine Will. Meditation helps to create the illuminating inner emptiness.

A subtle paradox along the way of my spiritual path is the question of intention. If there is specific intention, I am careful to question if impure ego has deluded me. If I have surrendered my ego to the Will of God, there usually is a general intention that exists without a specific goal. To have a specific goal-oriented intention, even for liberation, emanates from the idea of being a separate individual ego and believing I am in control. That simply is not happening. The freer I find myself from egoic memory and my identification with the

I am-ness, the easier it is, with great gratitude, to realize the infinite nature and expression of the Divine within myself and in all creation. For me gratitude is an inner experience-directed statement made only to God. In my experiential world, meditation in a Kundalini-activated system is far more than merely quieting the mind to transcend it. A Kundalini/Ruach Ha'Kodesh awakened and empowered meditation activates a tsunami wave of inner gratitude that is a whole other level of a spiritually transformative force for turning the body-mind-I Am complex into a luminescent vehicle of light.

Teaching: Meditation is food for the soul.
It is the ultimate spiritual nutrition.

I also found it supportive to study the great scriptures, because the wisdom and knowledge I receive from the Divinely inspired, written teachings, such as the Torah, the Vedas, Kashmir Shaivism's literature, and the Tao Te Ching also feed my soul and connect me to the collective historical world wisdom and expression of God through the written word. As previously mentioned, I did not start my spiritual path with an overt intention to become liberated. The awakened spiritual energy was simply intensely pushing me to wake up on every level. My primary focus was keeping up with the forceful fiery energy as it unfolded. That was and is precisely what happened and is happening in the unfolding of my whole spiritual life whether this soul-fire chooses it, or not. God expressed as the Divine Urge was and is clearly in control. If one doesn't feel the pull of the Divine Urge, then, indeed, the inspiration of one's teacher becomes a more critical part of bringing one to the place where that Divine Urge activates.

Teaching: Having the spiritual endurance to
keep up with, nourish, and honor the Divine
Urge is key to the liberation process.

What has come from this lifetime of spiritual experiences leading to liberation is a path newly labeled by me as the subtle ecstatic Holistic Liberation Way. Holistic Liberation is the cumulative summation of liberation consciousness which is the result of my being lived by the Six Foundations and Sevenfold Peace on every level which took me beyond the silent mind of my I Am-ness into oscillating between appearing and disappearing into the nothing with the subtle ecstatic unbroken fullness of the Eternal Presence remaining in the background.

Another important part of my liberation unfolding was developing the freedom to move in any direction (*hitpashtut*). I began to let go of any hesitations about actually doing what I felt was the most meaningful and spiritually expressive action. It is a sort of spiritual wildness, or crazy wisdom of liberation. As an awakened spiritual warrior, though free to move in any direction, I also learned to act in ways that are indeed guided by God and not dictated by my egoic considerations or even by religious beliefs and/or emotionally based, post-truth realities.

Teaching: An interesting Self Liberation side
benefit of being free to move in any direction is
that I found myself becoming free from the present
attempted mind control, which has gone on for
thousands of years empowered by different hidden
and also blatant forms of political correctness.

My holistic liberation journey continually reminds me that my "I-ness" is created in the image of God which cannot be seen but can be apperceived. I learned to let the fire of liberation burn through the ego box of self-comfort that previously tended to subvert me from the cosmic truth. This fire of enlightenment and desire for God has liberated me and will eventually liberate all of us. The fire of liberation can't be stopped. I have become a perpetual beginner with each new beginning as an opportunity to develop deeper liberation wisdom in every interaction in the endless play of consciousness and interaction with "Guru Tattva" – the world as the guru orientation.

Teaching: In the awakened life I have learned
to become a walker between the worlds touching
them all, but not blending with any of them.

Over the years, my direct experience, from meditation, from playing high school and college football, to hours of meditation, to following the Divine directive in developing a spiritual nutrition diet, to listening to the Divine Whisper guiding the return to my historic tribal roots at the end of the forty-day fast in 1983, living in sacred relationship and ultimately being guided by the Divine Urge has all been part of an ongoing holistic spiritual evolution that undoubtedly will continue at least as long as I am in my body.

Chapter 36

THE HEART OF THE HOLISTIC LIBERATION WAY

Teaching: At the heart of my path of Holistic
Liberation Way is faith. To live in faith is to live
in the direct apperception of the Truth beyond the
mind that there is only God. The Truth, which is
beyond the logical mind, is that God is the Many
and the One as creation and prior to creation.

My whole life has been based on faith since the age of four.
Every decision I have ever made and all I have ever done in
my life is based on faith in God. I realized faith was needed when I
was unable to understand the mystery of God rationally. Faith means
me believing when I do not even know why I am believing. I delve
into cosmic mysteries because I have faith in levels that are hidden

from me. Faith has opened up the gates of holiness for me and is the source of all holiness and mystical understanding which is the wild alchemical, magical world I live in. My redemption from the lack of faith in earlier years is dependent on regaining faith. Faith is the foundation of my spiritual growth because it has me ask the question in every situation: "How is this situation a spiritual teaching for me based on 'whatever God does is for the best?'" Despite my multi-leveled holistic scientific background, I lead my life through my pure and simple faith of believing in God as Truth without any sophistication or metaphysical teachings. I have chosen to live my life through the power and guidance of simple faith. My faith has never misguided me.

Teaching: Faith is based on the experience
of the truth that there is only God.

As this chapter and book ends, may you, the reader, be blessed with joy, love, peace, and faith in your awakening and liberation process. I pray that the experiences and teachings of my spiritual life experiences, development, and insights that I have shared with you serve to support you in your own unique spiritual evolution; and that you truly enjoy more and more the cosmic play of consciousness and the cosmic dance we are all intrinsically part of.

The writing of this spiritual autobiography represents an end to several powerful transformative cycles over the last seventy-seven years and, of course, the beginning of a new cycle. These endless interactions with the world have been a powerful purification by fire, moving "me" as a soul-fire along the liberation spectrum... beyond time and space, where there exists no future, present, or past... and actually only faith exists as knowing the Truth of God. For all this, I am extremely grateful to God for this grace and for the opportunity to share with you. It is much more fun to join God's liberation party than to resist it. Welcome to the party.

Poetry of Liberation

—ɯ—

Sunset at the Tree

Tonight, the Sunset kissed the fragrant beauty of the Rainbow
And the clouds cried tears of joy,
The earth beneath me smiled,
The heart exploded in love of You,
You have taken everything away
And made me wealthy;
With a wealth beyond the mind and expectations

—ɯ—

On the Silence of the Night

In the silence of the night
The song of the beautiful creatures of the night
Fill the air with Yah's praise
The starlight gently whispers
Sweet praises of Yah
Surrounded and penetrated by the Presence
Every cell resonates to the Divine Song.

—ɯ—

Becoming the River

The river bubbles,
And joyously sprays
Its love of God in every drop,
This one becomes the river.

Blessings, love, peace,
the guiding power of faith, and the bliss
of liberation on every level... to you.

—Gabriel

Gabriel at 77.

GLOSSARY

A

Abraham/Avraham Avinu—(Biblical) in Genesis he is described as Avram Ha-Ivri (Abram the Hebrew), the one who stands on the other side; first of the Hebrew patriarchs, and revered in Judaism, Christianity and Islam; the great liberated spiritual warrior patriarch and pre-founder of Judaism.

Achdut—(Jewish concept) direct apperception of the Cosmic Truth; in Yoga this path is called *anupaya*.

Adharmic—(Sanskrit) unrighteous, disharmonious, immoral; out of line with one's personal and greater spiritual perennial dharma; against sacred law.

Advaita Vedanta / Advaita—(Yogic/Hindu philosophy) Advaita Vedanta means "non-duality" in Sanskrit. Advaita is a school of Hindu philosophy and Self-Realization. Advaita Vedanta has become best known in the West through the non-dual spiritual teaching that there is only One Reality. Advaita is considered to be a philosophy or spiritual pathway rather than a religion, as it does not require those who follow it to be of a particular faith or sect.

Agaram bagaram—(Sanskrit) humorously self-effacing.

Agni Hotra/ Agnihotra (Vedic)—fire ceremony or healing fire; *agni* means "fire" and *hotra* means "healing.

Ahamkara—(Sanskrit) the term arises out of a 3,000-year-old Vedic philosophy; *Aham* refers to the self and *kara* to any created thing. It is generally used when referring to the attachment of the ego, or individuation principle, which must be transcended. Ahamkara is the boundary that separates us from the Nothing.

Ah Cah Tha triangle—(Yoga) a special chakra between the sixth and seventh known as the Soma or Amrita Chakra.

Ajna—(Hindu/Yoga) third-eye chakra; sixth chakra made more powerful through meditation.

Alma d'shikra—(Hebrew) the world of illusion; the Sanskrit equivalent is *maya*.

Amrita—(Sanskrit) means immortal or immortality; it is related to the Greek word *ambrosia*.

Amrita chakra—(Yoga) the Soma, Ah Cah Tha triangle, or special chakra located between the sixth and seventh chakras. Amrita means immortal/immortality.

Anahata—(Hindu Yogic) heart chakra or fourth chakra; it refers to the Vedic idea of balanced, calm, serene energy.

Ananda Kanda—(Yoga/Tantra) the Hrit or bliss chakra is analogous to the heart chakra.

Ani/Anochi—(Hebrew) refers to "I" or "I Am", the Eternal Presence.

Anupaya—(Sanskrit) the pathless path; experiencing the complete Oneness and unity of all creation.

Asana—(Yogic) means seat in Sanskrit and refers to a traditional Yoga posture.

Assiyah—(Kabbalah) the physical plane of existence; the world of action.

Ashtanga—(Sanskrit) having eight limbs; the classical eight-fold Yogic path as defined by Pantajali in the Yoga Sutras.

Ashtanga Yoga—(Yoga) a system of yoga transmitted by Sri K. Pattabhi Jois (1915-2009).

Atzilut—(Kabbalah) the world of emanation; the initial inspiration; Oneness awareness.

Avadhut—(Sanskrit) Yogi or mystic who is beyond ego-consciousness, duality and worldly concerns; a human spiritual ideal and example of non-dual Awakening.

Avant-garde—(French) experimental or unorthodox.

Ayahuasca—(Shamanism) a South American entheogenic brew used as a traditional spiritual medicine in ceremonies among the indigenous peoples of the Amazon basin.

Ayin—(Hebrew/Kabbalah) 16th letter of the Hebrew alphabet, means "eye" (pronounced EYE-yeen); in the Kabbalah it relates to "nothingness" contrasted with *Yesh* which means "something."

Ayurveda—(Sanskrit) means science of life; it is one of India's traditional systems of medicine.

B

Bal Shem Tov—Jewish mystic and healer, Rabbi Israel ben Eliezer (1698-1760) known as the Baal Shem Tov, was born in Poland and is regarded as the founder of Hasidic Judaism.

Bar Mitzvah—(Judaism) a coming of age ritual for boys in which he takes on the rights and obligations of a Jewish adult.

Berur—(Hebrew) clarification process of assessing reality versus illusion.

Bhakti—(Sanskrit) devotion to and dualistic love of God.

Brahma nadi (Yogic)—see *Nadi*.

Bilva/vilva leaves—(Hinduism) leaves considered sacred to Shiva, perhaps because of the trifoliate leaves which are said to represent the triple nature of the Divine, or trimurti.

Bitul hayesh—(Hebrew/Kabbalah) total negation of the ego; inner emptiness.

B'limah—(Hebrew) means nothingness. The term first appears in the Book of Job, and refers to the simple harmonious desire of God.

Book of Bhrigu—(India) or *Bhrigu Samhita* ancient prophetic books that contains information about the past, present, and future lives of many people. The books contain the soul patterns of anyone who is destined to find it, even those who are meant to become enlightened. It is said that the Vedic sage Maharishi Bhrigu channeled the text 5,000 years ago.

Brahma—(Hinduism) the creator of the universe; the first principle (*tattva*).

C

Chakra—(Sanskrit) also cakra; psychic energy centers or "wheels" in the body.

Cherokee—A Native American tribe that has well documented Jewish genes and may, like the Choctaw, be one of the Lost Tribes of Israel.

Chesed—(Kabbalah) the consciousness energy of the fourth sefirot known as loving-kindness.

Chey'rut—(Hebrew) enlightenment awareness.

Chit Kundalini—(Yogic) increased Kundalini energy intensity activated at the heart level to the third eye.

Choctaw—A Native American tribe that has well documented Jewish genes and may, like the Cherokee, be one of the Lost Tribes of Israel

D

Da'at—(Kabbalah) Associated with the third eye energy wisdom and location. Helps to integrate the right and left brain.

Dama—(Sanskrit) control of the senses or self-restraint.

Darshan—(Sanskrit/Hinduism) meeting with a holy person; beholding of a deity; a blessing.

Détente—(French) meaning "release from tension."

Dattatreya—(Sanskrit) the primordial guru energy; a three-headed figure of Brahma, Shiva, and Vishnu.

Devekut—(Hebrew) clinging to God; desire God merging.

Deveikut/Chey'rut—(Hebrew) God-merging and Self-Realization; the enlightenment awareness in Judaism.

Dharma—A word used in Hinduism as the cosmic law behind right action and right behavior, the right way of living. In Buddhism it is used to define cosmic law and order. Our main dharma is to know God. Our personal dharma is right livelihood that supports our liberation process; especially that gives us the spiritual lessons we specifically need in our path to liberation.

Dharmic—(Hinduism/Buddhism) sacred law; living in alignment with the law that orders the universe; following one's dharma is aligning with this principle.

Dharana—(Yoga) the sixth limb of Yoga and has to do with one-pointed concentration.

Dosha—(Ayurveda) one of three major body/mind types, of kapha, pitta and vata. There are 9 dosha variations; three primary life-forces govern the physical body; the mental body forces are called *gunas*.

Dristi shirsti—(Sanskrit phrase) the world is how you see it; the world is how you believe it to be.

Duality—the concept of good and evil; seeing the world as fractionated rather than as Oneness. (See: Advaita Vedanta)

Dhyana—(Yogic) the seventh limb of Yoga; the state of *Atman* or Pure Awareness.

E

Eros—(Greek) – the consciousness of Eros from a liberated perspective is living in a way which one rejoices in the incredible blissful inner experience of the ecstasy and erotic love of merging with the Divine in every moment and in every situation.

G

"G'neyvay da'at"—(Hebrew phrase) stealing of the mind through lies or deceitful actions.

Granthis—(Yogic) three controls or knots that regulate the balanced flow of Kundalini. The first is located below the base chakra (Brahma Granthi); the second is called the heart chakra knot (Vishnu Granthi); and the third is called the third eye knot (Rudra Granthi).

Gunas—(Sanskrit/Hinduism/Ayurveda) modes to existence. Three gunas developed by Hindu philosophy: *sattva*, *rajas*, and *tamas* define three personality tendencies and patterns. *Sattva/sattvic* in Sanskrit means purity, balance, or order; *rajas/rajasic* means active, energetic and willful; *tamas/tamasic* means negative, lazy, ignorant, self-destructive, but also solid.

Guru Tattva—(Sanskrit) means "the world is the guru".

H

Haniha—(Hebrew term) the energetic transmission that can awaken the Ruach Ha'Kodesh/Kundalini. It is called also called *S'micha m'shefa*. See: *S'micha m'shefa/Haniha*; also *Shaktipat*.

HaShem—(Hebrew) the main word for the name of God as Grace. Also known as "The Name".

Hey/Hei—(Hebrew) Hashem is usually written as Hei with a geresh: 'ה.

Histalkut—(Hebrew) disappearing or dying into the nothing.

Histalvut—(Hebrew) word referring to equal vision; seeing the light of the Divine in all people equally.

Hitpashtut—(Hasidic philosophy) the stripping away of materialism, abolishing selfhood, and aligning with Divine Will so that one is able to move in any direction and dimension.

Hoshek—(Hebrew) illuminated black fire letters on the nothing.

Hunka—(Lakota) is the making of a relationship that is a bond that never breaks.

I

Ida—(Yogic) According to the Yogic and Tantric philosophies, the three most important nadis are the *ida, pingala* and *sushumna*. Ida is the left channel, and can be experienced as is white or blue, feminine, and sometimes as cold. Ida represents the moon and is associated with the river Ganga (Ganges). Originating in *Muladhara* or base chakra, Ida ends up in the left nostril.

Inipi—(Lakota) a sweat lodge.

Ista Devata—(Hindu) one's primary guru energy and deity.

Ivri—(Biblical) a boundary crosser; Abraham, the original enlightened and spiritual warrior.

J

Jacob—(Biblical) patriarch, grandson of Abraham.

Janananda—(Hindu) Sri Swami Janananda Baba, a God-Realized man and second major disciple of Sri Nityananda.

Jnana Yoga—(Yogic) path of Self-Knowledge and wisdom; Yoga of the Mind.

K

Kabbalah—(Judaic) esoteric mystical teaching based on the Torah.

Kameshwara—(Hindu) a figure found in the *Ah Ka Tha* triangle; the male counterpart of Kameshwari.

Kameshwari—(Hindu) a figure found in the *Ah Ka Tha* triangle; the female counterpart of Kameshwara

Kanda—(Kundalini Yoga/Tantra) the kanda is slightly below the Muladhara or base chakra, and is the meeting place of the three main nadis (*ida, pingala* & *sushumna*); and is also known as *Yukta Triveni*.

Kashmir Shaivism (Tantra)—a branch of the Shaivite philosophical traditions that explains how the formless supreme principle or Shiva manifests the universe. A Tantric worldview of how to experience the world as the Dance of the Divine.

Kavod—(Hebrew) honor or respect, as in living with spiritual honor.

Keter—(Kaballah) the pure Divine Will.

Koach mah—(Hebrew) the power of "what"; a direct experience of the spark of God in all of material creation.

Kodesh HaKodashim—(Hebrew) the Holy of Holies within the great Temple; a physical place in which the holiness of the Divine is concentrated.

Kol D'mama Daka—(Hebrew phrase) referring to the small and silent voice of God.

Koshas—(Sanskrit) means sheath and refers to the layers of the mind.

Kriya—(Sanskrit) most commonly refers to a "completed action" technique or practice within a Yogic discipline; also, spontaneous movements that may occur when the Kundalini energy is awakened.

Kriyas—(Yogic) spontaneous movements that may occur when the Kundalini energy is awakened.

Kriyavati Pranayama—(Yogic) spontaneous breathing patterns.

Kundalini—(Hinduism/Yogic) the cosmic liberation spiritual energy that rests in us as pure potential, near the base of the spine below the *muladhara* charkra; it is also the cosmic spiritual energy in general. In Torah it is analogous to the *Ruach Ha'Kodesh*. It can be awakened as part of the liberation process with *Shaktipat*.

Kundalini Crisis—(Psycho-spiritual term) a psycho-spiritual crisis which may include breaks with reality, or/and psychosis which may appear to be a spiritual event.

Kundalini Shakti—(Yogic) see: Shakti Kundalini.

L

Laban—(Biblical) Laban the Aramean, brother of Rebekah, who married Isaac and bore Jacob. Laban was a master of the dark arts and was was spiritually defeated by Jacob.

Lakshmi—(Hinduism) the consort of Vishnu; Lakshmi is the goddess of wealth, beauty, fertility, good fortune and youth.

L'hitpallel—(Hebrew mysticism) becoming your prayer.

M

Mah—(Hebrew) means "the something".

Mahabharata—(Sanskrit) great epic poem about two branches of the family the Bharata dynasty, the Pandavas and Kauravas; it contains important information regarding the development of Hinduism and is traditionally ascribed to the sage Vyasa.

Mahadasha—(Vedic) an astrological term referring to significant astrological cycles in a person's life. A mahadasha cycle or time of life when a person is affected most heavily by certain cosmic energies of a particular planet.

Mahasamadhi—(Hinduism/Yogic) the way a Realized Spiritual Master leaves the body at death; the final *Samadhi*.

Manipura—(Yogic) means "city of jewels" and is the third or solar plexus chakra, located above the navel. This chakra is associated with the fire and the sun, and is generally shown with ten petals.

Mantra—(Sanskrit) a word or sound repeated to assist with meditation.

Masjid—(Islamic) Mosque.

Maya—(Sanskrit/Advaita) means magic or illusion; compare with *alma d'shikra*.

Mikvah—(Judaism) a bath used for ritual immersion and purification.

Mitzvot—(Hebrew) commandments, good deeds, or daily actions regarding one's spiritual duties.

Moshav—(Hebrew) means "settlement"; a type of cooperative agricultural settlement in Israel.

Mudra—(Yoga) sacred hand gesture.

Muktananda—(Hinduism) Swami Muktananda (1908-1982) is known as the Siddha Guru who awakened a generation of people. Baba Muktananda's name means the Bliss of Freedom.

Muladhara—(Yogic) means root and basis of existence; the base chakra located at the base of the spine.

Mussar—Jewish spiritual discipline of morals and ethics.

N

Nada—(Yogic) 10 Divine sounds.

Nada Yoga—(Yogic) the union of the individual mind with cosmic consciousness through the flow of sounds.

Nadi—(Sanskrit) means stream, channel or hollow stalk through which the Kundalini flows. There are 72 thousand nadis and three main ones: *sushumna, ida,* and *pingala.* Within the central channel of the sushumna are three additional subtle channels, the thunderbolt or *vajra nadi* which is solar, fiery and yang; the *chittra nadi* which is lunar watery and yin; and also, the *brahma nadi* which is the only channel that goes beyond the third eye to the crown.

Nefesh—(Hebrew) the most physicalized of the five levels of the soul, also considered the root of the soul or the root of the psyche.

Netzach—(Kabbalah) consciousness energy of the seventh sefirot with spiritual qualities of: persistence, victory, and perseverance.

Nirvikalpa Samadhi—(Sanskrit) merging into the black void.

Nisargadatta Maharaj/ Sri Nisargadatta Maharaj—(Hindu) guru who taught non-dualsim. His publication, *I Am That* (1973), brought him worldwide recognition. Nisargadatta left his body in 1982. He is best known as a teacher of Advaita Vedanta.

Nityananda—(Hindu) Sadguru Sri Bagawan Nityananda Maharaj or Bhagawan Nityananda of Ganeshpuri was Swami Muktananda's God-merged guru. Nityananda had the power to transmit spiritual energy (*shaktipat*) to people through non-verbal means.

Niyamas—(Sanskrit) the second limb of Patanjali's Yoga Sutras, the cosmic and ancient spiritual teachings of right living or ethical conduct. The Niyamas are the inner observances. (See *Yamas.*)

Non-dual—(*Advaita* in Sanskrit) Oneness—the essential unity of man, all creation, and God, as the Many and the One.

O

Ometz—(Hebrew) courage, specifically spiritual courage and leadership.

Ophanim—(Hebrew) Jewish roots of Yoga; sacred positions of the Hebrew letters.

P

Parshas—(Judaism) weekly Torah study sections; there are 52 parshas.

Para Kundalini—(Yogic) Kundalini awakening from the third eye to the crown. It is the most refined and subtle Kundalini. It needs to be activated before Self-Realization.

Pingala—(Yogic) According to the Yogic and Tantric philosophies, the three most important nadis are the *ida*, *pingala* and *sushumna*. Pingala is the right channel. Pingala is often experienced as red, masculine, and hot; it represents the sun and is associated with the river Yamuna. Originating in *muladhara* (base chakra), pingala ends up in the right nostril. From the base of the spine, ida and pingala alternate from the right to left sides at each chakra until they reach the *ajna* chakra where they meet again with the sushumna.

Pitta/Pitta Dosha—(Ayurveda) the pitta dosha is the hottest and fieriest of the three doshas in Ayurveda.

Prakashananda—(Hindu) Prakashananda Sarasvati (1917- 1988) was the first Indian disciple of Swami Muktananda to be acknowledged as liberated, and the author's second guru. Prakashananda was highly regarded within Muktananda's circle for his spiritual attainment and his loving demeanor.

Prana—(Yogic/Tantra) Life force; vital air.

Prana Kundalini—(Yogic) Kundalini energy from the base chakra to the heart granthi (or knot).

Pranayama—(Yogic) the practice of breath control, usually practiced after asanas; prana means "life force" and ayama means "to extend".

Pratyahara—(Yogic) sense withdrawal; the fifth component in the path of eight-limbed Yoga.

Puja—(Sansrit) derived from the word *Pu* meaning flower, is generally a ceremony where fruit or flowers are offered to an image or symbol of God.

R

Raja—(Sanskrit) means "king."

Rajas—(Sanskrit) passion, activity, active warriorship; one of the three *gunas* in Hindu philosophy.

Rajasic—(Ayurveda) energetic, active, warrior-like; spicy foods that increase energy are called rajasic.

Raja Yoga—(Yogic) the royal path to attaining a state of unity with mind-body-spirit.

Ram/Rama—(Hinduism) or *Ramacandra* is the seventh avatar of the God Vishnu and is considered an unparalleled warrior with the highest values.

Ramakrishna—(Yogic/ *Advaita Vedanta*) Sri Ramakrishna Paramahansa (1836-1886) was a liberated teacher of the philosophy of Advaita Vedanta.

Rasa—(Yogic) spiritual juice; Divine flow.

Ruach Ha'Kodesh—(Hebrew) the cosmic liberating spirit of the Holy One stored in the body waiting to be awakened. Compare with *Kundalini*.

Rudra granthi—(Yogic) energetic knot in the third eye that becomes open in the transformative process of liberation.

S

Sadguru/Satguru—(Sanskrit) means the true guru; truth itself.

Sadhana—(Sanskrit) daily spiritual practice.

Sadhu—(Hinduism) an ascetic, hermit, or holy man.

Sahaja Samadhi—(Sanskrit) a continual state of bliss and liberation even while engaged in daily life activities.

Sahasrara—(Yogic) crown chakra.

Sai Baba of Shirdi (Yogic)—also known as Shirdi Sai Baba (1838-1918); a spiritual master who lived a God-merged life. He is revered by both Hindus and Muslims, and taught by living example the importance of Self-Realization.

Samadhana—(Sanskrit) concentration of the mind or single-pointed concentration on the Truth.

Samadhi—(Sanskrit) deep spiritual bliss experienced when the mind is quiet and transcended; a totally silent mind that takes one beyond the mind. The two forms are merging into the light (sankalpa samadhi) and merging into the void (nirvakalpa samadhi).

Samskaras—(Sanskrit) karmic inheritances of often deep psycho-emotional scars; subtle impressions of past actions of past lives; impressions of earlier part of present life; and immediate results of one's actions.

Sankalpa Samadhi—(Sanskrit) merging into the white light.

Sanhedrin—(Judaism) the grand council of rabbis.

Satsang—(Hinduism) a sacred gathering or spiritual discourse.

Sattva—(Sanskrit) means light; it is also one of the three *gunas* developed by Hindu philosophy; relating to purity, virtue and wholesomeness.

Sattvic—(Ayurveda) pure living and being inner directed to the truth of the Self; light, nourishing. Sattvic foods and following the live-food lifestyle supports and maintains awakening a pure life.

Sefirot/Sephirot—(Hebrew) means "emanations" and refers to the 10 emanations in Kabbalah through which G-d is revealed.

Seva—(Hinduism) selfless service.

Shakta—(Sanskrit) a person who worships Shakti, the wife of Shiva.

Shakti—(Hinduism) primordial cosmic feminine energy.

Shakti Kundalini / Kundalini Shakti—(Yogic) the hand of God which takes you to the heart of God. The universal cosmic force that empowers life in general and spiritual life and liberation in specific. It exists both outside as the cosmic energy and stored in potential at the base of the spine.

Shaktipat—(Yogic) spiritual energy; the descent of grace or spiritual transmission that comes through a Shaktipat guru, and it may also be awakened spontaneously in rare situations. Shaktipat initiation is also known in Hebrew as *S'micha m'shefa/Haniha*; the awakening of the Divine force that is resting in potential within us. Once the spiritual energy is activated, it begins to spontaneously move through our body, spiritualizing every cell, every aspect of the DNA, every chakra, every nadi (which are the channels of the subtle nervous system), every organ and every tissue, so that all consciousness becomes activated into the next evolutionary stage. (See: *Haniha*)

Shaktipat/Haniha—(Yogic/Judaic) spiritual activation of the Kundalini that can ultimately lead to Self-Realization and ultimately liberation. (See: *s'mecha m'shefa*)

Shama—(Hebrew) to control and focus the mind.

Shatsampatti—(Sanskrit) the six treasures: shama, dama, shraddha, titiksha, uparati, and samadhana. *Shama* is mastery of the mind. *Dama* is mastery of the sense organs. *Shraddha* is faith. *Titiksha* is forbearance and persistence in the ups and downs of life. *Uparati* is dispassion in the face of life's challenges and experiences happening for our growth. *Samadhana* is one pointedness of the mind on the Truth.

Shekinah—(Judaism) denotes the dwelling and dance of the Divine feminine presence of God in all creation. Compare with *Shakti*.

Shema—(Judaism) a sacred prayer.

Shimbhavi Mahamudra—(Yogic) eyes turned upward spontaneously.

Shiva—(Hinduism) the third god in the Hindu triumvirate.

Shiva Lingam—(Hinduism/Shaivism) sacred stone thought to intensify vitality which represents the merging of Shiva (sacred male) and Shakti (sacred female) into the cosmic Oneness.

Shiva/Shakti—(Yogic) the Oneness of male/female harmony, also called He-Adam/She-Adam, or Aba/Ima

Shomer Shabbat—(Hebrew) a person who observes shabbat; in Yiddish they are referred to as *frum*.

Shraddha—(Sanskrit) faith and also devotion, specifically when aligning with the Divine Will.

Siddha Peeth—(Sanskrit) a spiritual center of an awakened, liberated, spiritual being; Swami Muktananda's first Siddha Yoga ashram in Ganeshpuri, India.

Siddha Yoga—the Yoga of the *siddhas*; a spiritual path founded by Swami Muktananda; a central element of the Siddha Yoga path is Shaktipat through which a seeker's *Kundalini Shakti* is awakened.

Simcha—(Hebrew) spiritual joy or gladness.

Simhasana—(Yogic) lion pose; a Yoga *asana* that exercises the muscles in the face and throat.

S'micha—(Hebrew) or *semikhah* means "to learn"; a rabbinical ordination.

S'micha m'shefa—(Hebrew) *Shaktipat* initation; the descent of grace.

S'micha m'shefa/Haniha—(Hebrew) the awakening of the Divine force that is resting in potential within us.

Soul mates—(Yogic) energetic compliment ideal for intimate relationships, especially for maturing the soul's evolution.

Stigmata (Judeo-Christian)—Holy wounds.

Sushumna—(Yogic) the three most important nadis are the *ida* (female), *pingala* (male) and the central *Sushuma*, which is often associated with the river Saraswati. Acccording to the Yogic and Tantric philosophies, within the sushumna nadi there are three more subtle channels known as the *Vajra, Chitrini* and *Brahma nadis* through which Kundalini moves upwards running up the spine from just below the Muladhara chakra to the *sahasrara* chakra at the crown of the head.

Sushumna Breathing—(Yogic) opening the inner flute; consciously breathing (as if from a straw) from the base chakra up the spine and then back down again while visualizing the movement of life force.

Sushumna nadi—(Yogic) the main *nadi* running up the spine that contains three other nadis: the *vajra nadi* (thunderbolt, or fiery/solar/yang); the *chittra nadi* (or watery/lunar/yin nadi); and inside of that was a thin line tube called the *brahma nadi*.

Svadhisthana—(Sanskrit/Yogic) meaning "dwelling place"; it is the second or sacral chakra and has six petals; the chakra is associated with water femininity and the moon.

Swadharma—(Sanskrit) living in daily liberation awareness; steady state of enlightenment.

Swarupa—(Sanskrit) when a person experiences a liberation moment.

T

Tamas—(Vedanta) ignorance, darkness, sloth and lethargy, but also stability; one of the three *gunas* developed by Hindu philosophy. (See: *Gunas*)

Tamasic—(*Vedanta*) lethargy, destruction, even chaos. Heavy foods that decrease the energy of the body are considered tamasic. The positive side is that tamasic energy is fixed, or unmoving.

Tantra/Tantric—(Yoga) Tantra in Kashmir Shaivism is experiencing the Eros of the Divine in all creation, which leads to a feeling of Oneness.

T'shukat deveikut—(Hebrew phrase) referring to the Divine Urge.

Tetragrammaton—(Hebrew) sacred name of God as YHWH (יהוה)

Tiferet—(Kabbalah) sixth sefirot of perfect balance, justice, beauty, love.

Titiksha—(Sanskrit) spiritual perseverance.

Tree of Life—mentioned in the Holy Scriptures, is the tree that God planted next to the tree of knowledge, good and evil. In the Garden of Eden, the Tree of Life bore fruit that sustained immortal existence; the mystical symbol of the thirty-two paths needed to be mastered for liberation. The Tree of Life is found in Judaism, Christianity, Celtic and Norse mythologies, as well as other world mythologies.

Twin Flame/ Twin Souls—(Yogic) two people from the same root soul who are very alike; they may share a mission but they are not ideal long-term intimate partners.

U

Uparati—(Sanskrit) contentment through right action and dispassion in the face of life's challenges and use of experiences to grow spiritually.

Urdhvareta—(Sanskrit) the upward flow of the semen, which creates natural celibacy.

V

Vairagya—(Sanskrit) non-attachment; seeing God equally in all people. Compare with *Histalvut*.

Vairagya/Histalvut—(Sanskrit/Hebrew) seeing God equally in everyone.

Vedas—(Sanskrit) means "knowledge"; the Vedas were written in Sanskrit and are a large body of religious texts originating in ancient India that inform the religion of Hindusim. The Vedas are also known as *Sanatan Dharma* meaning "Eternal Order" or "Eternal Path".

Vedic—(Vedic Religion) see: *Vedas*.

Vibhuti—(Hinduism) sacred ash often applied to the forehead or other parts of the body to honor Shiva.

Vishnu—(Hinduism) one of the most important gods in the Hindu pantheon along with Brahma and Shiva.

Vishuddhi—(Yoga) throat chakra shown with sixteen petals; the center of physical and spiritual purification. It comes from a Sanskrit word meaning especially pure.

Viveka—(Sanskrit) the ability to distinguish between the cosmic Truth of the One God and the myriad relative ever-changing truths of the material plane.

Vrittis—(Yoga) thoughts of the mind.

W-X-Y-Z

Yah—(Hebrew) Yah is one of the names of G-d and the first syllable in YHVH, or the Tetragrammaton, the four letters that form the name of G-d.

Yama/Yamas (Sanskrit/Yoga)—self-control; from Patanjali's Yoga Sutras, the cosmic and ancient spiritual teachings of right living or ethical conduct. (See: *Niyamas*)

Yatra—(Sanskrit) spiritual pilgrimage.

Yechudim—(Hebrew) seeing and connecting with and activating the spark of God in all of creation.

Yesh—(Torah/Kabbalah) means "there is"; in Kabbalah it refers to the "something" as compared with *Ayin*, or "nothingness."

Yod—(Hebrew) Yod is the tenth letter of the Hebrew alphabet (aleph-bet) and the numerical value is ten. Yod represents the world to come and completeness. It is the smallest of the Hebrew letters and is mysteriously suspended in mid-air. It is also the first letter out of the nothing.

Yogananda Paramahansa—(Kriya Yoga) an acknowledged yogi and one of the first Indian monks to come to the West (1893-1952); Yogananda introduced millions to meditation and Kriya Yoga.

Yukta Triveni—(Yogic term) known as the three rivers: *Ida, Pingala & Sushumna* that exists just below the *Muladhara*; it is the meeting place of the three main *nadis* in the *kanda* region just below the base chakra.

BIOGRAPHY

Rabbi Gabriel Cousens, M.D., M.D.(H.), N.D. (h.c.), D.D. (Doctor of Divinity), Diplomate Ayurveda, Diplomate American Board of Holistic Integrative Medicine is a living inter-faith holistic mystic who functions as a physician of the soul. Dr. Gabriel Cousens has been doing humanitarian and peace work throughout the world since 1965, including teaching and service in forty-two countries. Acknowledged as a liberated Yogi by his spiritual masters Swami Muktananda and Swami Prakashananda in 1982, Dr. Gabriel Cousens was empowered and directed by Swami Muktananda to give Shaktipat (energy to awaken the Kundalini) to as many people as possible. Co-founder of the first Kundalini Crisis Clinic in the world, Dr. Cousens is considered a world-recognized expert on Kundalini. He was ordained as a rabbi by Rabbi Gershon Winkler in 2008 and has encouraged the celebration of Shabbat in many countries around the world including such places in southern Nigeria where some of the tribes had previous awareness of their ancestors being tribally Jewish. He also teaches Torah- based Judaism as a mystical path to liberation. In addition, Dr Cousens is a four-year Native American Sundancer and Eagle Dancer and eleven-year Spirit Dancer (Ghost Dancer). Adopted into the Lakota Sioux Horn Chip Clan, Dr. Cousens was appointed head of Yellow Horse Clan by his Sundance chief. Dr. Gabriel Cousens was given the name Ta Sunka Hinzi (Yellow Horse) and also appointed as the Yellow Horse clan leader by his Sundance chief Kam Nightchase. Dr. Gabriel Cousens's unique contribution to the spiritual world today is the creation of the idea and teachings of spiritual nutrition and the formulation of the mystical path of Holistic Liberation Way, which emphasizes a natural way of living guided by the Six Foundations and Sevenfold Peace that can take one to liberation.

Dr. Cousens is also a Holistic Orthomolecular Physician and Psychiatrist, Homeopath, Family Therapist, Ayurvedic Practitioner, and has served as a lieutenant commander in the U.S. Public Health Service. He is a former member of the Board of Trustees of the American Board of Holistic Integrative Medicine and currently vice-president of the Arizona Board of Holistic Integrative Medicine (AHIMA). Additionally, he's a world leader in healing diabetes naturally. Dr. Cousens is also the founder and director of the Tree of Life Foundation, Tree of Life Center U.S., Tree of Life International Community, and the Essene Order of Light. He is the bestselling author of thirteen books. He is also a co-founder of a West African NGO called WARES (West African Rural Health Empowerment Society) and also Alianza de Corazón in Mexico (Alliance of the Heart), a group of humanitarian organizations in Mexico. He presently has established and supported more than 100 health and diabetes prevention programs, organic veganic farming projects, and orphanages in twenty-six countries. He received the Cesar Chavez Award in 2013 for his nutritional and diabetes education of migrant farmworkers in the U.S. He is happily married to Shanti Golds Cousens, father to Rafael (age 50) and Heather Cousens (age 47), and grandfather to Rhea (14 years old), Katja (12 years old), and Anaïs (10 years old). He lives part of the time in Patagonia, Arizona and spends the other part of the year in Moshav Mevo Modi'im in Israel.

For information about Dr. Cousens' work and his programs and to sign up for his newsletter visit:

www.drcousens.com

or

treeoflife.mn.co.